P9-DUX-433

THE
OMEGA PROJECT

ALSO BY KENNETH RING

Heading Toward Omega
Life at Death

THE
OMEGA
PROJECT

NEAR-DEATH EXPERIENCES, UFO ENCOUNTERS, AND MIND AT LARGE

KENNETH RING, Ph.D.

Foreword by Whitley Strieber

WILLIAM MORROW AND COMPANY, INC.
NEW YORK

MONTROSE REGIONAL LIBRARY
320 SO. 2ND ST.
MONTROSE, CO 81401

Copyright © 1992 by Kenneth Ring

Grateful acknowledgment is made for permission to reprint from:

Dream of the Earth by Thomas Berry, reprinted with permission of Sierra Club Books.

Earth Lights Revelation by Paul Devereux, reprinted by permission of Cassell PLC.

Confrontations by Jacques Valle, reprinted by permission of Random House, Inc.

"UFO Abduction Reports the Supernatural Kidnap Narrative Returns in Technological Guise" by Thomas E. Bullard, reprinted by permission of the American Folklore Society from *Journal of American Folklore* April–June 1989 (102:404).

Various articles by Michael Grosso, reprinted by permission of Michael Grosso, Ph.D.

All rights reserved. No part of this book may be reproduced or utilized in any form or by any means, electronic or mechanical, including photocopying, recording, or by any information storage or retrieval system, without permission in writing from the Publisher. Inquiries should by addressed to Permissions Department, William Morrow and Company, Inc., 1350 Avenue of the Americas, New York, N.Y. 10019.

It is the policy of William Morrow and Company, Inc., and its imprints and affiliates, recognizing the importance of preserving what has been written, to print the books we publish on acid-free paper, and we exert our best efforts to that end.

Library of Congress Cataloging-in-Publication Data

Ring, Kenneth.
The Omega project : near-death experiences, UFO encounters, and mind at large / Kenneth Ring : foreword by Whitley Strieber.
p. cm.
Includes bibliographical references and index.
ISBN 0-688-10729-X
1. Near-death experiences. 2. Unidentified flying objects.
I. Title.
BF1045.N4R564   1992
001.9′42—dc20   91-31638
                                                                      CIP

Printed in the United States of America

First Edition

1 2 3 4 5 6 7 8 9 10

BOOK DESIGN BY PATRICE FODERO

To Christopher J. Rosing,
without whose faithful friendship,
dedication, and computer wizardry,
the Omega Project could never have
been launched.

PREFACE

In January 1987, I received an unwelcome package in my mailbox. I was on my break between semesters at the university, and with the Christmas holidays recently concluded and my three grown children finally rerouted to their chosen cities of destiny, I was eagerly looking forward to getting back to work again. Coming in to the university that day, however, I remember I groaned audibly when I saw what lay in wait for me in the mail room. My box was stuffed with accumulated mail, as expected, and lying atop this unwelcome pile was a large mailer that looked decidedly as if it were the container of still another unsought book a well-meaning publisher had felt compelled to inflict upon me.

Academics, of course, are used to receiving steady supplies of such unwanted tokens of publishers' largess along with fervent, if brief, expressions of hope that we will be moved to adopt their unsolicited offerings for our classes, but since having become an author myself and often finding that I am swamped with more mail than I can cope with, I have come almost to resent anything that threatens to require a good chunk of my time. This package, I felt sure, constituted such a menace, and like a post-Christmas academic Scrooge, I'm sure I muttered dark oaths on seeing it.

In fact, I distinctly remember setting it aside in order to look at more personal mail first, and opening it only after I was done. It was, to be sure, a book, but I laughed when I saw its dust jacket. It featured a drawing of an insectoid-looking humanoid, with a sickly pale face dominated by a pair of large, impenetrable black buglike eyes. *Communion,* the title read, *A True Story*. I had never heard of the author, one Whitley Strieber. I quickly scanned the pages. Oh, brother, I thought, this is a book about UFOs! Still, I felt relieved—this one was obviously not going to eat into my time after all.

When I had opened the book, however, a little note had fallen out, and now I looked at it. Instead of the form letter I expected, to my surprise I saw that it was a handwritten message from my editor at William Morrow. As I remember, it said, in effect, that I shouldn't be put off by the cover or the content of this book (an advance copy), that it was very relevant to my work and thinking, and that I would do well to read it without delay.

I looked again at the book—this time with dismay. Despite my editor's exhortation, it was hard for me to understand what this book, with its horrid little alien staring at me from its cover, had to do with my work and interests. After all, for the past ten years, I had been researching and writing about near-death experiences, encounters of such sublimity and overwhelming joy that they could scarcely be imagined to be anything other than at antipodes to what this book appeared to be about. In near-death experiences, or NDEs as they are always abbreviated and usually referred to these days, there is often reported contact with a radiant, luminous figure—what Raymond Moody, one of the pioneers of NDE research, simply calls a "being of light"—from whom the experiencer feels nothing but the outpouring of the greatest love and compassion that he or she has ever known. What did UFOs, with their aura of tabloid looniness, have to do with experiences of such supreme transcendental power and profundity as NDEs?

Besides, as an NDE researcher in academe, I was used to walking uncomfortably close to the edge of professional respectability as it was. NDEs, like UFO stories, make good tabloid fodder, and when occasionally after the publication of my first book on NDEs, *Life at Death,* my own work was the source of such sensational (and misleading) tabloid headlines as, NEW AMAZING PROOF OF LIFE AFTER DEATH!, I would have to endure the reproachful and sometimes withering gaze of my department head as well as the good-natured, but often pointed, ribbing of my colleagues. Anyone who studies death in such a way as to even imply that surviving it may not be out of the question immediately runs the risk of no longer being taken seriously as a professional. And to intimate that the experience of death itself may, as Melville claimed, offer "a last wondrous revelation" is of course anathema to those who are convinced, as many academics are, that the only thing that happens at death is extinction. So, mindful of these attitudes and prejudices, I had tried to do my own work on NDEs, as much as I could, using scientific methods and statistical analysis and not to rely only on case histories and anecdotal reports. And over time I felt gradually rewarded by the increasing acceptance of the authenticity and importance of NDEs on the part of large segments of the professional community, as some recent surveys have shown,[1] and even among some physicians who were formerly inclined to be entirely skeptical about the existence of NDEs. Still, my early sensitivities to the professional costs of stepping over the boundaries of accepted scholarly concerns never entirely eroded, and I always exercised some degree of caution whenever I was exhorted by someone to peek over the edge of my own self-defined abyss. Even to innocent undergraduates who, knowing my reputation for the exotica of psychology, would sometimes approach me to sponsor their academically dubious projects, I would joke, "Look, even I have my limits, and I don't do ghosts and I don't do UFOs, so don't even ask me to consider it!" As a result, much as I was interested in NDEs and their spiritual implications, I went out of my way to avoid reading about spirits, seances, UFOs, and other similar professionally taboo topics.

Accordingly, you can appreciate with what distaste I considered my editor's injunction to me. Rather than rejecting his advice outright, however, I decided to temporize. I brought the book home with me (certainly no one was going to walk into my office and discover a book like that on *my* desk!) and let it lie on top of my bedroom dresser, where I put it in order at least not to forget its existence altogether. A few days passed, and then one evening I succumbed and took it into my study to begin reading it.

Like many others who have done so (the book was, of course, soon to become a best-seller, and remained at the top of the nonfiction charts for many weeks later that year), I was, despite my misgivings, swiftly in thrall to the author's fervid tale, and I quickly turned the pages, now quite oblivious of time or even of my initial reservations. *Communion* is, of course, the story of one man's experiences with nonhuman creatures who appear out of nowhere and with terrifying speed abduct him and put him through a humiliating and painful physical and psychological examination. Strieber's initial reaction, not surprisingly, was one of the deepest terror, and after he was returned from his ordeal (he knows not how), he was profoundly shaken and indeed suicidal. His anguish over these incidents (the first traumatic encounter loosed memories of other, previous ones) is palpable, but they soon lead him on a quest for understanding of these extraordinary events, and most readers, I suspect, are, as I certainly was, prepared to follow his passionate inquiry with deep interest and respect for his personal courage.

So I read on most eagerly, as one would a gripping novel (though Strieber's tale was billed, as you'll recall, "A True Story"), but for all my absorption in his book, I still couldn't discern any obvious points of connection with my own work. At least not at first, but as I got further into Strieber's story and particularly where some of the paradoxical-seeming *positive* aftereffects of his bizarre episodes began to emerge, the threads joining NDEs to UFO encounters like Strieber's were plain to see. What had blinded me, aside from my own prejudices, was my thinking that there could hardly be any commonalities between two categories of anomalous experiences, NDEs and UFO encounters, whose prototypes were so obviously discrepant with each other. What I had failed to see, however, and what Strieber's book was helping me to, was that these two very different types of personally shattering experiences could nevertheless apparently lead to *a similar kind of spiritual transformation*. Indeed, when Strieber talked about the kind of self-insights he had come to through the deep exploration of his encounters, his personal values, and his fears and concerns for the ecological well-being of the earth, and so on, he seemed to be speaking in the very phrases that I had heard so often from the lips of the near-death experiencers I had interviewed and, in many cases, with whom I had remained friends. And when Strieber expanded his focus toward the end of his book to consider the experiences and views of others besides himself who had had some kind of apparent UFO contact, it became clearer still that in describing the psychological and spiritual aftermath of his own encounters, he was doubtless speaking for many others. Now of course I could understand why my editor had been so insistent that I read *Communion* in the first place and what he knew I was in an almost unique position to see there.

Reflecting on all this, after finishing Strieber's book, helped to germinate the basic query that led to the research reported in this book. In its simplest terms, it is this: Are NDEs and UFO encounters (whatever UFOs may be!) in effect *alternate pathways* to the same type of psychospiritual transformation, i.e., one that expresses itself in greater awareness of the inter-connectedness and sacredness of all life and necessarily fosters a heightened ecological concern for the welfare of the planet? This question, of course, in turn suggested others. For example, in my second book on NDEs, *Heading Toward Omega,* I advanced the hypothesis that NDEs are a kind of experiential catalyst for human evolution, that potentially, at least, these experiences that we now know have occurred to many millions of persons across the globe are serving the purpose of jump-stepping the human race to a higher level of spiritual awareness and psychophysical functioning. Drawing on the inspired vi-sionary ideas of the late French Jesuit priest and paleontologist Pierre Teilhard de Chardin, I deliberately entitled my book *Heading Toward Omega,* in order to imply that the human race was advancing toward an end state of evolution that Teilhard had called "the Omega Point," and that NDEs could be under-stood as hastening that evolution. Might they indeed? This was obviously another possible link between these two categories of experiences. And, finally, if NDEs and UFO encounters could plausibly be shown to play some kind of catalytic role in the psychospiritual evolution of humanity, what forces could con-ceivably have "engineered" them into being? The philosopher Michael Grosso, who is also a deep student of the NDE, has not hesitated to speculate boldly about such unfashionable questions, and has made a cogent and well-reasoned case for the existence of something he, following the celebrated English novelist and mystic Aldous Huxley, calls *Mind at Large,* a kind of planetary or collective mind that is both an expression of humanity's deepest yearnings and transcendent to them.[2] The ultimate testability of such a formulation is of course beyond our means, but it does at least have the virtue of suggesting a novel idea: Could phenomena so vastly different as NDEs and UFO encounters somehow both be expressions emanating from a common source whose intent furthermore is to strive to awaken the human species to a truth it now desperately needs not only for its own survival but for the survival of all life?

Heady and perhaps unanswerable questions indeed, but my mind was fairly full of them when a day or so later I sat down to write Strieber a long, appreciative letter in which I outlined some of my then-nascent ideas about the possible parallels between our heretofore separate worlds of the NDE and UFO. A cordial reply was my reward, followed by a friendly phone call; and not long after, a visit to his home in New York was in the works. Our first meeting, on May 1, 1987, enabled us to share our experiences and views at length, and our exchange on that occasion, and those we have had when we have met subsequently, revealed that in fact by traveling very different routes we had been led to essentially the same arena of conclusions.

Sparked by our conversation at that first meeting, I observed that my near-phobia about getting involved in anything so fraught with opprobrium as UFO research is to the academic mind had been reduced to tolerable levels—now I only shuddered when I thought about it, but inwardly I had already decided my course. I was going to look into this. Strieber's book had shown me that there might be an unexpected avenue that led to the same destination NDEs conduce to, and in that sense one could say this book was truly the Alpha to my Omega Project, the study I shall describe in this book—which itself is the story of another road to Omega.

Heading toward Omega via UFO Avenue.

The tale I have told in this book begins, then, with my being drawn into the improbable world of UFO encounters and sensing for myself their possible connection with NDEs. Following this, the next several chapters are devoted to offering examples of these two types of extraordinary encounters in order to disclose their similar underlying structure; all of the accounts in this section have never before been published and all derive from the participants in the research conducted for this book. After I describe in Chapter 5 how this research was carried out, the next three chapters present my findings, which I have tried to express in straightforward, nontechnical language, leaving the statistical data in a separate appendix for the interested reader. Chapter 9 gives my interpretation of the overall findings of the study, and the last chapter, of course, my conclusions. By the time you reach the end, but possibly before, you will understand why I have chosen to call this book *The Omega Project*. You will also see that you, too, are taking part in it and are, in fact, its coauthor.

FOREWORD

by Whitley Strieber

Ken Ring's Omega Project represents the first time that anyone
has attempted a controlled examination of the perceptions of
people claiming alien abduction. The results are illuminating indeed, showing that there is some sort of core response both to
these excruciating perceptions and to the near-death experience.

Unlike the near-death experience, however, the "alien abduction" perception has been subjected to ruthless tabloidiza-
tion and pushed aside by medical and scientific communities
eager to distance themselves from the more absurd excesses
attached to the experience. It is greatly to Dr. Ring's credit that
he was willing to risk the inevitable media exploitation and de-
nigration of his effort on behalf of its value.

This is not a book by a scientist who has somehow been
seduced into believing in aliens. Indeed, this foreword has not
been written by an author who has claimed "alien abduction."
What I have claimed, and what Dr. Ring's study has found, is
that the perceptions that are popularly referred to as "alien abduction" have some readily identifiable and highly unusual aftereffects in the lives of the people reporting them. This means
that, like the near-death experience, the apparent alien encounter represents extremely powerful psychological material.

However, this experience has been for the past forty years
bound up in a most awkward conundrum of cultural politics,
and so has been almost impossible for serious scientists to address in a manner that would clarify it and dispel some of the
myths that surround it. Specifically, by describing their experi-

ences, victims have given rise to a folklore of alien encounter that has been seized upon by a press quite naturally eager for sensation. More sober minds have felt compelled to disparage these claims, and by so doing have also disparaged the validity of the underlying experience, whatever it may be.

However, it most certainly exists, and I can personally attest to the fact that it causes a great deal of human suffering. It is, in its essence, a culturally filtered reaction to some sort of stimulus—whether external or not remains unknown. Having had the experience many times, I can attest to its remarkable combination of subtlety and extraordinary impact. To come to terms with it, I went through five years of sheer hell, and still find it difficult to believe that the experience was not caused by an intelligence external to myself. Indeed, all of my internal references to it remain essentially *other,* despite the insistence of my intellect that this is almost certainly not the case.

I suspect that the cause of the disruption is indeed external, but that the form it takes is hallucinatory and culturally mediated. It would not surprise me if there was an intelligence behind it—but *alien* intelligence? That would be quite a surprise.

During the five years I struggled both with the experience and with a great deal of worldwide media attention, I learned the power of cultural conditioning. Despite the fact that I declared myself on behalf of keeping the question of the origin of the experience open time and time again, I was nevertheless introduced on my last major national television appearance as "self-proclaimed alien abductee Whitley Strieber." And despite the fact that the probable origin of the appearance of the phenomenon in the mind is the central theme of both my books on the subject, I have been more or less ostracized as a heretic from both the intellectual and literary communities.

Thus, my effort to throw the origin and nature of the experience into public question demonstrably failed; I ended up serving the very cause I sought to confound.

The reason for this is not some obtuseness on the part of the media or a failure on my part to communicate my position clearly. Rather, it is the sheer power and the convincing structure of the experience that has done it. I still receive upward of fifty letters a day, most of them from people who just want a confidential listener, and reassurance that they are not crazy. But these people are not likely to be convinced, even by the most definite science, that they have had anything but an encounter with enigmatic aliens.

Generally, they will have a close encounter with a UFO, as often as not in the presence of other witnesses. Days, weeks, or months later, they will begin to have a series of enigmatic experiences with what appear to be aliens. These will involve the most bizarre extremes of perception and sensation, ranging from being swept through walls and off into the sky, to—more commonly—losing time or packing hours' worth of events into very short time periods. These experiences need not happen in isolation; they are often shared.

As the folk culture continues to reinforce the "alien hypothesis," it becomes more and more difficult to suggest any other with any degree of public acceptance. Indeed, people from disparate backgrounds can often repeat tiny confirming details that have probably never been published anywhere, strongly suggesting that their perceptions are based on a commonality of some kind.

I believe that the "alien hypothesis" could well become so convincing that it will enter the mainstream of thought, and the idea that there are elusive aliens observing us will come to be seriously entertained and commonly accepted. However, I strongly suspect that the experience represents a response to some natural phenomenon, probably of an electromagnetic nature, and that the forms it takes depend upon the enculturation of the affected individuals. I say this because my own experience with the phenomenon has been extremely extensive, and I have been able to observe details of its intelligence that so strongly point to its human origins that I can only say that, if aliens are here, they have learned to mimic the inner mind of man.

The fascinating thing about the experience, and its importance, is that it is probably the primary source of all apparitional phenomena, from religious vision to UFO encounter, with near-death experiences, ghosts, poltergeists, and such tossed in along the way. Its prevalence in a given society is probably directly proportional to the degree to which individuals in that society are disturbed by its functioning. The fact that the UFO encounter is so widespread and so democratic would suggest that we are in the process of reconsidering the most basic tenets of culture. The coming of the UFO means, quite simply, that the curtain in the temple has been rent, and culture is about to undergo profound change.

The emergence of the UFO phenomenon paralleled the development of weapons of universal destruction and is, at its core, a foray into a sort of subconscious anarchy that, paradoxically, seeks some sort of control that will replace social systems that are being perceived as betrayers.

Similarly, Christianity sought to replace the god-emperor of Rome with a common man transformed, one who preached peace and neighborliness, and whose message eventually replaced the Roman sword and closed not only classical civilization but the classical way of mind.

Must the liberal, expansive, hopeful, and rational view that we have spent the past two thousand years achieving now be replaced by the cruel anarchies of the UFO phenomenon, with its message of doom and its depressing array of demonic or coldly indifferent entities? If the unconscious mind means to check the species with a new control mechanism, must we punish ourselves with these dreary apparitions? And I don't simply refer to the "evil" little gray men with the big eyes who are central to the folklore. I also include the somewhat less common angelic apparitions, which I must say that I find equally tedious. I have been awakened in the night by apparitions for five years now, and early on became tired of empty posturing. I expected more than this from my unconscious, and sought to enrich my experience. Enrichment is only available through understanding. My imaginal input, I can assure you, was sufficiently baroque to satisfy the most jaded consumer of the outré.

It is my hope that investigations such as Dr. Ring's will bring order to what is now a most disorderly situation. If there are indeed aliens present, they have done an expert job of confusing the issue. Perhaps their final disguise will be our own conviction that they come from within us.

I would not, however, dismiss out of hand the seemingly fantastic notion that actual aliens may have their origin inside the human mind. After all, is not the Garden of the Gods inside us also? Even Christ acknowledged this when he located the kingdom of heaven within.

Could it be that life itself is a mechanism by which some hidden, inner reality is touching and feeling its way into the physical world? Are we a medium of exchange, a communications device, an extraordinary construction designed to bridge the gulf between the physical world and something else?

Where do near-death experiencers actually go when they travel down that gleaming tunnel of culture into the arms of the Lord? They go to the same place that abductees go when they are carried or floated or dragged out of their beds. But it's nicer. Perhaps the dead live in a better nonphysical neighborhood than the aliens. But there is actually a sensible reason for the fact that the abduction experience is hard and the near-death experience generally more pleasant. The aliens are an inner mechanism designed to control the living, while the near-death entities are there to receive the dead into mankind's inner world.

The alien abductee is being forced to confront unrealized potential, while the near-death experiencer is being received into his own memories.

We go deep, we go down, we enfold ourselves in ourselves, seeking identity with the essence of our own expectations. We are like an ant trapped upon a hanging Christmas ornament: We have crossed our own path so many times that we cannot deny the reality of the trap. But we cannot see our way out. So we stop, we reach into the air, we feel blindly.

Such things as near-death experiences and alien abductions exist now because this is a desperate time. The culture has failed, and we know it, and we are desperate to somehow survive the consequences of the failure. Rome of the third century was a wide and prosperous empire, believed by its rulers to be eternal and unassailable. But portents were everywhere, the common people lived in constant expectation of the end of the world, and a story was passing from slave to slave that the son of a carpenter had usurped the emperor's claim to divinity.

A hundred years later the empire was dying, and the whole spirit of the world had forever changed. The civilization we are living in now will be similarly transformed in a hundred years.

There is a sense of hurry now, as if the leaves are racing before the wind. The old world is so impossibly huge, so tremendously poisonous, so bankrupt of ideas, and so strained by its own rigidities that there is virtually no chance that it will continue as it is now. The market economy will fail, deeply, profoundly, and utterly, and do so in the dual context of environmental disruptions brought on by its own excesses and a sweeping failure of interest in its products, the life it offers, and its outcomes.

I am not a millennialist, and I do not anticipate the extinction of mankind. I am impatient with talk of "earth changes," some mysterious force upwelling to right the wrongs that man has done. We are part of nature, and our destructions are no more unnatural or wrong than the lion's eating the gazelle. What is wrong is our view of ourselves as horrible, when in truth we are a great triumph.

The deeper levels of Dr. Ring's study indicated that there was some extraordinary enrichment available to abductee and near-death experiencer alike, that they were somehow touched by the light of the inner world, and that this light was opening, fruitful, and vastly entertaining. Such has been my own experience. Because I am an "alien abductee," I am full of anxiety. But I am also privy to great and enduring wonders. Instead of darkness, I see mystery without and within. My world is far more richly alive than the world of my friends who have been so unfortunate as to miss my experience.

It may be that the direction of evolution is toward immortality and away from the physical, that from the very first something has been seeking to escape the physical world. It escaped the bottom of the sea and went flying in the water, then it escaped the water itself, then it took flight above the land, and now it seeks finally to burst out of the physical altogether—which is the message behind all religion, behind all unexplained experience, behind all culture. Where are we going? Kafka, appropriately, said it most clearly: ''away from here.''

We are leaving, all of us, on a journey into the dark. We will go naked, afraid, and full of curiosity. Hopefully, we will also understand at last the exotic machinery that we ride. If Dr. Ring's pioneering leads to other work, and more work that is skillful and clever and open-minded, then perhaps we will not ride to the future in unidentified flying objects, but rather on the wings of knowledge.

ACKNOWLEDGMENTS

The research reported in this book owes its existence to the efforts and support of many individuals and several organizations.

My Medicis for the research project itself were the University of Connecticut Research Foundation, which awarded me a grant for my studies, and the Bernstein Brothers Foundation of Pueblo, Colorado, which provided additional funding. UFO-related research is, of course, not often funded for a variety of reasons, and is still considered so outré by most academics that university support for it is virtually nonexistent. Therefore, I would like to make a special point of expressing my appreciation to my own university's reseach council for its open-minded consideration of my research proposal and of course for its gratifying decision to fund my work. In addition, I would like to acknowledge the warm personal support over many years now of Morey Bernstein, the author of the classic book on reincarnation *The Search for Bridey Murphy,* who, through his foundation, also made a generous contribution to the Omega Project.

Whitley Strieber, the author whose book *Communion* galvanized my own interest in UFO research, was instrumental in several other ways in facilitating my study. Not only did he originally strongly encourage me to pursue my research interests in this field, but he and his wife, Anne, through their Communion Network, also provided me with the names of quite a few persons who eventually participated in the Omega Project. Of course, I am also indebted to Whitley for writing the Foreword to this book.

I had help from other researchers and writers as well in obtaining the hundreds of respondents who eventually took part in this study. Dr. R. Leo Sprinkle, recently retired from the

University of Wyoming, was extremely generous to me in many ways when I was starting out in this field, and helped me enormously by providing me with lists of attendees of his annual UFO conferences. Likewise, researchers Budd Hopkins and Joseph Nyman went out of their way to furnish me the names of additional respondents from their own research files, and my debt to them is equally great. Finally, my good friend and long-time colleague John White also assisted me by making available lists of persons who had attended *his* annual UFO conferences in Connecticut.

To obtain persons who had either had near-death experiences or an interest in the topic, I drew mainly on my own files, but I also received assistance from the International Association for Near-Death Studies, formerly located at the University of Connecticut, which supplied me with additional names. Barbara Harris was especially helpful in this regard.

These days scarcely any research effort is an individual undertaking, and in my case, would have been entirely unthinkable without the support of my research team, headed by Christopher J. Rosing, my project coordinator. My indebtedness to Chris is expressed in my dedication of this book to him, but no words are sufficient to convey his absolute indispensability to this project. He made everything possible. He and I, however, were also helped inestimably by several graduate and undergraduate students: Barbara Rosen, Kristie Davis, Kevin Nelson, and Gretchen Gaughler. I particularly want to acknowledge Barbara Rosen's contribution in helping to construct the original version of one of the questionnaires in this study, the Home Environment Inventory, in which task she collaborated with Dr. Barbara Sanders, my wife, who is also a psychologist at the University of Connecticut (though she was not involved in this research project as such).

Concerning the ideas expressed in the book itself, I owe a special word of thanks to my friend and mentor of many years, Dr. Michael Grosso, whose conversations and writings have been an ever-rich source of provocative and useful insights, many of which have come to play an important role in may own thinking about the kind of extraordinary encounters with which this book is concerned. My debt to him will be particularly obvious in the last chapter.

To him, and to a few other readers—Dr. Sukie Miller, Dr. Patricia A. Trautman, Rachel Elkin, Alise Agar—of my manuscript, I would like also to express my appreciation for their comments, from which *I* benefited even if my book didn't always show the imprint of their suggestions and strictures. Those of my editors, Elisa Petrini and (originally) Matt Campbell, did have more impact on the final manuscript and made it a better one than it would have been without their careful attention to it.

I wrote my book on my Mac SE computer, who (and I say "who" deliberately) performed faithfully and flawlessly even when I didn't. I confess that, like so many before me, I have become addicted to my computer and can no longer conceive of a life without one. For this, I thank another old friend, Dr. Ronna Kabatznick, who several years ago insisted that I join the twentieth century and buy my own PC. (It was she who also browbeat me into acquiring an answering machine; for that, I *don't* thank her.)

Carol Valone, an unfailingly generous-hearted and exceptionally competent secretary, pitched in with various forms of assistance, including, at this very moment, photocopying the manuscript for me. She's the tops, and also faxes.

I have saved for last the largest group of people, and ultimately the very ones without whose participation there could have been no Omega Project. These are the hundreds of persons who took the time to fill out our questionnaires and upon whose answers I have reached the conclusions expressed in this book. Many of these persons, beyond completing our questionnaires, also took the trouble to write to express their appreciation for the study or to provide additional information to me. To all of you, my deepest thanks for all that you have shared with me and, through this book, with those who will now learn more fully about the world of extraordinary encounters and their equally extraordinary effects.

Storrs, Connecticut

CONTENTS

OMEGA PROJECT

CHAPTER 1

ANOTHER ROAD TO OMEGA

*We must assume our existence as broadly as we in any way
can; everything, even the unheard of, must be possible in it.
That is at bottom the only courage that is demanded of us:
to have the courage of the most strange, the most irregular
and the most inexplicable that we may encounter.*

—Rainer Maria Rilke

The real is what will strike you as really absurd.

—W. H. Auden

For most of its checkered history, the field of UFO investigation has elicited far more laughter than laudation. Certainly, the response of most scientists and scholars to the matter of UFOs has long ranged somewhere between amused mockery and outright scorn. And who can blame them—or others—when the standard educational source on the subject, the weekly tabloid at your local supermarket, features its usual lurid and ludicrous headlines on the latest "amazing" UFO absurdity (8 FOOT E.T. SEEN AT BUS STATION PANICS TRAVELLERS!). It *is* to laugh. And when one considers all the stories one hears about "UFO buffs" searching the skies for signs of wondrous lights that portend some sort of supernatural salvation ("the space brothers will beam us up in the event of a nuclear attack") and waiting to migrate to the nearest UFO landing site, is it really possible to avoid a feeling of pitying condescension for such pathetic and benighted souls? No wonder that the field of UFO studies has almost from its inception in the late 1940s been smeared with the brush of ridicule and its phenomena consigned to the twilight world of the tabloids and the late-night world of talk shows devoted to the sensationalism of the paranormal. For years, then, the prevailing wisdom on UFOs has been the skeptic's view: This is not a matter to be taken seriously. At best, it is the stuff of science fiction; usually, it is simply harmless fantasy; at worst, it is fodder for grandiose delusions.

All this, however, is beginning to change. A Gallup poll taken in 1987 shows that a majority of Americans (who express an opinion) believe that "UFOs are real." Furthermore, the more educated one is, the *more likely* one is to hold that UFOs exist.[1] That same year, Whitley Strieber's book *Communion,* which vividly describes his own purported encounters with what he calls "the visitors," whose manifestation into Strieber's life is clearly connected with UFOs, was the number-one nonfiction best-seller in America for several months. And his was not the only UFO book to achieve substantial success in the national market; there were at least two others.[2] Media coverage has similarly broadened and in some cases reflected a more serious and open-minded attitude toward UFO phenomena than has been customary. For example, *The New York Times,* traditionally hostile to the subject, published a balanced article in its Science section in 1987. Similarly, *The Washington Post* printed an in-depth report of a June 1987 national conference of UFO investigators. During this same period, some of television's best-known news and news-magazine programs, such as *20/20* and *Nightline,* among others, thoughtfully explored facets of the UFO issue. And perhaps most important from the standpoint of scholarship—though this is less well known to the public at large—increasing numbers of scientists and academicians have quietly been investigating UFO-related topics and have founded new refereed professional journals, such as *The Journal of Scientific Exploration* and *The Journal of UFO Studies,* with impressively credentialed editorial boards to provide a rigorous forum for UFO research.

As a result of all these developments—and other signs of a greater and more sympathetic professional involvement that I haven't mentioned here—it seems safe to say that the UFO phenomenon is at last beginning to emerge from the shadows of obscurity and derision into the full light of increasingly respectful and probing attention. As has happened before, the mystery of the UFO is once again hovering over us and is exciting our imagination and curiosity in ways that even a decade ago few would have predicted.

Why is this? What is responsible for this heightened wave of interest that seems to be reaching its crest as we move closer to the dawn of a new millennium? Why is it that now the UFO question has finally presented itself in a form that can no longer just be cavalierly dismissed or simply laughed away?

It isn't merely that literally millions of persons—the estimates range as high as *19 million*—in the United States alone have now reported that they have seen what are to them inexplicable aerial phenomena, though clearly the sheer volume of such observations and the cumulative publicity given to them must be considered as important factors associated with the current climate of receptive attention being accorded to UFOs. More significant than those many sightings, however, is a particular and peculiar type of UFO-related *experience* that apparently increasing and persuasively large numbers of persons are beginning to describe. In my opinion, it is chiefly the widespread and independent reports of this kind of personal experience with UFOs that have forced us to reckon seriously with the UFO enigma.

I am speaking of course of the so-called "abduction experience." It is this type of encounter with apparent alien entities—shattering in its consequences if literally true, fascinating in its psychology even if it is not—that seems to be primarily responsible for inaugurating a new era in UFO studies and has triggered the searching reappraisal now under way. Because of its importance, this phenomenon will also be at the center of my own investigation of the UFO-related experiences I examine in this book, and in Chapter 4 we shall have occasion to consider a substantial number of such episodes in detail.

From what I have confessed in my Preface, you will already know a bit about how I myself got sucked into this deepening UFO current against all my previous inclinations and certainly against my conscious desire, and in fairly short order found myself washed onto the shore where I was to meet the man who had quickly become the most famous "abductee" of the modern era, Whitley Strieber.[3] That meeting was, as I have said, the real beginning of the research study I have called the Omega Project, and was to take me along a very different and much stranger route than I had come to know from my previous decade of explorations of the near-death experience.

HEADING TOWARD OMEGA VIA UFO AVENUE

My conversation with Strieber that first day of May served to reinforce my hunch that there were important but heretofore unsuspected similarities to be found between persons who had survived NDEs and those who had endured the kind of UFO trauma that Strieber had described in his book. Strieber himself encouraged me to pursue this line of research and, generously, even offered to be of help by providing me indirect access to a list of many persons who had already written to him in order to relate similar incidents. I would of course need precisely this sort of person for the study that was beginning to take shape in my mind, but it was obvious that before I could begin it, I would have to learn quite a bit more about the field I had so long resisted even hearing anything about—the academically disreputable but now intriguing world of UFO studies, known to its adherents as "ufology."

In fact, even before my meeting with Strieber, I had begun to take my first tentative, and somewhat clandestine, steps into this formerly forbidden domain. A couple of months earlier, I had learned that there was a well-known UFO investigator, Larry Fawcett, the coauthor of a highly regarded book on the problem of government secrecy about UFOs,[4] who lived in a nearby town only a few miles from the university. That semester, as it happened, I was teaching a small seminar that dealt primarily with near-death experiences but did occasionally stray into other exotic subject matter. In any case, after determining that my ever-intrepid students were not adverse to my idea, I called Fawcett and asked him whether he could give a talk to my class on his work. Happily, he readily consented, and though I didn't fully realize it then, I was about to take my first irreversible steps onto UFO Avenue.

Before his presentation, Fawcett had lunch with me and my wife, Barbara, like myself a professor of psychology at the University of Connecticut. As we were both neophytes and Fawcett immensely knowledgeable about the dark world of government secrecy concerning UFOs, he easily held us spellbound throughout lunch. I didn't know what to make of the stories, claims, and rumors he discussed so amiably that afternoon (both at lunch and later in my classroom), but I must have betrayed a deep interest in what Fawcett was saying. As we were concluding our lunch, he gave me a conspiratorial look, smiled, and said, "You're really interested in all this stuff, aren't you?"

Fawcett suggested that because I was especially fascinated with the kind of experiences Strieber had had—what ufologists now call "abduction episodes"—I should get in touch with two friends of his, Bob and Betty Andreasson Luca, both of whom had been subjected to such ordeals. I already knew a little about Betty Luca because Strieber had mentioned her in his book. Betty had been the subject of one of the most extensive and well-publicized UFO investigations in the 1970s, and the first book describing her case, *The Andreasson Affair,* by Raymond Fowler, a well-regarded UFO researcher, had created quite a stir in the UFO community, and to some degree in the public at large, when it was published in 1979. The Lucas—Betty had remarried after the book appeared—lived in Connecticut, Fawcett told me, and suggested that though they were currently no longer active in UFO circles, they might consent to give an informal presentation to my seminar.

Needing no further encouragement, I called them up, and not many weeks afterward, my wife and I again found ourselves at the same restaurant where we had met with Fawcett, this time listening with rapt attention to the story of what had occurred to the Lucas (Bob had also had an experience similar to Betty's, but not quite so extensive) when they were abducted, and to the then-strange tales—involving tapped telephone lines, mysterious black helicopters, bizarre psychokinetic effects, apparent poltergeist incidents, and other anomalies— that had been their lot ever since. I would soon enough hear and read the claims of many such events in the lives of those who have had UFO encounters, but listening to them that day from Bob and Betty, two obviously sincere and thoughtful persons who were as puzzled by what had happened to them as my'wife and I were, had a particularly strong impact on me.

I had long been aware from my studies of NDEs that no book or other indirect source could ever succeed in fully communicating the emotional authenticity and personal compellingness of transcendental experiences. I would, for example, customarily observe in my undergraduate lecture course on NDEs that at the beginning of the semester a number of students, who had at that time only read or listened to me speak about NDEs, would evince an attitude of deep skepticism or at least serious reservation about the reality of these experiences. In the third week of the semester, however, I typically invite two or three near-death experiencers (or NDErs, as I shall call them from now on) to share their stories with the class. Hearing such narratives in person is usually a revelation to these students, and most of them from that point on don't need any further evidence that NDEs are real. But what dissolves the doubt of the doubting Thomases in these classes is not, I think, so much what these NDErs say as it is something about the convincingness of their very presence. Not just their testimony, then, but their way of being and relating to others almost compels one to conclude something like: "I don't really understand what happened to these people, but obviously something very important and profound did; at the very least, I am now sure that they are not making this up."

Something like these thoughts was now my own response as I, somewhat in the role of the skeptical student myself, listened to Bob and Betty describe their lives since their UFO encounters had taken place. After lunch, when my guests came into my class, I could also sense a similar reaction taking shape in my students' minds. Betty is by training an artist, and in recounting her own very detailed and elaborate abduction scenario, she made use of slides she had prepared to illustrate the various stages of her encounter. These were an effective accompaniment to her recitation and made it clear beyond doubt that something indeed very strange—and strangely wonderful in her case—had happened to her and that, furthermore, for her at least, there was no question of its reality.

So it was that by the time I saw Strieber at the beginning of May of that year, I had already, thanks to Larry Fawcett and the Lucas, been induced to tread, if not bravely then at least resignedly, onto UFO Avenue. And once I had definitely resolved to go on this journey, stemming from my meeting with Strieber, things speeded up quickly.

Since I had by then formulated the research project I meant to do pretty clearly, I needed to prepare for my involvement with the field of UFO studies by grounding myself in its literature, and so I plunged into it with alacrity. At the same time, I was making initial telephone and eventual personal contact with a number of leading researchers and writers in ufology, and beginning to attend UFO conferences where not just the formal presentations but also the opportunity for all-night marathon discussions of UFOs and abductions helped to provide me with some of the remedial education I eagerly sought. Before the year was out, I was deeply immersed in the field, had ongoing contact and conversations with many of the investigators and scholars who had come to dominate and helped to shape modern ufology, and had even begun to teach an experimental seminar on UFOs at my university. During this time, as a preliminary aspect of the research I was planning, I was also interviewing various persons who had by then come to my attention and who had undergone bizarre UFO encounters, often of the abduction variety. Still others had begun to write me or send me tapes of their UFO experiences, and in some cases extended phone conversations with these persons were required to discuss aspects of their experiences that were still troubling them.

Eventually, I felt confident enough about my background in ufology to speak on the subject at the conferences I had been attending, and also began to publish articles in the field. I was, to be sure, still the new kid on the UFO block, but at least the people and sights of the neighborhood were becoming more familiar to me, and I no longer felt like a complete stranger there myself. And the more I delved into the varieties of UFO encounters that I was studying, the more convinced I became that my initial intuition was correct: There were hitherto unnoticed links between NDEs and UFO encounters, as well as among the people who were having these experiences.

All I had to do now was to prove that my hunches were not merely in my head. My initial explorations had been completed, and the way was now clear to conduct the research that would show me whether I was onto something. Surprisingly, even the funding for my project was not long in coming, and with it, I was set to begin.

THE OMEGA PROJECT

The Omega Project tells the story of the surprising linkage between NDEs and UFO encounters, and it is a book that I believe many will find full of surprises and unexpected commonalities between persons who have undergone either the one or the other type of experience. The empirical heart of this book is a survey I undertook of such persons. Hundreds of participants in my research filled out an extensive battery of questionnaires that was designed to explore two broad areas: factors that predispose certain individuals to have these experiences in the first place and how they are affected by these encounters. The results of this inquiry, as you will soon read for yourself, are startling, even shocking, and they give us an entirely new understanding of the nature and significance of these encounters, and answer a great many questions about the type of person who is susceptible to them. For what my study shows quite unmistakably is that there is a distinctive psychological profile for the person who is especially likely to report such experiences—*and that it is the same for near-death experiences and those who have UFO encounters.* The findings presented in this book, in fact, make it plausible to suggest that there is what I call *an encounter-prone personality,* a type of individual who is particularly likely to be vulnerable to a variety of extraordinary encounters such as those I have investigated here. This is a book, then, that deals with the psychology of extraordinary encounters and attempts to explain why they tend to happen only to certain people.

But don't be misled into thinking that my study merely attempts to *explain away* these encounters in purely psychological terms. Nothing could be further from my intent or interpretation of my results. *The Omega Project* also considers, you remember, the *effects* of these extraordinary encounters, and just as with NDEs, it is these findings that ultimately reveal their "message" for humanity at large. For what emerges from a study of the aftermath of these experiences, as distinctly as a church bell sounding over the countryside on a quiet Sunday morning, is indeed an intimation of things to come. It has nothing to do with an invasion of flying saucers or even with life after death. It is concerned, instead, with the future evolution of our species and with the fate of our planet. As you will see, the speculations about human evolution—a *psychophysical* evolution—that I advanced in my previous book on NDEs, *Heading Toward Omega,* are supported here, for the first time, with empirical evidence. What I have found is only an indication, a trace in the sand, as it were, but it is enough to suggest that something is indeed happening to us as a species as a result of these extraordinary encounters, and we would do well to mount further studies of their remarkable effects and ponder their meaning even more deeply than I have tried to do here.

Having now reviewed the influences that served to shape this study, as well as having previewed something of its aims and findings, we have but one task left before I can introduce the Omega Project itself. As you will appreciate, a full understanding of the purposes and results of this research is not possible without a certain prior familiarity with the two types of extraordinary experiences that represent our special focus of concern, i.e., UFO encounters and NDEs. Accordingly, as a necessary prologue to the research story to come, the next three chapters will acquaint you with and illustrate the essential features of these two modalities of experience.

CHAPTER 2

VARIETIES OF UFO ENCOUNTERS [1]

*. . . the phenomenon remains obscure, hovering mythically
in a twilight zone between the physical and the psychical,
between space-time objects and dream images, between fact
and fiction, between this world and other worlds. From this
twilight zone UFOs present themselves not simply as a phenomenon to be seen, but as a challenge to all our customary
ways of seeing.*

—Tony Nugent

I . . . heard this loud noise and it woke me up. I turned and
looked at the bedstand and saw the alarm clock [it was 3:00
A.M.]. The sound was a vibration—powerful. The house felt
like it was being pulled off of the foundation. It was very
frightening. . . . I saw a bright orange light going at a very
rapid pace back and forth. Shining on the outside. My heart
sank. . . . My daughter cried out, "What is it, Mom?" . . .
The light came back, the house just shook. I have never
been so frightened.

My first experience happened in . . . Alaska. In the back of
my grade school. I saw a moose at the top of a hill, so instead of walking home, I investigated the moose. When I
got to the top of the hill and into the woods, I couldn't see
the moose, but instead saw a shiny, metallic round craft. I
then found myself inside somehow and saw two seats and a
control panel of colorful, festive lights. I sat down and then

heard footsteps behind me. A being with large eyes and about four feet tall telepathically said, "Do not be afraid," and I wasn't. He took my hand and took me to a chair in another room and sat me down and flashed different colored lights over my head and telepathically repeated, "Remember the light." When that was done, he led me to the control panel and I sat down and suddenly I saw the tops of the trees, then I saw the earth, and it was so beautiful. I did not want to return. We came back to the same spot as we left, and then I found myself outside the craft, and I walked home and excitedly told my mother that I had seen a moose!

I awakened from a dream or what I thought was a dream. Under hypnosis . . . I recalled being taken aboard a spacecraft. I was on a surgery table in a well-lit round laboratory-type room. I was paralyzed—couldn't move anything but my head. The encounter was terrifying. I have some real concern—fear [and] anger about whether they [the entities] have the right to do that without our consent.

The foremost fact about UFO encounters, as these accounts from Omega Project participants demonstrate unequivocally, is their variety. As a class of experiences, they will quickly be seen to cover an enormous range both in *types* of encounters and in subjective *reactions* to them. Where type of encounter is concerned, for example, the spectrum extends from simple sightings of an anomalous, inexplicable light in the sky to seemingly preposterous forms of apparent alien-human contact. Reactions to these perceptions and events are similarly diverse and run from excited and positive feelings of attraction through perplexed but lively curiosity to the most anguished expressions of terror. The *quality* of the experience is likewise variable: Sometimes the encounter seems distinctly dreamlike, even hallucinatory; in other cases, it has the character of an actual physical event, seemingly as real as a clod of earth held in one's hand. Adding still further to the aura of ambiguity surrounding these encounters are the conditions governing their recall: In many instances, the experience is remembered spontaneously and without difficulty; in others, it only surfaces when it is apparently cued off by a stimulus that serves as a vivid reminder; in still others, the encounter is only recalled, and often with great emotional upheaval, with the aid of hypnosis, where, as is well known, confabulation can easily occur.

For all these dimensions of variability in UFO encounters, however, there are certain fairly typical features concerning their general character and the context in which they tend to occur in a person's life. Of these, the following four will be of particular interest to us here.

First, there is, not surprisingly, often an eerie quality associated with these encounters. For example, there may be an anticipatory sense that something unusual is about to occur. In some instances of this kind, there may be a distinct feeling that one is being looked at or is already under a vague yet disconcerting kind of surveillance. The onset of the encounter itself is often marked by an unusual alteration in consciousness—almost as though one has been swept up into some sort of a time-space warp where the ordinary boundaries of reality have been temporarily breached. Furthermore, inexplicable events may not only occur in connection with the encounter, but follow it as well, adding still more to one's sense that something truly incredible has indeed just taken place.

Second, a surprisingly high proportion of first encounters are reported to occur in early childhood. The age of five is the most often spontaneously mentioned time of life from which these episodes are retrospectively dated.

Third, these encounters, whatever their form, tend not to intrude only once into a person's life. Instead, multiple encounters are the rule. Moreover, such encounters for any given individual do not necessarily adhere to any single type; here, too, variation is more common than not.

Fourth and finally, UFO encounters frequently take place within a personal context that is already or soon becomes rich with other anomalous events. That is to say, a person who reports a UFO episode is also likely to have had other odd things happen to him or her as well. Thus, the UFO encounter is not typically an isolated kind of occurrence in an individual's life;

instead, it appears to be part of a larger pattern of unusual experiences, often of a psychic nature.

From what I have said so far about UFO incidents, you may already at this point be inclined either to discount the meaningfulness of these experiences or to question the mental health of those who report them. If so, I would caution you that such a quick judgment, though understandable, will in the face of further facts we have yet to consider turn out to be insupportable. For it will be evident, as we will shortly see, that underlying this extraordinarily diverse array of difficult-to-credit perceptions there seems to be a genuine *phenomenon* as robustly consistent as it is inexplicable. Not just "believers" in UFOs, but skeptical and in some cases even hostile scientists and scholars who have taken the trouble to sift through this set of reports, have in most instances found themselves willing to concede that, whatever UFOs themselves may be, there is unquestionably a cause for these encounters that cannot be reduced merely to the vagaries of human psychology.

Of course, it has long been known that UFO sightings themselves have sometimes been found to be unmistakably correlated with radar signals, that in some instances careful analysis of photographic evidence supports their existence, that apparent electromagnetic disturbances sometimes occur when UFOs are seen over the affected area, and that not infrequently an alleged UFO leaves definite and otherwise puzzling physical traces on the ground that can be subjected to scientific measurement. Yet all that evidence notwithstanding, there is still reason to believe that the kind of UFO encounters that will be of especial concern to us in this book reflect a factor that cannot cavalierly be dismissed as only some sort of aberration of minds under stress. And this has to do with the fact that, despite all the variations we have been at pains to make clear, there is still a distinctive and undeniably meaningful *patterning* to these experiences. Thus, beyond the distracting and confused hum of human idiosyncrasy, one seems nevertheless to discern the voice of a phenomenon that is, against all our modern prejudices, finally succeeding in making itself heard.

Toward what end is, of course, the major conundrum we will be struggling to answer throughout this book.

Now, however, in order to piece together the pattern that I
have implied is inherent in these encounters, we need to begin
to listen to the testimony of the persons who have actually
undergone them. All of the excerpts to follow in this chapter
come from the written statements of persons who took part in
my research project, and none of them has been published previously. To protect the anonymity of my respondents, however, pseudonyms are used where necessary. In covering the
full range of these encounters, it will be convenient to start
with instances of UFO sightings and then to follow a progression that will lead us, by the next chapter, into accounts of
what appear to be episodes of full-blown abductions of the kind
that Whitley Strieber's *Communion* made so familiar to modern
readers.

UFO SIGHTINGS

Melvin Page was a thirteen-year-old newspaper boy in Ohio when
he had an experience that erupted into his youthful consciousness with a shattering intensity. It was still dark on the morning
of May 12, 1967, when Melvin started his route on his bicycle.
He comments that though it was seemingly an ordinary morning, he felt somewhat strange and even had the curious feeling
that he was being followed while making his deliveries. Nevertheless, his morning passed uneventfully—until toward the end
of his route he approached a certain apartment. "To this day,"
he comments, "I can go to this one building, for I will never
forget it." Reading his full account, one easily understands why.

> I walked up on the porch and placed their paper inside the
> screen door. As I turned to step off the porch, I looked
> down at the ground. This is when I noticed that I was stand-
> ing in a circle of light. At this point, I thought I was just
> tired. I rubbed my eyes and stepped down to the sidewalk.
> My bike was approximately twenty feet away on the main
> sidewalk. I took several steps and stopped. I'm not sure
> why, I just stopped. Again, I looked down. Again, I was
> standing in a circle of light. The circle of light (white) was

probably about 10–15 feet across. I knew I wasn't right. I thought maybe I was dreaming. Then I seemed to hear this very slight humming type of sound. It was just barely audible. Then I looked up! There it was!!!!

There was this huge round disc hovering above the apartment I just walked away from. I took several more steps. The disc followed me! It wasn't any more than 25–35 feet above my head. When I stopped in the middle of the sidewalk (halfway between the apartment and my bike) the disc moved directly overhead. It had different colored lights that flashed on and off in a circular motion; clockwise I think, very rapidly. The bottom part of this disc seemed to have a lowered circular portion in the center. This was where the lights were. I'm not sure how large the entire disc may have been. I may have only seen a portion of it, I'm just not able to recall for sure.

About the time the disc became motionless, I found that I wasn't able to move my body. I've always assumed this was due to pure fear. By this time I was totally terrified. My entire body went totally numb. After this point, I can't remember much at all. I don't know how long I stood there. I had no sense of time. The next thing I do remember is a sensation of feeling returning to my body. I was able to think how terrified I was again. I could move my arms and legs again! Oddly enough, I was still looking up.

All of a sudden, the disc moved slightly side to side. Quietly! This was all it took! I burned rubber to my bike!! As I looked back up to the sky, the disc was rising straight up (I think). It stopped for a moment. (I can't even guess the height from the ground.) All of a sudden it shot up somewhat in a northwestern direction at a 45-degree angle up to the heavens. It disappeared from sight within seconds. To say the least, I went home totally terrified. I don't even remember if I finished my route.

Wayne Heald was only nine when he had his UFO encounter, but, as with Melvin, he, too, was terrified. Here is his story:

Attending summer camp in Virginia, I awoke late one night—in a screened-in (no windows) cabin—to a series of flashing lights on the ceiling of the cabin. Sitting up in bed, I turned to my right and saw a smallish, bell-shaped craft on the ground no more than 25 feet away. A strobelike series of lights flashed with an almost vacuum-producing speed—red, green, yellow, white. I was absolutely terrified. I was certain my face had been seen through the screen mesh. Covering my head with the bedsheet I forced myself to remain as still as stone for fear that if I moved one muscle they would hear it and "capture" me. Although I did not once see any being or intelligence, I was apprehended by an overwhelming sense of presence—one which seemed malevolent at the time but in retrospect was probably a nine-year-old's natural reaction.

I have a perfect recollection [Wayne is now thirty] of an awake state during this episode. I recall the measured breathing of the four other kids sleeping in the room with me. I remember the cold air on my shoulders, the strange sound (or lack of it) coming from outside. I do not remember falling back asleep, and in fact have always considered it amazing that I should have done so under the intensity of the moment.

The next morning I made a terrible fuss with the camp counselors over their disbelief and demanded to speak to the owners of the camp about my experience. They allowed me to, and the owners had me call my parents who calmed me down. That was the end of it.

Of course, not all UFO encounters are harrowing, and neither are they only reported by single individuals who alone see a UFO. Many sightings in fact are associated with *positive feelings* and are witnessed by more than one person. To illustrate such an instance, consider next this report of a forty-year-old college graduate:

> My ex-husband and I were driving from Boulder, Colorado to Lamar, Colorado where we were living at the time. We were just a few miles south out of La Junta at approximately 7:30 to 8:00 A.M. when we both observed an object to the left of the road at about 350 yards from us S.E. We pulled off to the side of the road where the object was (a barbed-wire fence obstructed us from moving any further toward it). We stopped our VW and just looked at the object. I mentally gave a "greeting" but don't know why. The object was approximately 350 to 400 feet up in the air and at least the size of a football field. The object was elliptical in shape and its exterior looked to be a bright metallic gold or platinum. No movement emanated from the object and there were no windows or lights which we could see.
>
> No clouds were in the sky at this time and I might add the sky was very blue. At no time did we feel we were in danger, but we did get a very vivid impression that whatever we were looking at was watching us in return. About 30–35 minutes passed. All of a sudden a few scattered, very white little clouds appeared. Then one large, massive very white cloud came in from the west traveling east over the object. When the large cloud passed over the object, the object was gone as though it was never there.
>
> On the way to Lamar, after the incident, a feeling of calm and peacefulness came over me that I have never experienced before or since.

A psychotherapist from Massachusetts describes a very similar reaction to a UFO she and her husband witnessed:

> I was with my husband. It was in the early evening. There were three glowing balls (large) side by side, 200 feet from the ground. We stopped the car, and I felt a deep urge to be

near them! So I went to where they were, just directly underneath, it seemed. There was no physical sensation. Only a profound, transcendent feeling of "I know you"—of peace, brotherhood, and that they were there for me. There was telepathic communication, which later in deep meditation was revealed again. Having to do with our joint cooperative mission, in service to the planet, and more.

To this point, though I have presented only four brief narratives, you may already have noted some suggestive correlates. For example, the scary UFO incidents were both recounted by small boys (though both are now of course grown men), whereas the positive encounters came from adult women. Lest you think these differences are significant, however, I had best disabuse you now: As you might well suppose, little girls can also sometimes be frightened by UFO encounters, and mature men can be strangely comforted by them. In a word, there is no necessary correlation between the age and gender of respondents, on the one hand, and the type of reaction they may have to seeing a UFO, on the other.

In the following case of a joint sighting of a UFO, a woman and her husband had a similarly strong response to their experience as well as comparable aftereffects. But while this narrator's remarks echo the deep positive feelings that we have encountered in our last two instances, the incident she describes adds something new to these accounts, i.e., *visual and photographic evidence* of actual physical deformations at the alleged site of the UFO.

Hazel Underwood is a fifty-three-year-old college-educated owner and manager of a radio station in Georgia. Like the last two reports, her account also contains reference to confirmatory observations by her husband, but here there was other corroborative testimony as well, which, as we shall now see, was what led her and her husband to have their own life-altering experience during the summer of 1987.

On the morning of July 14 of that year, Hazel received a call at her radio station from a woman who claimed that she, her husband, her sister, and *her* husband had all had a vivid close encounter the previous evening after returning home from a country picnic. The caller informed Hazel that in the field where the UFO had been sighted, "there are three areas where the grass has been mashed down." Intrigued, Hazel decided to conduct her own on-site investigation. A few hours later, in the early afternoon, she and her husband, having taken their cameras, arrived on the scene. Observing the field for themselves, they saw:

> . . . three rectangular depressions in the grass. My husband stepped each area off. . . . The first was 9 x 9, the center depression was 9 x 12 and the rear depression was also 9 x 9. He also stepped off the distance from the front to the rear of the depression and it measured 69 feet. We both got our cameras and took pictures. After the pictures we made we could see that the formerly bright green grass was a light lavender in the depressed areas. On all sides of these areas and in between these "landing pods," which I decided to call them, the grass was still green and waist high.

Not knowing anything about UFOs I had the feeling that "it" would come back again and somehow I knew exactly where I had to be to see it. We live near the Savannah River and there is a bluff about one-half mile from the river where the trees had been clear cut about two years before. I "knew" that if we went to that spot *that* night, Tuesday, July 14, we would see it. I don't know how I knew where to go, but I did.

[Later that evening] we drove to the river. . . . As we neared the bluff the truck passed behind a clump of bushes that partially obscured my vision. But out of the back side of my right eye I saw a huge red light coming over the bluff. I told my husband, "Back up, cut your engine and cut your lights." There it was, a quarter mile away. It came over the bluff just at tree top level and was moving as smoothly as a bird. No sound, no engine, no wings, and moving at about the speed of a bird. It was a huge object with a large red light at the front, a big red light in the center, and another large red light on the end. It was cylindrical in shape, or so it appeared from the side. When you see something like that, it's so awe-inspiring you literally go blank. We didn't think to grab the cameras out of the truck when we got out, and neither of us said one word to the other. We just stood there and watched it. It did have about 8 or 10 small white lights underneath the center belly of the craft and while we were watching it there was a blue-green emission from the center of this group of lights that lasted for just a few seconds.

As it flew over the bluff and flew slowly past us, I was seized by the impulse to try and follow it. I turned and ran down that unpaved, unlighted road in the Savannah River swamp trying to keep up with this object. I had tears in my eyes and I did not even realize that I was running until it hit me that there was no way I could ever keep up with it. Then, suddenly, every light went out at once, like you had flipped a switch, and it just vanished with no sound at all. My husband and I both felt more calm and peaceful looking at that craft than we ever have at any time before. It has changed my outlook on life. . . . My husband says that he feels as I do.

The foregoing accounts are sufficient, I think, to convey a sense of the numinous, and indeed sometimes frightening, power that a UFO sighting can have on its beholders. Certainly not always, but often enough, such an encounter compels extreme emotions and elicits either an almost trancelike fascination or a paralysis of terror. In either case, the witness is held virtually spellbound in the grip of a truly awesome, mind-numbing spectacle.

Not only is one's consciousness profoundly altered by such a sighting, but both before its onset and after its usually mysterious disappearance, one's mind and sense of self-awareness may be far from normal as well. We have already had some clear hints of the peculiar disturbances of mood and perception that may precede and accompany these sightings, so it remains

MONTROSE REGIONAL LIBRARY
320 SO. 2ND ST.
MONTROSE, CO 81401

only to give a few brief examples of their sometimes equally strange aftermath to complete the picture.

One of the most commonly reported aberrancies following UFO encounters is a period of "missing time"—that is, an interval of time for which one appears to be amnesiac. For example, a forty-five-year-old attorney stated that following his seeing a fearful light in the sky (which he is now convinced was a UFO) while driving in his automobile, he found that he had arrived at his destination inexplicably two to two-and-a-half hours late. "I couldn't account for the missing time," he comments. Another respondent, this one a thirty-six-year-old college graduate, described a puzzling UFO encounter one evening at her farm that was witnessed by a visiting friend, herself, and their two children. They were alerted to something unusual by the frantic barking of her dog, and all of them saw a brilliant white light ascending over some nearby trees. Though it was a cold January night, they all raced out to see what now appeared to her, and seemingly to the others, to be a small ship marked by pulsating pastel colors. "During this time," the woman mentions in her narrative, "I felt such an incredible connection— like they were communicating something." Afterward, they all went back into the house, talking about what they had seen, and started to draw pictures of it.

> We looked at the clock and it was ten minutes of ten. The next thing we knew, Romi [one of the children] started talking about how she felt like she was coming out of a meditation—another consciousness—[while] I was fixed on the white light that was from the lamp reflecting off the window pane. We looked at the clock and Jason [another child] said it was ten minutes of twelve. Two hours had elapsed—and we all do not know what we did.

The general literature on UFO encounters, as is well known, is replete with such stories as these featuring a missing-time motif.

Time disturbances, however, are far from the only anomalies to occur in the wake of a UFO sighting. Unusual incidents, bizarre encounters with other human beings, and peculiar electrical or electromagnetic effects may also be part of the pattern afterward, suggestive that the distinctive spell cast by the perception of a UFO may linger even after the apparent object itself vanishes. A case in point was furnished by a thirty-eight-year-old woman with a Ph.D. in neuroscience.

She and her sister were driving near Boston when they both observed an unusually lit flying object. They stopped to take photographs, and while they were parked:

> . . . we met (only I remember this) a man who acted very strangely. My sister saw the object speed away rapidly after I took the photo (but I didn't notice this). It is possible that both of us could have a memory gap. We followed the object for quite a while trying to figure out what it was. A truck driver followed us in a harassing manner for a while. There was a green light in our car twice. On the night after this experience there seemed to be some odd activity in my apartment. My alarm clock kept going off even though I didn't set it. There were noises and an object flew across the room.

The nature of these alleged events may, of course, push your tolerance for weirdness beyond its limits, and you may therefore elect to believe that this woman, Ph.D. or not, is either describing things that just couldn't possibly have happened or that there is a prosaic explanation for what actually did happen. At this point, however, it might be prudent to suspend one's judgment here, because what is *really* peculiar is just how frequently events like these are described by other respondents, as we will later see. Could they *all* be self-deluded or otherwise mistaken? Or is the world of UFO-related phenomena simply stranger than we might suppose?

Before we can even address questions like these, of course, we need a great deal more information—and that, to be sure, will be forthcoming in later chapters. For now, it is enough to note that the examples I have given here of UFO sightings, all provided by well-educated respondents, are fairly typical of the thousands of such cases that are to be found in the general literature of ufology. What these observations may represent is still an open question, but the fact of their occurrence, and in great numbers, can no longer be doubted by anyone who takes the trouble to examine the body of evidence patiently collected over many years by UFO investigators.

For us, however, there is now only one further point about these encounters that especially deserves our notice. As we have seen, several of these narratives state or imply that the witness had a strong sense of an intelligence or a presence associated with the UFO (or lights) he or she saw. In some cases, there was a distinct feeling that there was "a something" with which one was already in communication. Yet (apart from the excerpts presented to open this chapter), in the cases we have reviewed, nothing—certainly no human or other being—was ever definitively described that would directly support such inferences.

But of course you must remember that we are only at the beginning of our exploration of the variety of UFO encounters. What comes next confirms what our previous accounts have only hinted at, and thereby confronts us with an entirely new and even more baffling kind of UFO-related episode.

CLOSE ENCOUNTERS OF THE THIRD KIND

In studying UFO encounters, it is a natural step to move from instances where a presence is only implied to those where a nonhuman being of some kind is actually seen. In ufology such cases are known as *close encounters of the third kind,* a term originally proposed by the father of modern ufology, J. Allen Hynek, but of course made famous by the popular 1977 Steven Spielberg film of the same name. Again, the general UFO literature of the last two decades is full of accounts of such seemingly wild tales, though by now their sheer numbers alone suggest that, whatever such perceptions may represent, they are something other than the products of mere imagining.

Our respondents, too, report such incidents, and we will sample just a few of them here so that their distinctive features will be clear. As with sightings, this kind of close encounter can take place even in a young child's world, so we will again start with some examples where children are involved.

When Lori Demara—who like Hazel Underwood is now a college-educated radio-station manager—was about five years old, she recalls a strange incident taking place in an open field:

> I remember standing in the middle of the huge spiral my dad had mowed in a field for me. I was looking up. A bright metal craft came straight down. Next thing I remember is a small white creature (man?) talking to me. He had huge black eyes and was bald. He talked to me about my destiny which was related to cleaning up [the] earth's environment. Then I was walking back to my home.

Helen Martinez was also five when she had her first close encounter. In her case, however, she does not mention the actual presence of a UFO. Nevertheless, as we shall see, in some of her subsequent experiences, a UFO clearly precedes her seeing a nonhuman creature.

> I was sleeping in [a] bottom bunk bed [and] was awakened when I felt the presence of something standing next to me. It was a short grey-white being with a large head leaning over me. I then blanked out.

A more extended childhood episode, with a curious confirmatory coda, was provided by Lisa Terrell, now a forty-one-year-old illustrator with a college degree. In the summer of 1959, when Lisa was nine, her family went to Germany in order to visit an abandoned castle that had once belonged to her ancestors. While there, following a picnic, Lisa happened to enter some nearby woods. Not long after, she sensed she was under surveillance:

> I began to have a sense of being watched. I suddenly found myself face to face with a strange being. He was about my height, luminous and wearing what appeared to be a lumi-

nous reflective suit without seams. He had a triangular face with large cat-like eyes. I had the sense that he was surprised I could see him or had found him. Also, I had the sense that he was a scientist and had been examining plants or something. I'm not sure how I got these impressions, but I did. I had the sense of a great intelligence and a curious neutral nature. I also had the sense that something about me surprised him. I call him a "he" [though] I don't know what gave me that impression as he was devoid of any sexual characteristics. He also seemed mature, not a child even though he was my height.

I'm not sure exactly what I felt—wonder, fear, curiosity, and a sense of looking into something I wasn't supposed to know about. After that, everything went blank, though the vague impression of many lights remains. The next thing I remember is being back with my family and feeling very strange. The family get-together proceeded with boisterous singing, but I felt weird and found it difficult to participate. I was frightened by the experience, but told no one. I was terrified of telling my mother, who often accused me of being overly imaginative.

For a week after this encounter, Lisa was plagued by dreadful nightmares and other disturbances. She remembers becoming more psychic and entering spontaneously into what she simply calls "altered states of consciousness." Altogether during this period, she says that "I felt I was in a different reality." Finally, with the arrival of her grandmother a week following the incident, Lisa felt herself returning to her normal state. Her relatives convinced her that she had been sick and had been hallucinating. In 1988, however, she learned otherwise:

A year ago I was talking to my brother, Henry. We brought up the castle in the conversation and I said that something very weird had happened to me that afternoon. To my shock, Henry said, "You mean the little monkeylike creature?" I didn't know he had seen it. He apparently suppressed the memory until I referred to a weird incident at the castle. That statement triggered the following memory: He and my other brother, Tim, decided to catch up with me after I left the group (Henry was 5 and Tim was 3). Henry saw me above the path on an embankment. He also saw the profile of a strange little creature like a monkey wearing a white suit. It was peering at me. His impression of the creature was that it was sinister. He said he saw it take me away. After that he doesn't remember anything.

The last case involving a child was actually narrated by his mother, who, along with her husband, also saw some diminutive creatures, this time clearly in conjunction with the landing of a UFO. This incident took place in September 1976, when she was twenty-three and her son just three years of age. The mother, a college graduate, reports it with what seems a curious matter-of-factness despite her obvious emotion at the time.

We were living on a 3-acre wooded tract of land. House faced a clearing, was bordered by a bayou. "Ship" (circular with lights) landed in clearing. My son ran out to play (beings were about his size; he was 3 at the time). I was terrified; my husband was curious. They wanted to take my son; they said he's smart. My husband said no, but they could visit. They've been back twice to "check" it out. My son is indeed smart—psychological testing puts him at near-genius level. We don't speak much of this to him except when he asks questions.

Beings were about 3 to 3 and ½ feet high, spindly fingers, but soft, and skin was wrinkly like a SharPei puppy. They didn't seem to have any awareness of clothes, and they didn't seem overly curious about us. The nearest I can describe it is the ones looking at my son were like a disinterested doctor doing a medical exam.

As the preceding narrative illustrates, these small UFO-connected creatures are seen by adults as well as children, and as the last two cases suggest, these beings are difficult to dismiss as mere hallucinations since they are collectively perceived. Still another instance of a jointly witnessed close encounter of the diminutive kind was furnished by Hank Reed, a thirty-one-year-old construction worker living in Michigan.

One night in the fall of 1979, Hank and his then-girlfriend (now his wife), Glenda, were parked on a deserted dead-end road, necking. It was pitch-black, about 3:00 to 3:30 A.M., when they were both startled by the sudden appearance of what first seemed to be a car. Since a car could not have driven by them, as Hank's own car was blocking the end of the road, they couldn't believe their eyes at first. Gradually, however, they discerned that it was not a car that was parked there, but a bell-shaped craft of some kind that was furthermore giving off a definite, somewhat eerie, light. Hank and Glenda were now huddled together in stark fear, Hank trying to calm his frantic girlfriend. In a few moments, they both saw something stranger still, and I will quote here only a brief description of what it was:

> The most extraordinary encounter was of a small individual approximately 3 and ½ to 4 feet in height and who had a very much human-like form. However, the head seemed to be slightly larger in proportion to the rest of the body. It was wearing a snug-fitting body suit and was holding in one hand what looked like a small metallic pail.

Supplementing Hank's written account of this incident is a much more extensive version on cassette tape. His genuine puzzlement over, and the sincerity of his plain-spoken oral rendition of, this event would, I'm sure, be obvious to any listener.

As we sample these cases, the similarities in exactly *what* is perceived begin to mount, and a general scenario of sorts emerges. Before I try to sketch out this pattern, however, we need to consider two last cases here, each of which will provide some additional important details. The first one involves an encounter of a woman, now thirty-six, which contains an odd set of parallels to that of Lisa Terrell, whose story we presented earlier in this section.

At the time of her episode, however, Laurie Watkins was a good deal older than Lisa. She had in fact just turned twenty, but like Lisa, she was out in the woods, camping with some friends. They were on the outskirts of Laurie's hometown in New York on a warm August night, laughing and talking. Finally, around midnight, Laurie and her friends decided to turn in.

> I remember going to sleep around midnight or a bit after. About 1 and ½ hours later I remember feeling frightened (we were camping under the stars—no tents—just a tarp for the ground and sleeping bags). I felt something was near us. I felt very, very frightened. I saw between 6–10 figures walking near us. They were walking (floating) on a very slight incline. They were small (about the size of a 2–3 year old). They were greyish-silver (skin color) with very large heads, incredibly large black eyes, small mouths. They were wearing something like a long greyish garment (I can't remember seeing feet). I remember one of them came toward me. He— I felt it was a male—came as close as to stretching out his hand to touch my face and shoulder. I felt at this point that I was so entirely paralyzed by fear that I was going to die. It is very hard to control your body and mind in that state. I really wanted to die at that point (or forget). I remember another being motioning *not* to touch me. I think it sensed my fear would have caused me harm (physical)—dying. . . . Then they began to move away from us. They were near my friend Nancy, too.

> I didn't talk, but Nancy after a few minutes said, "Oh shit." I didn't speak. After a few minutes I said, "Nancy, are you okay?" She said, "I had this horrible dream." I said, "Me, too," and we *never* spoke of it—until 4 years later.

> We both had gone to visit our families during Easter. . . . I called Nancy and asked if she'd like to visit. She came over—

we chatted, laughed, caught up on our lives. . . . Then, I finally said to her, "Nancy, what did you see in your dream?" She began to explain what she saw and I couldn't believe it! Her dream/encounter(?) was the same as mine. She explained their size, physical features. I think we laughed out of nervousness.

Our last case takes us back to another episode in the life of the child, Helen Martinez, whose first close encounter, when she was about five, I cited briefly toward the beginning of this section. It is now six years later and, like a modern Orpheus, Helen is about to be tested in the UFO netherworld:

I was standing in my grandparents' backyard during the day with my cousin. The sky was overcast. Behind a cloud we saw a silver disc, which put out a beam of light down toward us. A small being came from around the garage. He was small and grey-white in color and also had on a uniform. Next thing I remember I'm inside a craft. There's a humming sound in my head. I'm being led down a corridor. There is a metal grating on my right. I keep thinking, I'll be all right if I don't look at their faces. But I do look.

Unfortunately, Helen's narrative abruptly leaves off here, so we never learn the consequences of her peering at the faces of the beings she found herself with or about what happened next. However, since Helen was obviously alive in order to report these childhood encounters in the first place, we can be sure that she survived her youthful ordeal! In fact, Helen's form provides abundant information that she has continued to have peculiar experiences throughout her life, some of them seemingly with UFO motifs, with the last one occurring as recently as 1988.

Nevertheless, Helen's second encounter, as well as some of the other cases we've reviewed in this section, gives us ample hints concerning what we might well come to expect if these episodes were to continue the dramatic course that only begins with the sighting of the diminutive beings who give these incidents their distinctive flavor. Before we try to anticipate this narrative line, however, let me take a moment to sum up some of the recurrent features of these close encounters we should be sure to keep in mind.

First, there is the matter of the creatures themselves. Despite the variety of ages, circumstances, and personal reactions of the witnesses, their descriptions of the appearance of these beings are remarkably uniform. They are invariably said to be small in size, like children, and, where we have more detail, usually characterized as having big, prominent black eyes in a head that may, like a fetus's, be disproportionately large in relation to the body. In coloration, they are usually said to be either white or gray or grayish-white, and they appear to affect tight, formfitting suits like uniforms.

Similarly, there is a consistency with respect to the *behavior* of these creatures. Typically, they tend to impress the observer as somewhat detached, sometimes almost clinical—"like a disinterested doctor," said one of our respondents. And though their appearance may cause the witness to feel naked terror, they do not seem to be malevolent, as in the case of Laurie Watkins when she felt that one of the creatures acted to protect her from further fright. Instead, they just seem to go about whatever their unknown business is, and may even be startled by the unexpected encounter with a human in their midst.

Of course, to anyone hearing this for the first time, it is risible and sounds patently absurd. But, on reflection, the very fact that there is such consistency in these descriptions—especially in view of the extreme emotions these encounters usually engender—is *prima facie* evidence that *something* other than idiosyncratic perception under stress is involved. The additional fact that these creatures are sometimes seen by multiple witnesses, even when the latter may not be aware of their shared experience at the time of the original sighting itself, bolsters this argument still more.

Indeed, there is even stronger support for this position than I have so far mentioned. If one looks beyond the few examples of close encounters that I have provided from my own research to the much vaster UFO literature dealing with them, one soon finds *hundreds* of cases where such creatures have been described.[2] To be sure, the widespread incidence of these reports—which come from many parts of the globe—doesn't in itself compel any one interpretation of these encounters, but it does at least suggest that there is certainly a phenomenon that stands in need of explanation.

Second, there is the behavior of the witnesses themselves to consider. For one thing, I have already commented on the powerful emotions that these encounters arouse—understandably enough if you were for a moment to imagine that an event like this happened to you in a subjectively undeniable fashion. But while the emotional quality of these encounters for the witnesses is self-evident, there is another important feature of their accounts that is easy to overlook. And because this is something that may in the end prove crucial for our interpretation of these episodes, we need to linger over it for a moment here. It is the matter of the gap.

In reviewing many close-encounter and UFO-sighting cases—and not just those presented for illustration in this chapter—one soon notices evidence of peculiar discontinuities. These are indicated by such expressions as "the next thing I knew," or "what I remember next," or "suddenly I found myself," or "and then I blanked out," and so on. The use of such bridging phrases is of course open to several interpretations, but one of them would be that these experiences may be *inherently discontinuous* rather than linearly unfolding events. However that may be, the very structure of these UFO stories is itself reminiscent of other narrative forms with which we are already familiar.

Think, for example, of fairy tales with their charming use of the devices of discontinuity for literary effect. Or, perhaps closer to everyone's nocturnal home, consider dreams. The quick shifts of scene, the piling up of incongruities, the distortion of time, and all the other strange facets of our dream life that each of us knows so well are suggestively similar to the narrative form of UFO tales.

Am I suggesting, then, that these UFO accounts are nothing more than dreams that may occur in the absence of sleep?

Hardly. Rather, they seem more like dreams that one has *awakened into* and that, in some unknown way, have come to interpenetrate ordinary reality, resulting in a kind of double vision, which, eventually, returns to normal. But if this is some species of dream, it is far from those we are familiar with, because at the very least it would then have to be some sort of *collective dream* since many people are reporting similar, and similarly bizarre, encounters.

Clearly, there are deep enigmas here, and it is far too early in our inquiry to think that we may be even close to unraveling them. All the same, it will prove useful to remain aware that there may be *some kind* of connection between the structure of dreams and fairy tales on the one hand, and UFO narratives on the other—even if we cannot yet say exactly what it is.

With these considerations in mind, we are now ready to return to the issue of the narrative line these close encounters of the third kind imply. From a dramaturgical point of view, it seems clear enough that they represent the phase of the *initial encounter with the alien*. There has been a drastic rupture in the plane of ordinary reality, and one experiences a momentous ontological shock wave. The glimpse of the alien promises more shocks to come, the continuation of an unknown undertaking that is only signaled by the sight of the alien. And we have already had hints in the accounts we have reviewed in this chapter of what may follow. The alien, "like a disinterested doctor doing a medical exam," threatens to take one away into his world for his own arcane purposes. The witness who first sees a riveting light in the sky, and next beholds a wondrously multicolored craft, and then, finally, catches sight of an alien creature, has already been psychologically prepared for the next stage of his adventure: the inevitable ascent into the UFO overworld—the space-age version of the perennial hero's journey.

CHAPTER 3

CLOSE ENCOUNTERS OF THE FOURTH KIND

Among the Buryat the shamanic apprentice is visited by the Utcha, his shamanic ancestors. They take his soul to heaven and place it before the assembly of the Saajtani, who torment him in a horrible fashion, poking around his belly with knives, cutting whole chunks of flesh off him, and throwing them about. During these tortures the shaman can hear his heart beat, but his breath subsides and his skin becomes dark blue. The spirits cook his flesh to "ripen" it. The initiate acquires his inner knowledge during this procedure and becomes conversant with the rules of shamanic wisdom.

—Holgar Kalweit

. . . aboriginal shamans have a powerful and consistent tradition of ritualistic initiation, the elements of which bear amazing similarities to many modern-day UFO abductions and contact accounts.

—Bill Chalker

After contact comes the journey. It is, in most cases, an almost archetypal *journey of initiation* with its familiar invariant triadic sequence: separation, ordeal, and return. In the UFO literature, the stage of separation is usually called *abduction,* since in the main (though, to be sure, not always) the individual feels that he is suddenly taken away against his will or certainly at the very least without his consent and without warning. He is, then, spirited away—an old-fashioned but oddly apposite phrase—to an utterly unfamiliar world where he is subjected to a kind of ritual inspection and testing that has an obvious, if sometimes rather distant, kinship to the dismemberment motifs in traditional shamanic initiations. In the context of the UFO journey, this stage of the experience is usually referred to as *the examination,* and has the form of a medical probe of the sort that you might imagine would take place only in second-rate science fiction. The final stage of the journey, *the return,* usually to the same physical location, is often marked by feelings of confusion, disorientation, time loss, and memory impairment, but there is also ordinarily the sense, however dimly apprehended, that something extraordinary has happened that will leave a lasting imprint on one's life. In modern ufology, stories with this narrative structure, which have now become rife, are called *close encounters of the* fourth *kind.*

Such encounters, for some, have a dreamlike quality, though experiencers often put the word *dream* in quotation marks or otherwise imply that to label it a dream does not do justice either to the vividness of the episode or to its psychological impact. Others may recall the experience only with the aid of hypnosis, during which strong emotions and apparently long-suppressed memories may surface. Still others, however, remember the events of their abduction from the start without the need of any prompts or inductions. Here it is important to note that whether the abduction is recalled as a dream, or through hypnosis, or spontaneously, *the nature of the episode is identical.* Through careful comparisons between those who remember their encounter directly and individuals whose accounts have come from hypnotic sessions, it has been established that there are essentially no substantive differences between these two groups of respondents.[1] Therefore, though UFO investigators often do use hypnotic techniques to elicit and explore close encounters of the fourth kind, these procedures in themselves cannot be said to *create* these stories in the first place. In short, there are plenty of cases where persons spontaneously relate UFO abductions in the same manner as those who have been hypnotized.

Where do these encounters take place? Many seem to occur in a dreamlike context or when an individual appears to be awakened from sleep by a nonhuman nocturnal intruder. Perhaps surprisingly, such encounters are not infrequently retrospectively reported by young children, who assert that their first experience (many individuals, as I have said, claim to have had multiple experiences of this kind) took place around the age of five. Since such instances are numerous in my own research, it seems appropriate that we begin our survey of these encounters by drawing on these narratives.

CLOSE ENCOUNTERS OF THE FOURTH KIND IN CHILDREN

We shall begin with several examples of encounters that have the explicit or implied form of a dream or dreamlike experience. First from a woman who now holds an M.S. in education and who was perhaps four at the time of her journey:

> The experience I recalled as a dream. I remember when I was a little girl, I remembered this experience and always wondered whether it was true. I dismissed it as a dream because it was so unbelievable. But my memories of it are pretty vivid. I remember I would meet this little person. He was about my size—small—and "little" like a child. He was all white, but try as I may, I cannot remember his face. I felt it was a male—although there was no telling by his features. Mostly what I remember is coming home in the early hours after I was in his ship. I just recall thinking that he would come to give rides in his ship—for fun. After I left the ship (don't know how I did this), I remember seeing him next to me and then somehow he was in his craft and lifted [off]. The craft was small, and I was always wondering why there was a blueness [and a] shimmering appearance. Maybe it was illuminated in such a way that I didn't understand because I had never seen anything like it before. I know he came more than once because I looked forward to seeing him and riding in his craft. I have visual memories of flying over our vineyard to our house and where I was set down

to say goodbye. I was not afraid at all. I never told anyone until I was an adult.

In this case, obviously, we have a recollection of what appears to be a totally benign and enjoyable experience with no hint of trauma. While there are occasional reports of this kind both in my sample and in the UFO literature in general, the following instance of a childhood encounter is more typical and has a more ominous tone as well as making specific reference to features that define this kind of journey. It comes from a woman, now fifty-one, with an M.S.W.

The first experience was when I was a child of about 5. For years I had a recurring dream of standing beside a field when a hole opens up in the ground in front of me. The dream ends with me looking into the hole. I was just standing there looking at the hole. Under hypnosis I stepped into the hole and walked down a short tunnel. The tunnel widened into a small waiting area where there was a bench just at the right height for a 5 year old. I sat down and waited. A tall black featureless being came through a doorway, walked to me and held out his hand. I took his hand and went back through the doorway with him. He placed me on a table that appeared to be about 3 to 4 feet high. He laid me on my back and took one big hand and held my upper body flat on the table. The other beings were behind him looking at instruments on the wall. I was held this way for several minutes. When the being turned to look at the other two, it was as if he lost control over me and I jerked out from under his hand, fell off the end of the table and ran for the door. When I got to the door, I knew I wasn't supposed to go any further. I stopped and turned around. The being who had been holding me came to me, took hold of my left arm and looked into my eyes. I was looking at where eyes would be on a human but I don't remember actually seeing eyes. I feel something was communicated, but I don't know what.

The implied aim of the examination in the foregoing account is made explicit in the one that follows, furnished by a woman administrator who also holds a master's degree. In her case, however, no hypnosis was ever used to ferret out the story of her encounter.

I have only recently recalled part of my experience at the age of 5. I was aboard a spaceship. I recall being physically examined with much time being spent around my genitals. I was told that I was there because I was special. I was also told that my parents were not aware that I was gone. The beings were kind and friendly. They were all black and had an antlike appearance with large black eyes. Before being returned home, I was told I would see them again.

The next set of cases features encounters that take place when a child remembers being in bed at the outset, but those could, of course, also still be regarded as dreams. Our first account, from a thirty-six-year-old mother, conveys a strong impression of the ordeal aspect of these encounters:

At age 6, while in bed for the night in my own room, I saw a strange-looking "man" at my window. It was a second floor room, but there was a landing outside that window. I was scared as the "man" didn't look right. He was small, about my height, with a big funny head, and with no hair and scary, *big* black eyes. He knew my name, he called me out. I suddenly wasn't afraid anymore. I got out of bed and went out the window with him. I just kind of went through it. Outside there were two or three more of them. The next thing I know I'm in a big room, dimly lit, lying on a table on my back. They're doing things to me, some of it hurts. Only one seems to be "working." The other two are watching closely, and there's one in the corner that's just standing there. He's dressed differently also; he's wearing black, something like a cape. He just seems to be guarding. Next, the three that were "examining" me, help me over to a vertical, round, flat thing and they somehow attach me to it.

I'm *very* frightened, I seem to know what this thing is. I don't want to get on it. It starts to spin, it's a horrible, awful feeling. That's all I remember. I originally remembered this as a dream except for the "man" at the window.

A forty-nine-year-old Ph.D., a mathematics professor, remembers this incident when he was five years old. It shows that following the ordeal, the candidate may be given special instruction and teachings, as in classic initiation rites.

. . . in 1946, I unaccountably awoke in the middle of the night, walked out alone and watched calmly as a UFO approached and drew me aboard on a light beam. The creatures stripped me and subjected me to various unpleasant, invasive procedures, including opening my head and tampering with various things there. Then I had to get in some sort of transport device, and was led to a sort of theater or auditorium, where most of the seats were taken by identical little old ladies. The room darkened, and scenes appeared on the wall while a creature "lectured" telepathically. They showed a view of their home planet, devastated, and said they had to go out into space to find places where there was the kind of life that could help them, and Earth was one of the places they found. (At age 5, I knew nothing about planets and space, and immediately became very interested in these subjects, to understand what I had been told.) After a long "conversation" with the alien (I spoke aloud, but his lips never moved), I went to another room and was shown things that were yet to happen to me. There is a gap in my recall here, but eventually I ran down a ramp and back into the house and into the bed—just in time [for] it was already getting light.

A more elaborate nighttime encounter was described by Sheldon Mack, now a thirty-two-year-old college-educated librarian. As with the preceding account, this event also took place when he was five.

I was woken up by two beings who had oval, hairless heads, round dark eyes, and dark coveralls. Each took an arm of mine and floated me out the window. The height and the butterflies-in-the-stomach feeling panicked me, [so] they made me unconscious. (I was made unconscious several times throughout this, usually at particularly upsetting moments.)

I was brought to my school, where I had begun kindergarten recently, escorted up a ramp into a dark elliptical-shaped object that sat in the schoolyard. I was in a state of confused disorientation throughout this, possibly externally induced, and I almost never saw, directly, their faces (they seemed to have a way of blurring my vision of their faces). They took me to a room that had a table on it. I was placed on the table, and what I gather was an examination took place. I was unconscious throughout most of it, my body moved into several positions. Eventually, I was awake and sitting up. (Somewhere in here, an eye-shaped object was brought up to my face, terrifying me; I went unconscious. . . .) I asked them if this was some [kind] of entrance procedure for kindergarten, were other kids brought here other nights? They said no, it was just me. During this, I realized that they were responding to my questions as I thought of them but before I said them aloud. This amazed and delighted me. . . .

An interval of play in the schoolyard ensues, followed by an abrupt transition (indicated by the parenthetical admission "I'm unclear of the exact order of events") that finds the boy trying to escape "their floating craft." This compels an immediate response from the formerly playful beings:

They forcefully (out of alarm) grabbed and dragged me away. . . . Eventually, the one in white told me it was time to go. I asked if I would see them again. He said (either verbally, possibly telepathically, I'm not sure) they would when I was older (or bigger), but I wouldn't remember them. . . . [Eventually], two beings took an arm either side of me and floated me up. I felt the butterflies/fluttery feeling in my stomach, was frightened of heights, and went unconscious. I assume they then took me home.

A final bedtime encounter, this time unambiguously frightening, was described by a thirty-two-year-old college-educated artist. Greta Lincoln, like several other children whose stories we have already read, was also five years of age when she suddenly found herself awake one night.

I was 5 years old sleeping with my brothers—my parents were sleeping in the room next door—in a basement apartment. The memory of this experience just came back to me [in] November of 1987 during a rebirthing therapy session. Prior to that I drew a picture of a space ship like nothing I had ever seen and then a picture of an alien being—then the memory came. It was quite terrifying—terror was the feeling I relived.

As I stated, I was sleeping and awakened for some reason to see seven strange looking forms at the foot of my bed— approximately 4 feet tall, large black eyes round shaped, greyish white skin, large head, very thin body, long arms, fingers and toes. They then seemed to raise me out of the bed without touching me and stayed below up the stairs and outside. There was a very bright light coming down from the sky which seemed to draw us up into it. Next thing I saw was being in a very sterile white room lying on a table with these beings around me again. I was very frightened and one who seemed to be in charge touched my forehead and I immediately felt calm and saw a picture of my brothers and parents sleeping like they didn't know any of this was happening. The beings then started to examine and probe my body with long thin metal instruments scanning over my body and some were inserted vaginally and rectally. The only memory I have after that is being back in bed and screaming like I saw lightning flash and saw a skeleton head in the bedroom window. I could never sleep without the closet light after that for the next 15 years.

Not all encounters, of course, take place during or, as these last respondents would claim, after an abrupt awakening from sleep. Others are reported to occur when the individual is fully conscious and is going about his or her business in an outdoor environment. Our final two childhood cases illustrate just how such incidents can take place in a state of ordinary, sensory-based consciousness.

David Masters was ten years old and living in a small town in Texas when one night he and a friend decided to stir up a little trouble. The resulting adventure, however, turned out to be quite different, and far more devastating, than David could ever have anticipated. Now thirty-eight, David tells his terrifying story, a portion of which he was able to recall only through hypnotic regression, as follows:

At the age of ten, a friend of mine and I climbed out the bedroom window of my parents' house in the middle of the night. We intended to run around the neighborhood committing many acts of vandalism, which was about the only sport we could participate in at the time. When we were running back into my backyard after throwing some rocks on a neighbor's roof, the landscape suddenly lit up as if it were high noon. There was a sound like thunder. I looked at my friend's face. He was facing to my left rear. His countenance was that of a person in shock. I turned to my left rear to see a HUGE saucer-shaped spacecraft hovering 300 to 500 feet above the ground.

[The next portion of David's narrative is based on his hypnosis.] The next thing I remember is a small craft about the size of an automobile landing in the yard near where we were standing. Three "people" got out of the small craft. Two of these guys were 4 to 5 feet tall and grey-colored. The other one was brown-colored and much larger than the other two. My friend was standing agape, struck dumb. I began to run. The big brown guy was on me in a flash, forcing me back to the small craft. I resisted and was shocked repeatedly with an "electric" sort of gadget. I continued to resist. They shocked me into unconsciousness. They did so brutally, viciously. I came to and allowed myself to be forced into the small craft. We then lifted off, silently and smoothly, and proceeded up to and into the large craft.

My next recollection is that of being fastened to a metallic sort of examining table. A dark green woman was sitting on my chest, her legs to my right side. She manipulated me sexually with her hand. I had a child's orgasm, with little or no ejaculation. They then fastened a contoured, dark-colored plate to the front of my face. I couldn't see what they did at that time, though there were a number of strange sensations. I was then placed in a small closetlike room which had a seam in the floor. The floor opened up, a multi-colored energy field appeared around me, and I dropped out of the craft into the night sky. I was 300 to 500 feet above the ground. I slowly floated back to earth in my backyard.

[Conscious memory again.] I stood next to my friend and we watched in awe as a V-shaped formation of large round shining objects moved directly overhead to over the horizon. These things moved at a speed that there are no words to describe.

Our second instance of an outdoor encounter concerns a little girl, of the usual age (i.e., five), who one day became lost in the woods for eight hours. Now twenty-seven, she remembers:

. . . following my dog into the deep middle of the forest. He was wagging his tail. It seemed that he was following someone or something. Under hypnosis I remembered being taken aboard a spacecraft by three MEN. They seemed like men even though they looked different. One of them—I call him the "leader"—I felt as if I knew. I was examined—sexually, too, but never to completion. The older, wiser being communicated that I was much too young for that type of examination the other two wanted to perform. They wanted to put something inside of me with a long thong-like instrument. The "leader" objected. He was very loving and not as clinical as the others.

I remember [afterward] waking up in the woods without my dog and following a ball of light out of the forest. I was very deep in there. . . . It was just beginning to get dark when I found my way out. EVERYONE was searching—all the neighbors, my mother, my grandparents, the cops. And my dog ran to me and licked me all over.

My question is, where was my dog during my experience? He seemed to lead me in but he was nowhere around when I awoke on the ground. I was unharmed and have always remembered this incident. It was the first thing I recalled under hypnosis. I don't need hypnosis to remember it now. It is very real and vivid.

I have now presented enough of these stories of close encounters of the fourth kind in children for you to be able to see for yourself what their basic structure is and how their recurrent elements tend to cohere in the same general pattern. It need hardly be mentioned that, at face value, they are manifestly absurd. Even granting that there may be real aliens in our midst, most of these tales contain features that seem like either the purest dream imagery or the worst sort of science fiction. All that is of course obvious, but to say these narratives are literally incredible and often ludicrous as well is not *necessarily* to imply that they are without psychological meaning. After all, all of them *do* seem to share a largely common set of motifs and, perhaps just as striking, many of them take place, if we are to believe at least this of my respondents, at the age of around five. Such regularities suggest that, despite the *content* of these encounters, there is something systematic (and not merely idiosyncratic) that underlies them. In addition, as I remarked at the outset of this chapter, these are stories that fit a well-understood archetypal form, i.e., the initiatory journey. Therefore, we shouldn't, I think, fall into the trap of dismissing these narratives merely on the basis of their surface content; instead, we need to probe more deeply into the reasons governing their underlying structural uniformities.

But at this point we are by no means finished with these abduction stories. The fact is that what begins in childhood continues into adulthood. Abductions, therefore, tend to be repeated occurrences. Moreover, young adults who recall no earlier such incidents may suddenly find that they, too, are the targets of these unsettling, and even frightening, encounters. Accordingly, we must turn our attention next to adult incidents of this kind.

CLOSE ENCOUNTERS OF THE FOURTH KIND IN ADULTS

It will come as no surprise to learn that the abduction scenario in adults follows much the same course that we have already come to know through our review of childhood accounts. Therefore, to dim the unwanted specter of unnecessary repetition, I will present somewhat fewer cases in this section and will select those that illustrate certain important features or aftereffects that have yet to be brought out. As before, however, I will divide them into dreamlike, sleep-related, and outdoor encounters.

Our first brace of incidents, those that typify the close encounter as dream, will disclose an unexpected effect heretofore not revealed by any of our childhood cases: the presence of inexplicable physical marks or pain manifesting in the immediate aftermath of a "dreamed" abduction. We begin with a description furnished by a thirty-six-year-old high school graduate whose experience took place in 1987.

In February of 1987, on a Saturday morning, upon awakening, I told my husband, Harry, of a very vivid dream. . . . In the "dream," I was awakened by two people—one male and one female (looking very much like us except that their eyes were set far apart and very, very dark). I remember looking at the clock—it was approximately two A.M. I reached for Harry and was screaming to him that someone was in the house. . . . They told me (mentally) that "it was no use to try to get his attention" because he couldn't hear me. Then, without any effort, they seemed to pick me up and they brought me down the hall and out the front door. I had the feeling of floating because my legs didn't seem to be moving. My next memory is of being in a brightly lit, cold, hospital-like room. Everything looked like stainless steel. The same two beings that brought me there were still with me along with several others (all dressed in tan-colored coveralls). They started to put needles (?) right under my right breast below my ribs. I told them they were hurting me and that is the last thing I remember until I woke up and started telling my husband.

When I went to the bathroom to get dressed I noticed marks under my breast. Under closer examination I noticed that they were three small blisters in the shape of a triangle.[2] It really frightened my husband and me. I couldn't concentrate on anything all day. Later that night when taking my bath I noticed that the blisters had dried up somewhat and turned black. (Now they are still visible like burn scars.) When I was bathing, I started to shave my legs and I noticed that the back of my leg was sore and when I looked, the very same mark was on my upper calf. Now I really started to worry.

In an addendum to her account, this woman notes that at the time she was writing—two years after the incident already described—she found "the exact same marks" under her left breast, directly across from the other marks. "Same size, same pattern," she comments.

Our second case here comes from another high school graduate, now thirty-nine, who had his "dream" when he was twenty-two.

. . . about November 1963 I had this "dream." I woke up on a table. There were two frail-looking beings standing next to it. I could see them from the waist up. They were greyish-white and both almost identical except for size and very slight facial differences. One said, "Don't be afraid, we're not going to hurt you." And I was very calm and very curious. They had tremendous Deep Black Eyes, and I felt assured. Then one said, "What shall we do with him?," and the other [said], "Let's give him these and see what he does with them. . . ." I was then back asleep and thought, "I wish I could wake up from this dream," and I did—but I was not back in bed. I awoke back on the table. They said (they really did not speak; I don't think they had mouths like ours), "You will not remember any of this when you awake!" [Then] they put me back to sleep and I thought, "I must remember this, I will remember." I then woke up in bed with pain on each side of my head. It was about 4 A.M. I woke my wife and told her of the dream. I felt as though something was placed in my head. I also remember something about a fiber being pushed into my head through my eye socket.

The next pair of cases, which relate to encounters reported to occur at night when the respondent was *not* asleep, illustrate how profoundly different the reactions to and interpretations of these interventions can be. As with the immediately preceding testimony, these persons likewise aver that they had physical markings or injuries following their episodes. In the second case, we will also become more fully aware of another frequent, troubling consequence of adult abductions—the presence of symptoms indicative of posttraumatic stress disorder. More evidence of this reaction will also be available from the next set of examples we will consider toward the end of this section.

Our first instance here—of a benignly perceived close encounter—is unusual in one respect. It comes from a woman who was sixty-four years of age at the time it occurred. Although this woman describes other UFO-related incidents in her life, beginning in her early forties, it is relatively rare for "examinations" of the sort we've been considering to be reported by older persons. Instead, the demographics of abductions show them to be predominantly a phenomenon of childhood and young adulthood.[3] Hattie McDowell, a college graduate, is now a seventy-five-year-old minister and teacher of metaphysics. On the night of April 12, 1979:

> . . . I woke up in my own room to feel someone's hand on my back. I reached around and tried to push it away and then turned around to see two beings leaning over me. One had a rather large hypodermic syringe with a long needle attached to it which he/she held in a gloved hand. As I tried to push the hand away I was told there was no use to resist and my hand was pushed gently but firmly down to my side and my head pushed down on the pillow. The communication was by mental telepathy. I felt relaxed and was not aware of anything else until I woke up as they were going out the door.

> I did notice that my room had a soft glow about it and I could see that the beings had on suits designed with a series of inflated rings like the auto tire advertisement except they were smaller. I feel sure the hypodermic needle was used to either inject a fluid or take fluid out of a region in the lower mid-right side of my back. For the next few days, I had a mildly uncomfortable sensation in that area but nothing more.

Hattie's reflections on this experience are especially of interest and not what one might expect:

> As I thought about this experience I wondered if these beings are doing some sort of medical research for the good of humanity, for the good of their own people, or for my own good as an individual whom they are using for a specific reason. I have been asked if I felt they were infringing on my own self authority, and I do not. They have always been gentle with me and I feel that this, whatever it is, is some-

thing that I have agreed to at some time in the past and maybe before I was born.

Hattie's charitable and accepting attitude couldn't contrast more starkly with that of Claire Chambers, a thirty-one-year-old college-educated writer and researcher, whose outrage over her repeated encounters constitutes the strongest expression of anguished protest we have yet heard from any of our respondents. The specific incident in question took place sometime during 1982.

My boy friend (age 35) and I were both removed from my bedroom in the night. My large dog attacked and injured one of the aliens. I fought also, but was rendered unconscious. I awoke (in the craft I assume) in a strange environment lying on a table helpless with total paralysis. One alien was by my head and attempted to frighten me with his large eyes. Three other aliens were working on my body. I was terrified and in great pain from the physical procedures they were doing to my body. At one point, I almost strangled and choked to death. I screamed, "NO! STOP! WHY?" over and over. There was no response from the alien life forms.

Claire then comments:

In my many encounters where I have always been kidnapped from my home, the aliens have shown no compassion. I have several times felt them exhibit FEAR when I have hit them as they do feel FEAR. They are physical beings with physical bodies. Their reaction behavior patterns do *not* indicate an intelligence as high as I would expect from their technology. In various ways, they are mentally and emotionally INFERIOR to humans. I have been kidnapped by them from 1969 to January 6, 1989, with wounds and injuries examined by four different doctors. These experiences have been dreadful, terrifying, and I would like them to stop!

Finally, she attests:

1. I do not drink alcohol.
2. I have never taken illegal drugs.
3. I had *no psychological problems prior to* the 1982 abductions but had anxiety after that.

Our last three examples in this section concern situations where the encounter took place in full waking consciousness in an outside environment. We begin with a case that continues one of the themes of Claire's account, that of serial abductions. In this instance, however, we return to a woman whose childhood close encounter at the age of five we have already presented. She is the fifty-one-year-old woman, the holder of an M.S.W. degree, whose story we presented on page 67. She is now twenty-six years old, has just been married within the past month, and, as her episode unfolds, is driving in the state of Ohio.

I was driving from Columbus to Marion when I felt compelled to turn into a state park area. I drove into the park about a mile, stopped the car and got out. A bright light was hovering high in the sky over the trees. I stood beside the car and stared at the light. It descended into the trees in front of me. I walked through the trees to the UFO which was sitting on the ground *not* glowing. I went into the UFO.

There were two tall beings inside who seemed to welcome me and attempted to reassure me that they were completely harmless. They were all black, and I cannot recall any features or clothing details. I seemed to be waiting tongue-in-cheek until they finished. They then walked to the door and indicated that I was free to leave. I went out, walked to my car and left without looking back.

On the way home that night my car stopped at the side of the highway. I got out of the car and walked into an empty field where a UFO was hovering. I walked to the bottom of a ramp, stepped onto it and was taken into the craft. I had a physical exam which included a vivid pink light which focused on my chest. The experience may have been one where I came close to death because under hypnosis I begin to hyperventilate when I try to explore what happened with the pink light. It seems as if my chest may have been opened but there was no physical evidence of this. My clothes were not removed during this time.

One week later, I drove to Marion and again the car stopped and I went into a craft. It seemed as if this was a follow-up of the week before. No beings were present when I entered. I undressed and climbed onto a table against the wall. Three needles attached to tubes came out of the wall. One went into my upper arm, one into my waist and one into my hip. After they retracted I sat up to get my bearings for a while and then got dressed and headed for the door. At the door I knew I had to wait. I sat on a seat by the door and waited. A tall, totally black, featureless being came through a doorway at the other end of the room, walked to me and stood looking down at me. I have no idea what was communicated to me. I then left and went to Marion.

If you have taken the trouble to reread or happen to remember this woman's childhood experience, you cannot help noticing some very curious similarities between her rendering of this third incident and the one she reports at age five. In both, for example, she sees "a black featureless being" who comes "though a doorway." And also in both accounts, prior to leaving, she realizes when she gets to the door that she has to wait. The black featureless being then communicates something to her, but what it is she doesn't know.

There was a tragic, but presumably unconnected, event that followed this set of three encounters in late 1965. She mentions that her husband was killed in an automobile accident three months later.

Our next case took place in the New Mexico desert in 1976

when the respondent was thirty-nine. Tom Murillo is a heavy-equipment operator with a grade school education. The traumatic aftermath of his encounter will be evident.

I had gone out into the prairie southwest of town after a family quarrel. I parked my truck and left the radio on as I walked around near the truck. I must have been there a while when I heard a rustle around the sagebrush near me. I looked up to see a tall figure . . . I called out and got no answer, to which I started calling him bad words. Then the figure left and at that time I sensed something, but too late to get away. I heard this whirling noise above me to which I couldn't move at all. As an elevator formed, a tube engulfed me and I was raised up into the spacecraft where I was inserted into some kind of tube-like space. I floated through some kind of passage which took me to a big room where I landed on a glass-like table.

I lay [there] for a few moments till these four tall aliens came into the room. They observed me for a while, then started their examination on me. A scanning device was used all the time. This device went around the glass table—above, sideways, under the table—and all the time I couldn't move a muscle except my eyes. All the data picked up by the scanning device was fed into a strange-shaped grey screen where I was fortunate to see my insides. My heart, my stomach, and other parts. I just lay there as I was examined. I felt scared but sensed they were not out to harm me. I could pick up somehow some thought waves of a friendly nature. I know now that I did communicate with them but my frightened state didn't help me any. They continued to examine me. One thing they were real interested in was my ten fingers on my hands and my toes. They kept coming back to these areas of my body.

Now here is how the aliens looked from my point of view. Over 7 feet tall, greyish color, [they] had 3 finger hands, were friendly, wore that flexible armor-type suits worn by the knights of old. I couldn't see their faces due to their strange helmets which must have been one way, vision-wise.

After what seemed like hours, they stopped and conversed among themselves. . . . Then they dressed me up (I forgot to mention I was undressed before they started to examine me). I was then lifted up [and] inserted into the same passageway, [then] sent to the tube-like elevator where I was set free on solid earth to find myself with no sense of direction whatsoever.

As I stood there scared, [I tried to] move and couldn't. As I started to gain my self-control, I looked around the moon-lit prairie searching for the truck, which I finally saw a few feet away as the moon shines on the windshield. I then broke to pieces as my whole body shook uncontrollably. I cried, "Oh, God, why me?" I couldn't calm myself as I cried like a baby . . . I was still shaking a lot, but I finally started my truck. It died on me several times till I started crying again. I finally half-controlled myself and started the truck and made it home. I don't know how but I did get home.

Our final story of an outdoor abduction and examination will have some notable commonalities with Tom Murillo's account, both in terms of the form of the paralysis described and the immediate aftermath of the experience. John Barker, a high school graduate, is a seventy-one-year-old retired truck driver who lives in Ohio. When he was thirty-six, he saw his first UFO.

It was in the fall of 1955, about 8 o'clock in the evening. I was walking down the street, the sky was clear, stars were shining bright, and the moon was full and bright. I looked up at the moon . . . and lo and behold, here comes a little red ball of light coming through the sky aiming straight at me!!! It was just a pin dot way out in the sky when I first saw it. Then it turned Bright White Hot in color. It looked like someone was welding in the sky, it was so bright. Then as it got closer to me it seemed to cool off and turn reddish.

It stopped over the top of me a couple of hundred feet and then fluttered like a leaf and made one, two, three wopples [sic] and stopped about 50 feet above me. It couldn't come any lower because the high tension electric lines were under it. It was 75 to 100 feet in diameter. I didn't see any portholes or windows.

Then, the next thing I know, it felt like I was floating up!!! I'm completely paralyzed, the only part of my body I can move is my eyes. I could look around. Up close the metal of the craft looked like fresh-cast aluminum. I saw no bolts or rivets, just smooth metal. Also, as I got very close underneath it, I saw a circle of electric sparks about 3 to 4 feet high, and then everything blanks out.

I come to, and I'm standing in the middle of Franklin road, between 7th and 8th streets, with my back to the traffic. When I came to, I'm in a state of shock!!! They scared hell out of me, whoever they are. I did not see any person or head or body. I vaguely remember seeing two hands, and they were checking my penis. That's all I can remember of them.

When I came to standing in the street, I looked around and saw another UFO in United Metal's storage yard. It was standing on end, starting up and out of the storage yard. It was about 30 feet in diameter and had six flaming exhaust [sic] coming out of it . . . It looked like they had special lights shining on it to make it stand out. I'll tell you this, it was a fantastic beautiful machine. Then it went up over United Metal . . . [and] was gone in the blink of an eye. I then looked at the one that was above me, and it was still there but slowly going up. It was sinister-looking in the dark sky now. Then it went out of sight. Neither of these things made any noise. They were silent, no noise at all!!!

Since this event every several months I would get a strange sickness. Violent chills and a fever that lasted for several hours. This went on for thirty years. . . . Also for years off and on I have a nightmare that I'm on a shiny steel table, paralyzed *cannot* move and making a grunting noise. Also, I cannot talk. My wife will wake me up and say, "Okay, Dad, it's okay." And I'll wake up.

The accounts in this section of adult close encounters of the fourth kind clearly add some distinctive elements to the archetypal pattern—that of the initiatory journey we've now grown quite familiar with—or serve to heighten the significance of some of those we've already noted. For example, in reading the foregoing narratives, we can more fully appreciate just how incredibly oddly these experiences *begin*. In the case of outdoor encounters, respondents find their cars apparently stopping of their own accord, and witnesses then behave as though they themselves are in a trance. Or they may find themselves suddenly floating upward only to discover they are then completely paralyzed except, as our last two examples made clear, for the eyes. Once they are in the grip of the creatures who have captured them, whatever the context of the inception of their encounter, we can see some other consequences set into motion. For instance, it appears that if they resist the examination procedure, they will be forced to submit anyway, resulting in considerable anger and deep resentment afterward. On the other hand, compliance sometimes brings reassurance, as though one is in the hands of a kindly physician who wants to set one's mind at ease as much as possible before a painful or strange procedure is about to be performed. In any event, an attitude of submission during the examination seems to leave respondents with better feelings about the possible motives of their captors, as Hattie McDowell's testimony suggests.

To anyone who hasn't been forced to endure one of these encounters and who only reads about them, they must have an utterly fantastic, unreal quality, and, as I have noted before, one's natural tendency is to laugh them away or, if one is feeling more expansive, simply to marvel at the inventive power of the human imagination and let it go at that. But then there are those respondents like Claire Chambers who insist with matter-of-fact directness that their alien captors "are physical beings with physical bodies." And Claire is hardly voicing an isolated opinion. The UFO literature is full of similar claims on the part of experiencers. I myself have sat with a man of high education and obvious intelligence who has spent many long hours reflecting on his own close encounters and concluded that, though he doesn't understand how it can be, his episodes did indeed take place in the physical world. And yet such opinions, though they are common, are not universal among experiencers. For instance, consider the statement of one of my respondents, not previously quoted, a thirty-five-year-old college-educated sales administrator who underwent an abduction. After a prolonged personal inquiry that involved a hypnotic regression with a well-known UFO investigator, she confessed, "Let me stress one thing: I myself don't know if it is my imagination or if it is real. I still don't know today." And there are many others like her, too, who voice similar uncertainties.

In the face of such perplexities, it is easy to feel that any attempt to unravel the tangled knot of the meaning of these encounters is destined to result in one's simply becoming more ensnarled in it.

Until one remembers one additional feature that only our adult narratives in this chapter have made us aware of: the *aftereffects* of these episodes. As we have seen, our respondents often indicate that they notice otherwise inexplicable physical signs of their strange encounters immediately afterward, some of them apparently of some medical significance. Others comment on persisting pains, while still others report psychological symptoms indicative of posttraumatic stress disorder. And once again, what can necessarily only be *suggested* by the few examples I have cited in this chapter is amply illustrated in the UFO literature at large: significant physical and psychological aftereffects of close encounters of the fourth kind are in fact widely reported.

Obviously, then, these experiences, whatever their ontological status, *are real in their effects*. Something, though we don't yet know what it is, *has* happened to these people—because it has left its mark on them. Jacques Vallee, one of the most distinguished of contemporary ufologists, has for many years contended that we can only hope to understand the UFO phenomenon in terms of its effects, and in this book I mean to show the relevance of his edict to UFO encounters specifically. We will therefore hold tightly to this thin, but strong, Ariadne thread representing these aftereffects in the hope that it will eventually lead us out of this labyrinth of confusion to our goal of understanding what significance these UFO encounters have for us and for the persons who have directly experienced them.

And in following its trail, we will before we are done come to see that it will bring us to some surprising conclusions, ones that are indeed almost paradoxical in the light of the aftereffects we had cause to consider in this chapter. Some hint of what is to come, however, will be found in the following chapter where we turn, finally, to the other variety of extraordinary encounters with which this book is concerned, near-death experiences.

CHAPTER 4

NEAR DEATH EXPERIENCES

But first a hush of peace, a soundless calm descends;
The struggle of distress and fierce impatience ends;
Mute music soothes my breast—unuttered harmony
That I could never dream till earth was lost to me.

Then dawns the Invisible, the Unseen its truth reveals;
My outward sense is gone, my inward essence feels—
Its wings are almost free, its home, its harbor found;
Measuring the gulf it stoops and dares the final bound!

Oh, dreadful is the check—intense the agony
When the ear begins to hear and the eye begins to see;
When the pulse begins to throb, and the brain to think
   again,
The soul to feel the flesh and the flesh to feel the chain!

—Emily Brontë

While in the hospital in June of 1983, I was so ill my doctor and his associates thought I wouldn't leave the place alive. One night, long after the night nurse had come by to check on me, a strange feeling came over my entire body. I knew I was dying. I could actually feel the energy of life leaving. The beginning of a glow appeared in the upper left corner of the room. While watching it, [I] seemed to [see it] envelop the entire room and transform it into the beginning of a tunnel. I began moving through the tunnel which beared [sic] off to the left and slightly downward, the glow ever increasing and just far enough ahead that you couldn't actually see its source. To my immediate left there seemed to be a window, much like a passenger train has, travelling alongside. On the other side stood my wife and children. Upon reaching the end of the tunnel, I was aware of a presence to my immediate right *mentally* offering me a choice to either go on (from the tunnel's end) or return. I knew I could respond ONLY ONCE—my decision would be *final*. Mentally choosing to return, the experience ended. The following day, my condition was *greatly* improved and continued to do so each day after to the amazement of everyone.

We are a long way from the world of the UFO abduction. Instead, we now find ourselves in the rarefied realm of the near-death experience, which in the typical case involves an encounter of almost inexpressible sublimity. The man whose words you have just read—a thirty-eight-year-old engineer from Maryland—speaks for literally tens of thousands of such experiencers and makes it clear at the outset that in almost every way the NDE seems to be at antipodes to the type of UFO encounter we have just finished considering. With the NDE, we are in a different world, indeed.

To begin to appreciate the differences even more clearly, let me present two further instances of this second type of extraordinary encounter of concern to us in this book. First, from a forty-three-year-old woman, with a master of science degree, who had her NDE in the aftermath of the birth of her only child in 1984:

Due to a prolonged and difficult labor, I experienced severe complications postpartum. Thirty minutes or so after [Patty's] birth I hemorrhaged, lost blood pressure and became unconscious. Soon I left my body through the top of my head and hovered in the corner of the room near the ceiling with an aerial view of the medical staff who were attempting to revive me. I felt no pain—rather I was relieved to be free of my physical body. I felt great compassion for my husband and daughter, but no attachment and no regret at leaving them.

I floated for a while and then was drawn down a long dark passageway with a very clear bright white light at the end. Soon I was enveloped and felt reunited with many familiar but undefinable entities. I felt a total knowing, an absence of conflict, complete peace.

Soon I was communicated with—very clearly but not exactly in words. I was "asked"—are you ready? I certainly was! I had never been so happy! I considered for a moment, then responded, "Yes, if you think Earl [husband] can take care of Patty. At that moment, I re-entered my body through my head with a sickening thud. It was awful returning like that. I tried to tell people of my experience but they laughed or looked at me sadly. I stopped talking about it and got very depressed in the following months.

The second account comes from a sixty-eight-year-old cartoonist who was hospitalized in Michigan for a clot in his leg during the summer of 1985. As he recalls:

I was there for about five minutes when I began gasping for air. Within seconds I was engulfed in a warm darkness and fully aware that I was dying. A voice or a thought entered my mind: "Be calm, breathe slow, breathe steady." At the same time, I was above my body, seeing my left shoulder and upper arm . . . from a strange angle. I then saw my upper torso looking down, as if I were hovering over it. My thoughts were that this is very interesting, but what next? The soft darkness was beautiful. There was an assurance that all was well and that there was nothing to fear. I had never known such a peace and acceptance. I felt that I was beginning a wonderful adventure. How long I remained in this state is hard to tell. The first indication I was back in my body was feeling a board being placed under me. I was at peace and unconcerned. They say I was in a coma for three days [and] that I had suffered heart failure with no heartbeat for several minutes.

I now know that just as there is the miracle of birth, there is the miracle of dying.

From the three narratives I have so far presented, we can in fact detect most of the recurrent features that together make up the stable and coherent pattern known as the prototypic or core near-death experience. Since this particular pattern was named and identified by Raymond Moody in his 1975 book, *Life After Life,* it has been corroborated by scores of independent researchers in the United States and Western Europe who have collectively interviewed and otherwise studied thousands of persons who have reported NDEs.[1] Indeed, the thousands of NDEs summarized in the literature in near-death studies are presumably only a small fraction of those that have actually occurred. George Gallup, Jr., for instance, has estimated, on the basis of an extensive poll taken in the early 1980s, that there may be as many as *8 million* persons in the United States alone who have had this kind of experience.[2]

What, then, is this classic NDE pattern that departs so radically from that associated with UFO encounters, especially of the abduction variety? To begin with, NDErs often report a tremendous feeling of peace, ease, and security at the onset of the experience. When perception becomes possible, they tend to find themselves "up above" their physical body, which they can plainly see below them, as a detached spectator would. Next (although typically in an NDE, there is no clear sense of time), they may feel themselves to be moving through something like a tunnel or dark void toward a radiantly beautiful light. As they progress toward the light, they are engulfed by it and feel bathed in a pure, unconditionally accepting form of love. At this point, they may become aware of a presence (however, they won't necessarily see any figure as such) who may ask them to make a decision whether to continue further or return to their physical body, though occasionally the presence will enjoin them to "go back." Sometimes this aspect of the experience is accompanied by a rapid and full panoramic review of one's life. In other cases, NDErs will encounter the "spirits" of deceased relatives who may either beckon them to enter their realm or inform them that it isn't their time, they must return. In any event, however, the experience is brought to a resolution, NDErs do, of course, eventually find themselves back in the physical world where they may feel either exhilarated over what they have experienced or depressed or angry about the fact that they are no longer "there," but faced with the prospect of living in the ordinary world again.

Certainly, as I have said, such an encounter would seem to have little connection with the terrifying episodes of UFO abductions whose patterns we are now well familiar with. At the level of direct experience, this seems incontrovertibly obvious. And yet, at a deeper level of analysis, there will be found to be, astonishingly enough, a common link between these two categories of extraordinary encounters. Specifically, as soon as one begins to consider these two types of experiences in terms of their underlying *form,* that is, *their archetypal structure,* their relationship is clear.

In discussing UFO encounters, especially those involving abductions, you'll recall that I said that they take the form of an *initiatory journey,* marked by the classic stages of separation, ordeal, and return. In this context, it is immediately evident that something similar also holds for the NDE. Here, too, the individual is separated from his usual physical environment by virtue of his life-threatening crisis and is immediately thrust into "another world." True, it is a very different domain from that the UFO abductee is forced to enter, but it is akin to it in its undeniable nonordinary reality and in its numinous power. And it unmistakably represents an *initiatory* ordeal as well, for as Holger Kalweit, a deep student of shamanism, reminds us, "initiation always signifies death and resurrection,"[3] which is of course the very hallmark of the NDE. Following this stage, the NDEr, like his UFO counterpart, is obliged to return to his original physical environment and is, as we shall come to see, also profoundly shaken and transformed by his otherworldly encounter. Thus, *both* NDEs and close encounters of the fourth kind (hereafter for convenience abbreviated CE IV) have the *structure* of initiatory journeys, even though their specific *content* and emotional charge are patently at variance.

This underlying similarity of form, as well as the surface differences, of these two types of experiences can perhaps best be appreciated by perusing the chart on page 94.

We have, of course, already illustrated and commented on all of these features pertaining to CE IVs, so to complete our survey of NDEs, the only thing that remains for us here is to do the equivalent for the corresponding features of these experiences. In fact, it will be sufficient for our purposes to provide information on only the first ten factors (with the first, *precipitating event,* usually implied) listed in the chart. Since it will be expedient to try to exemplify more than one factor at a time, when possible, the excerpts to follow will be selected on these grounds, and for that reason will usually represent only a fragment of a fuller account. As before, all the narratives given in the remainder of this chapter (as was the case for those that introduced it) derive from a new sample of NDErs who participated in the research done for this book and whose accounts have not previously been published. Finally, the persons whose descriptions I will be presenting next come from only about a *fifth* of my entire sample of NDErs, but they are representative of the whole.

FORM OF SEPARATION AND INITIAL RESPONSE

I'll begin with a complete, but brief and succinct, account of an NDE furnished by a forty-seven-year-old homemaker that includes a clear statement concerning how the ecstatic feeling-tone of the experience may be intertwined with the sense of being swept up into a transcendental domain:

> My experience came about during the premature arrival of my last child. It was a case of placenta praevia with much hemorrhaging. [The] actual NDE occurred while being

A COMPARISON OF FEATURES OF THE TYPICAL NDE WITH THOSE OF THE TYPICAL CE IV

	NDE	CE IV
1. Precipitating event	Life-threatening crisis	Sudden capture
2. Form of separation	Swept up into a light-filled realm	Taken away to an alien environment
3. Initial response	Peace, security	Fright, terror
4. Perception of reality	Hyperreal	Dreamlike, fantastic
5. Nature of beings	Beings of light, spirits of deceased relatives or friends	Hideous alien creatures
6. Nature of encounter	Compassionate self-examination; insights of profound spiritual import	Clinical physical examination; awareness of obscure alien purposes
7. Sense of encounter	Total affirmation	Violation
8. Motivation regarding encounter	To remain	To be set free
9. Determination of return	Personal choice, externally imposed injunction, or not indicated	Under control of alien beings
10. Emotions upon return	Disappointment, regret, sorrow, resentment, but also exhilaration	Relief, panicky confusion, anger, hatred
11. Memory of encounter	Usually intact	Often impaired
12. Immediate aftermath	Variable, strong emotions	Posttraumatic-stress symptoms
13. Frequency	Usually only once	Often recurrent episodes
14. Occurrence	Usually in adulthood	Often in early childhood

prepped for C-section. Suddenly, [I was] engulfed in overwhelming peace and aware of spiralling upward through a
dark comforting tunnel which gave a sensation of velvet walls.
[The] upward end of the tunnel had [a] luminescent glow of
light and as I stepped into it, there was soft music. I found
myself separated from vague forms on the opposite side of
a stream of water and the Light emanating through this scene
shimmered in iridescent pastels. Then came Voices telling
me I had to return to complete my mission.

Another respondent, a clinical psychologist with a Ph.D.,
tells a similar story of her movement into a realm of light. In
her case, however, though she, too, was hospitalized at the time
of her experience, it was the direct result of an anaphylactic
shock reaction following the injection of a dye for an X ray.
She remembers:

As my diaphragm began to paralyze, the walls of the room
and the heavy X-ray equipment began to move at a very
rapid speed away from me. At almost the same moment, a
beautiful golden light filled the room and I felt a Loving
Presence fill all the space—everything, people, objects. I
started to move rapidly toward something I knew was white
light but did not see anything other than the golden glow
filling the room. At that moment, I knew I had a choice to
go forever into the Light or stay. An enormous sadness filled
me, like nothing before or since.

Still another woman, this one a thirty-nine-year-old registered nurse, tells what it was like for her to nearly die of
congestive heart failure. Recently hospitalized for a heart attack and then released, Jessica Havens was forced to return to
the emergency room of the hospital when she found herself unable to breathe. Her account of her NDE is particularly striking
for its expression of the feeling of rapture that often accompan-
ies the beginning of these experiences.

I knew I was dying. . . . I felt I was "falling backward"
into darkness and total silence. . . . Suddenly, I was sus-

pended in total light—bright but not glaring. *PEACEFUL and ABSOLUTE JOY*. I was dressed in a flowing, glowing light and floating right beside me was someone else. He—and I don't know why I say "he"—was also covered in light. We communicated but not in words. It was absolute joy. The communication was concerning whether I wanted to "go back" or not.

Finally, a thirty-year-old man provides a vivid and more encompassing statement concerning the feeling aspect of NDEs in the following narrative. In his case, he had collapsed in his office, located, conveniently enough, in a hospital. When he was in the intensive-care unit there, he first became aware of observing himself from the outside:

> I was out of my body looking at it from the side. I didn't see anyone else there, just my body. From my waist down to my toes, my body was a deep charcoal black. From my waist up, including my arms and head, it was a brilliant, glowing, breathtaking white light. It was brighter and whiter than looking at the sun, but it didn't hurt to look at it.

> I felt myself floating toward this beautiful light. It wasn't as if I was going back into my body, but I was going through it to be engulfed in this light. I have a hard time describing the feeling I had at this time. I compare it to how it must feel for a baby [to be] floating in his mother's womb before delivery. I had no responsibilities, no worries, no problems. I didn't think of anyone, I was just obsessed with the serenity of the light. The peacefulness was wonderful. It's a selfish feeling when I think back because I didn't think of my wife, Sallie, or the kids or my folks, no one. Just peace, serenity, quiet, floating, carefree—it was beautiful.

After reading such descriptions, the contrast to the terror-filled onset of abduction experiences needs only to be mentioned to be appreciated. But still another striking contrast will appear in the next stage of the NDEr's journey, though it is one that at the same time will also have a curious, almost amusing, parallel to the harrowing situation the typical abductee finds himself in.

PERCEPTION OF REALITY

In the literature on NDEs, there is frequent mention made of the fact that, as far as the experiencer is concerned, the *reality* of the events witnessed is beyond doubt. For example, in my own interviews, I have had NDErs say to me with the greatest feeling, "This experience was more real to me than you and I sitting here talking about it," or "My experience was more real than life itself." Other researchers, of course, have heard similar sentiments expressed by their own respondents.

Nowhere is this sense of the hyperreality of NDEs more evident than in the phase where the experiencer finds himself out of his body and somehow able to look upon it from this external perspective. The subjective acuity of visual perception here is not only as astonishing as it is inexplicable,[4] but in a number of instances has proved to be veridical (i.e., accurate), thereby demonstrating that it is certainly no mere hallucination.[5]

Of course, since many of these out-of-body experiences (or OBEs, as they are now usually abbreviated) take place during operations or other medical procedures, we find ourselves with an unexpectedly ironic situation on our analytic hands. Abductees, as we now know, often report that *they* have been subjected to various medical-like examinations, and, as we have seen, their descriptions of this aspect of their encounters tend to be laced with rather fantastic and even lurid elements, and frequently seem to have a dreamlike quality to them. Accordingly, it should prove to be instructive to compare the accounts of NDErs who find themselves in somewhat similar circumstances while still definitely in *this* world.

Although sometimes NDE-based OBE perceptions of oneself are overglossed with a transcendental sheen, as in the case of the man quoted in the last section, more typical are statements that are striking because of their sheer, almost laconic matter-of-factness. As an example, consider the comment of Vince Hermann, a thirty-one-year-old respiratory therapist who lives in Florida. When Vince was not quite seventeen, he was almost killed in a serious automobile accident. As is common in cases in which many years have elapsed since the near-death incident, his recall is sharp:

> Even after almost thirteen years I can still vividly recall crossing over. The warmth, the security. Initially, I remember being able to see the doctors and nurses working around me. As if I were everywhere in the room. Able to see from all angles. I distinctly remember looking into my eyes—inside my head. I felt confused about why they were so engrossed with an empty shell.

Here is another example, this time from a thirty-three-year-old, college-educated technical writer:

> I remember [before her NDE] being aware of tubes and "accessories": in my arms, up my nose, and down my throat. Several people wearing green uniforms and masks were gathered around me, gently trying to reassure me that everything would be all right. Someone held a rubber mask over my face (I remember this distinctly because it smelled awful) and asked me to breathe deeply.
>
> I obviously became unconscious, only to wake up abruptly to find myself hovering face down, looking at a small child on an operating table. My first thought was that these adults were going to get mad at me for leaving the table. But they were working so furiously over the small body that no one even noticed me.

It's clear, of course, that our narrator is recalling a near-death incident when she was a little girl. A very little girl, in fact. For she claims to remember this event taking place when she was approximately only eighteen months old!

Lest this allegation seem fantastic, however, let me assure you that there is now abundant evidence that adults can indeed sometimes accurately describe actual occurrences that they were never told about that took place in their childhoods at ages even less than eighteen months.[6] In the specific context of NDEs, there are already numerous studies that collectively and convincingly present many instances of childhood NDEs,[7] some of them dated at ages comparable to that of our example, and even one case indicating that an NDE undergone at the age of six months was still recalled when the child was three and a half.[8]

Finally, let me present an illustration from one of my adult NDErs that will serve to represent the kind of precise and realistic visual OBE perception that is widely reported in the general literature. Its contrast with the vague and inchoate impressions of UFO abductees will be so obvious as not to require comment.

In 1952, a twenty-one-year-old U.S. soldier serving in the Korean War was wounded and flown to Japan for surgery. Now a speech pathologist living in Connecticut, Harold Jaffe still remembers the details of his operation vividly:

Spinal column surgery . . . Ineffective spinal anesthesia in midsurgery required rapid use of gas/shots from a panic situation. I heard later that the combination "went green," i.e. sour. I recall lapsing into unconsciousness (having been awake and alert during the first hour of surgery). I "sensed" my heart stopping—thought, "HEY, you guys are losing me." The next moment I was "floating" against the canvas roof of the O.R. tent, looking down on "me" stretched out on the table, face down, still being operated on.

The surgeon was alerted to cardiac arrest; several people shouted at once. A heavy, muscular black Air Force sergeant rushed in on call. "I'm not clean, sir," he said. "To hell with that, flip this man over!" He waited for a second for the surgeon to pack the wound, then fork-lifted me onto my back. I clearly "saw" an x-shaped scar on the top of the sergeant's scalp—even though my vision without glasses is 20/400. The medical team frantically worked on my body to resuscitate me. I saw the anesthesiologist (female, lieutenant, Air Force) wiping tears, shaking her head, saying, "Oh shit, oh shit, he's gone!" I "yelled" to her that I was still here, but she couldn't hear me. (Now I recall that my "being" at the roof top had no form, no mouth—only consciousness, vivid, painless, unimpaired hearing and vision and thought.)

I felt myself being sucked back. Many days later I regained consciousness. . . . Weeks later I spoke of my experience to my surgeon, hoping he wouldn't think I was crazy and declare me Section 8. Surprised that I could describe every detail of my "death" and [be] aware of the black corpsman's x-shaped scar on his scalp, my doctor only shrugged and said, "Well, nothing surprises me anymore."

NATURE OF BEINGS

Again, when beings are encountered during NDEs, they are typically very different from those met with in UFO abductions. In general, they are all-loving, seemingly omniscient, and filled with compassionate regard for the NDEr. Though sometimes perceived as a truly Godlike personage (or only merely sensed as a "Loving Presence," as we have already learned), or in angelic form, such beings may also appear as familiar but already deceased relatives who come to guide and direct the individual in his journey. To illustrate this variety of benevolent figures in near-death encounters now, let me begin with a homely instance, again told from the no-nonsense retrospective standpoint of a child, this time of twelve years.

In the summer of 1945, Wayne Thornton had a bad case of pneumonia, and there was some question in his physician's mind whether he would make it through the night. During the night, Wayne began having a typical NDE, however, and found himself moving toward a point of light, which rapidly grew larger:

Either I am moving toward it, or it is approaching me. It is fair to say I feel no discomfort; on the contrary there is a sense of absolute peace and *no* thought of fear. Anyway, I enter the light and I emerge not far from the house standing next to a little stream . . . I step across and immediately the stream begins to get wide . . . The narrow stream now looks like a mile wide and I am standing on some kind of a plain.

I see this guy with a long robe and a shepherd's long staff with the crook on top. I do not know him, but have the feeling he is one of my grandfathers. They have both died before I was born. We are soon standing face to face and he tells me, without speaking, that "It is not time yet" and "You have work to do," meaning me.

An example of both perceived angelic and human figures appearing together for the benefit of an NDEr was furnished by Hannah Markham, a thirty-eight-year-old college graduate who, when she was eighteen, attempted suicide by swallowing twenty-five sleeping pills and then slashing her arm with a razor blade. Fortunately, she was discovered while still unconscious, and rushed to a hospital where she had an OBE as the medical team attempted to resuscitate her. Later in her experience, she remembers:

. . . tumbling down through a tunnel about three feet wide. There was a light toward the end of the tunnel but before I could reach it, two figures appeared outlined in light. They communicated with me through my mind, telepathically. I recognized one of the figures as being my father. He confirmed and agreed with everything conveyed by his companion who seemed to have great authority, like an angel or one of God's helpers.

In the next section, we will continue with Hannah's account in order to show the benign and compassionate nature of the interaction that ensued, and the understanding this person took away from her encounter with these beings.

To conclude this section, however, let me cite at least one brief case where the NDEr clearly perceives what is for her the figure of a revered divine being. Estelle Farmer is now a retired legal secretary living in Ohio, but in 1980, when she was fifty-five years old, she had an NDE while undergoing surgery. During it, she had a typical OBE, but later found herself floating and then drawn to a tiny white light:

> The light came closer and closer at a high rate of speed. It then took on the shape of a man in a white robe. The man hovered at about 20 feet away. He spoke no words but I knew it was Christ.[9] . . . Christ has a very kind, loving compassionate face but at the same time you know He is in command.

In what I have said so far about NDEs, we know only that NDErs are sometimes asked by the beings they encounter either to decide for themselves whether to return to life or, as in the first example in this section, they are summarily ordered to do so. In fact, however, there may be a great deal more information conveyed to NDErs during these telepathic interactions— information that appears decidedly to have a deep impact on them later on. In the next section, we will focus, then, not merely on the character of the beings met but on what they communicate during these NDEs.

NATURE AND SENSE OF ENCOUNTER

NDEs often provide experiencers an opportunity to see and examine their lives in a new context, one of unconditional acceptance, affirmation, and all-compassionate love. These at least are the qualities they sense so strongly from the beings in whose presence they find themselves. Yet something else happens during these exchanges that is even more remarkable. It isn't just that NDErs bask in the quite literal light of the love and acceptance they receive; rather, it is as if they are *infused* with it, and having absorbed it into themselves, they come immediately to have greater *self*-acceptance and compassionate understanding for themselves, and eventually for others, too.

These effects are brought out in a few bold verbal strokes in the case of Lisa Walker, a thirty-six-year-old lab supervisor who had her NDE in January 1979. She had vomited and aspirated after coming out of surgery, and immediately found herself high above her body in an area of brightness:

> . . . and "God" was within this brightness. I felt loved beyond all judgment, an "Agape" type of love, and completely accepted. This "God" communicated to me—no words, just kind of pushed knowledge into me—that I had had a rough past but he/she was delighted at my handling of my life, and that I was OK . . . The God was gentle, but I knew I had to go back. He/She showed me a glimpse—a glimpse of the future; I'd already had the condensed life review when this entity told me I was OK. As all this went on, my understanding of *everything* was growing.

Children who have NDEs experience the same effects, though, to be sure, they are conveyed in a setting and in a manner that conforms to a child's understanding. Here is a simple example from an NDE that occurred to a girl at age seven:

> I was in a garden. I was among large bright flowers the size of sunflowers (like giant dahlias). A presence came to me. I felt completeness, love, perfect peace, bliss. The presence knew all about me and loved me anyway.

In the last section, I presented the case of Hannah Markham, who, as a teenager, had attempted suicide. You will remember that during her NDE, she encountered a being whom she took to be her father *and* another figure of a distinctly different mien, "like an angel or one of God's helpers," she said. This figure conducted Hannah through a self-examination of the life that had led her to her suicide attempt:

He made me understand that I had black marks against me because fear had prevented me from doing things that I should have done. (It was also explained what these beings were saying about the black marks against me. They were saying that statement to make a point. They didn't mean I had black marks against me that I would be punished for.) I was urged to change my attitude, and to have a more positive outlook on life on earth, even in tough and hard times. I would have to face what I had tried to escape. Without the option of refusal, I was compelled to return and felt myself sucked back into my body. Now, when I apply the advice given to me by this shining being so full of knowledge and wisdom, I am able to love life on this planet more.

The theme of love—self-love (in the sense of self-acceptance), love for others, love for the planet, love for the divine cosmos—is in fact the constant refrain in these NDE hymns. NDErs almost without exception are wont to say that it was the message of love that was the most important gift and indeed the very essence of their encounter. And it is this same love that they wish to make known and share with others, truly to give the most precious thing that they themselves have received.

These insights are made clear in our last account, provided by a commercial pilot who had his NDE in Orlando, Florida, in January 1988. He had been standing outside his aircraft when he was struck down and nearly killed by a fuel truck. Once in a nearby hospital, he underwent emergency surgery for ruptured arteries and other internal injuries. Sometime after this, he had his NDE, and eventually, like so many others whose near-death stories we have heard, he, too, found himself standing in a light:

> It was like standing in total darkness in front of a well lighted porch at night. I looked into the light and I saw what I believed to be a face. . . . I cannot remember tears, but if they were possible, the emotion was so strong that they would have been falling like a waterfall. I looked upon the face

again and I was filled with a feeling of love, peace and knowledge. At the same time, the light moved from in front of me through me to behind me. The NDE ended here . . . I think if I took one thing away from this experience, it was that the most powerful force that we all have is love, and before this I had no idea what love was, only what I had been shown in the world.

THE RETURN

The encounter with the light or its emissaries is obviously the apogee of the NDE and, emotionally and spiritually, it stands at the furthest remove from the nadir of terror that CE IVs inspire in those caught in their paralyzing vise. Therefore, it will come as no surprise that whereas the abductee struggles to get free, the NDEr, if he or she has any felt choice in the matter, usually yearns to stay. A few representative brief passages from our NDE narratives are all we need here to make this clear:

> I remember pleading with God, and saying, "Please let me stay." He never answered, just smiled with that loving and kind smile on His face.

> I understood . . . that returning to earth was part of my task, although I wanted more than anything to stay there.

> My desire was to stay right where I was. Almost instantly I felt cold. I screamed, "But why?"

> I remember feeling light as air, free, no pain, happy to go. Not wanting to come back . . . I resented being sent back.

Of course, not *all* NDErs feel sent back against their will and ardent desire to remain. Some, who feel that the choice is truly theirs to make, freely elect to return to physical life, usually, however, for the sake of others. The case of a seven-year-old-girl cited in the last section provides a good example. Picking up where we left off:

> Not with words the presence communicated, "So you've decided to go back." I communicated the same way of putting thought into the presence. I said, "Yes." The presence said, "Why?" I said, "My mother needs me." At that moment I started down a tunnel. When I could see the "light" no more, I woke up.

Sometimes the presence causes the person to reflect before making the choice, as in this example furnished by a thirty-three-year-old woman who had her experience at thirty:

> As soon as I asked the question ["When am I going to get to the light?"], a voice spoke to me telepathically and said, "What would be so important to you that would make you want to stay?" I automatically thought, "My best friend and my cats." While in the tunnel, I felt a being which was so loving and knew my every thought. As soon as I answered the question, the tunnel faded away like clouds dissipating. I was then again in my sick body.

In this example, you might have found the reference to this woman's cats amusing, but to anyone who has a pet or who loves animals, it is perfectly understandable. And though it is usually the case that NDErs who choose to return for the sake of others do so for other human beings, this isn't the only instance where attachment to one's animals was a factor in influencing one's decision to come back. In the case of Lisa Walker, the lab supervisor whose narrative was quoted at the beginning of the last section, her experience was brought to its resolution by this realization:

> Then I knew that (believe it or not!) the *dog* needed me. She would, actually; she was *mine,* a one-woman dog, and would have had to be put to death if I went—no one else could control her. [Lisa's main avocation in life, then and

now, is raising and taking care of her dogs.] And as soon as "God" put that thought to me, I was back, barfing and crying all over the place.

With some NDErs, however, the desire to return can be overwhelming. In my experience, this is usually when a mother feels that she simply cannot abandon her young children. This reaction is illustrated in our last example of this decisional process here, that involving a woman, now twenty-six, who had her NDE when she was six-and-a-half months pregnant. During her vision, she found herself in a domain with several deceased family members and friends who urged her to:

". . . step up" and join them. I started to cry and said I was not ready to die as I had a three and a half year old boy I deeply loved and wanted to raise. [They persisted in entreating her, however, but] . . . I continued to protest I wasn't ready and they said I could return to earth. When I really awakened, tears were still streaming down my face.

Regardless of whether one chooses or agrees to return, is sent back against one's wishes, or simply finds oneself living in a physical body again, it is of course necessary to come to terms with the fact that one has had to relinquish a treasure beyond price. For most NDErs in the immediate aftermath of their experience, coping with both what they've lost and what they are now faced with is emotionally very trying.[10]

If everyone could have this feeling I think it would be like Heaven on earth. . . . I felt as if I had been in another dimension, maybe spiritually many, many light-years away from this planet and felt like an alien back here.

Dr. Ring, when I came back . . . I felt *horrible pain*. . . . After this experience . . . life seemed very difficult to adjust to. It seemed as if I was a stranger living on another planet. I felt so different, and have never truly felt the same since this incident happened. . . . No longer is this earth my home.

I was *cold,* and felt severe pain, anger, disappointment, and very frustrated.

I . . . got very depressed in the following months. I was ashamed to be sorry to be "alive" in this world, sorry to have left that lovelier one, guilty that it meant I didn't love my daughter enough to want to live.

And yet, for all the expressions of post-NDE regret and yearning, there is also sometimes this kind of reaction:

I awoke many hours later to discover myself on a respirator in Intensive Care. I was *overjoyed* about my experience and in spite of realizing I was very ill again, I wrote on a slate board to my sister and husband about it.

CONCLUSIONS

Our survey of the various major facets of NDEs has shown repeatedly how they represent on almost every point of comparison the polar opposite of CE IVs. Not only is the content of the two experiences vastly different, to say nothing of the emotional response to them, but the very *quality* of these two categories of extraordinary encounters also stands in blatant contrast to each other—NDEs are subjectively highly real, even in their transcendental aspects, whereas UFO alien encounters have a curious dreamlike or even fantastic flavor. While it may be true, as I have argued, that they both have the structure of *archetypal initiatory journeys,* the *worlds* that they open to their respective travelers seem, perhaps quite literally and not just metaphorically, to reside in altogether different universes.

That much, at least, seems obvious. And yet, what is obvious may not be true. As a case in point, consider the following narrative. When you read it, please decide into which of our two categories it should be placed.

Beryl Hendricks is a thirty-nine-year-old college-educated woman who operates a day-care center in New York State. In 1977 she had a benign tumor removed from her breast, but in the early summer of the next year, she discovered another one "about the size of a golf ball." Resolving to call her physician the next day, she remembers going downstairs that night to join her husband on the couch. She *doesn't* remember passing out there, though of course her husband witnessed it. He took her pulse and found she had none, as he later told her.

Meanwhile, Beryl had entered a nonordinary reality:

The next thing I remember was looking out of a round window and seeing the blackest blackness with tiny white sparkles (I later realized I was experiencing deep space). I felt cold—colder than I have ever experienced. I was unconcerned about my predicament and I turned my gaze from the window (to my left). There was a bright white light directly above me with four–seven thin, tall figures around me (I later realized I was on some kind of operating table). I was given two messages (telepathically):

1. Look and see—it is gone.
2. Follow your husband (we had been experiencing marital difficulty at the time).

All of a sudden, I was tumbling head over heels (figuratively—as I was out of my body) and saw the earth as geometric green and [was] shown land masses, changing, getting closer and closer, not unlike an airplane crashing, [traveling at] unbelievable speed, and finally falling from the couch to the floor; vomiting relentlessly.

Two hours passed, and when I washed the vomit off, the lump was gone—totally . . . In the ten years since this experience my health has been excellent and I have (with my husband) found a close personal relationship with God.

What on earth—or in heaven—do we have here? Is this an NDE or some kind of UFO encounter? Clearly, it has elements of both, and just as clearly it threatens to confound our neat dichotomy between these two types of experience. In fact, it is what I have come to recognize as a "mixed motif" case, and as that phrase implies, it is not the only instance in my files. Among my respondents, I have found others who in describing what purports to be an NDE begin to talk about UFOs and aliens in the same context. Furthermore, there turns out to be a small but respectable number of persons in my sample who report having had (though, to be sure, at different times) both an NDE *and* one or more UFO encounters.

Episodes such as Beryl's and the other mixed-motif and dual-experiencer cases to which I have alluded do indisputably give rise to some tantalizing possibilities. Could it be that the world of the NDE and that of the UFO abduction, for all their differences, are not, after all, universes apart, but a part of the *same* universe? And, second, could it be that NDErs and UFO experiencers have more in common with one another than we have heretofore suspected?

Now that I have raised these questions, it becomes obvious that, of course, all we have had to consider in the last three chapters are *reports* of experiences—of, indeed, some very extraordinary kinds of experiences. But all these reports come from *people,* and aside from a few demographics, we know absolutely nothing about them or the matrix of their lives out of which these remarkable encounters emerged. Who, then, are the people who have narrated these fascinating—and disturbing—tales? What are their backgrounds, and what, in more general psychological terms, do we know about them, anyway? And, finally, what, if anything, might our two categories of experiencers have in common?

These, naturally, are precisely the questions that the research conducted for this book was designed to answer. And before we are done, we shall indeed determine the exact relationship, now murky, between UFO encounters and NDEs. On our way to the answer, however, we are in for some surprises.

CHAPTER 5

THE OMEGA PROJECT

We have studied abduction stories individually and collectively with considerable care, but abductees remain the terra incognita of this phenomenon for now. Yet we cannot hope to gauge the value of the stories as evidence without some knowledge of the tellers as persons. Patterns in their psychology could tell us much about the shared predispositions of abductees, or the shared consequences of their experiences.

—Thomas E. Bullard

Thomas E. Bullard, a highly respected folklorist at Indiana University, is widely regarded as perhaps the preeminent student of UFO abductions in the world today. His two-volume work, *UFO Abductions: The Measure of a Mystery,* a survey of over three hundred abduction cases, published in 1987, set such a standard for scholarly excellence and methodical thoroughness that it has quickly become the one indispensable reference for anyone who seeks to understand the nature and dynamics of these perplexing encounters.

Recently, at a small invited conference for professionals at Virginia Polytechnic Institute, Bullard began his lecture on the topic of abductions with a lament. Even after all this time, he observed, we still know too little about the psychological makeup of persons reporting such experiences. And he is unquestionably right. Considering the mushrooming interest among ufologists in abduction episodes over the past five years or so, there has been a surprising dearth of attention regarding the psychological background and characteristics of those who have described these improbable, but thematically consistent, incidents. Even the one clinical study usually cited in this connection[1] is inconclusive regarding the extent to which abductees may have psychological problems, and its findings remain controversial and subject to varying interpretations.[2]

Even when we broaden the focus to include psychological studies concerned with people who have reported a variety of UFO encounters (including abduction episodes but not restricted to them), the picture isn't much clearer. The early work of Leo Sprinkle,[3] a veteran UFO researcher, which involved the administration of various personality tests, has recently been extended by his colleague June Parnell.[4] Their collective findings led these investigators to conclude that UFO experiencers were on the whole mentally healthy individuals with no obvious neurotic or psychotic symptoms, but a close inspection of their findings does also support a less sanguine interpretation. For example, UFO experiencers do appear to have stronger tendencies toward moral self-righteousness, suspiciousness, alienation, and even schizoid thinking. Although some researchers[5] concur with the views of Sprinkle and Parnell, several psychiatrically oriented commentators[6] take a far less charitable position and suggest that some form of mental illness may be present in persons claiming UFO contact.

This lack of agreement among various psychological and psychiatric experts about the mental health of those reporting UFO experiences of various kinds cannot help, at least for now, but revive our earlier doubts about such individuals. To put it bluntly, do strange people have strange experiences?

When we turn our attention to near-death experiencers, we find ourselves floating in a similar sea of ignorance concerning their psychological makeup and mental health. In their case, however, we are confronted with an additional puzzle. It has long been known that approximately only one of three persons who survives a near-death incident will later describe having had an NDE of some kind.[7] But why only one in three? Why should some individuals experience an ineffable light and a feeling of divine love when they nearly die, whereas others, who presumably come just as close to the brink of biological death, remember nothing? This question has stumped researchers from the beginning. Indeed, when I first met Raymond Moody in 1977, I made a point of asking him about this. His reply was as candid as it was pithy: "Ken," I remember him saying, "I haven't got a clue." And the answer to this conundrum has continued to elude NDE investigators to the present day.

Nevertheless, it will pay us enormous dividends if we can continue to tug at this unyielding knot, for, as we shall come to see, once it is unraveled, we shall have the solution not only to the mystery of differential NDE recall among near-death survivors, but to the type of person who is likely to report UFO encounters as well.

In my view, the reason previous research has failed to reach resolution over the matter of the psychology of those who report anomalous experiences such as UFO encounters and NDEs is that most of it has been, explicitly or otherwise, directed to issues of general psychopathology. This, however, is a red herring. The trail we really ought to be following is one that inquires into *specific psychological characteristics or childhood histories* that can be shown to *predispose* persons to report such unusual experiences in the first place. From here on, then, I would like to lead you onto the trail of such an inquiry and suggest that in pursuing it, it will be helpful to consider our two categories of extraordinary encounters together. I say this because it will soon be evident to you that the same factors that conduce toward remembering an NDE are also involved in fostering awareness of UFO encounters.

Now what might such psychological factors be?

We shall start with one that has almost suddenly swept into ufological and even NDE circles as the explanatory candidate of choice for those who are skeptical of the reality of these experiences. In the jargon of modern psychology, it is the trait now known as *fantasy proneness*.

A principal attempt to explain both NDEs and UFO encounters in strictly psychological terms has been made through invoking this concept of fantasy proneness—that is, the spontaneous tendency to enter into a state of rapt absorption focused on a world of self-created fantasy. For example, in the early 1980s, Sheryl Wilson and Theodore Barber, the two psychologists who first proposed the term and studied fantasy-prone women in their own research, suggested that NDErs might well come disproportionately from these ranks.[8] Likewise, in the often overheated world of UFO debate, there has already been a great deal of discussion and controversy over what role this psychological propensity might have in generating reports of UFO encounters.[9] For instance, two of the foremost proponents of the fantasy-prone interpretation have made a plausible case that Whitley Strieber, who was in fact a well-known author of horror fiction before writing *Communion,* is a prototypic fantasy-prone personality.[10]

The difficulty with evaluating the hypothesis of fantasy proneness, however, stems from the fact that almost without exception the commentators who concern themselves with it are long on opinion but present little or only selected anecdotal evidence in support of their position. As a result, we have almost no useful data by which to settle the point.

It was in part because of this unsatisfactory empirical state of affairs that the research to be reported in the next three chapters of this book was undertaken. One of the main purposes of the Omega Project, then, was to assess through careful and systematic study the relevance of a number of psychological factors, such as fantasy proneness, to the question of genesis and form of extraordinary encounters. As implied, however, fantasy proneness is only *one* such possible predisposing factor. Let us now consider some of the other candidates.

Clearly, one possible characteristic that might sensitize individuals to extraordinary encounters is the ability to respond to *paranormal experiences* in general. In UFO studies, for example, a number of researchers have argued for years that a notable proportion of persons claiming UFO encounters appear to be psychically gifted.[11] Recently, the English ufologist Jenny Randles has renewed interest in this possibility by asserting that many abductees have a personal history of paranormal experiences that may provide an important interpretative context for their abduction episode.[12] In near-death studies, there have already been several investigations showing that NDEs appear to stimulate the development of psychic awareness,[13] but whether NDErs are psychically gifted to begin with has remained unclear.[14] Accordingly, another of the aims of the Omega Project is to determine the degree to which NDErs and UFOErs (the abbreviation we shall henceforth employ to signify those who have reported some kind of UFO encounter) were, as children, already more open to the realm of paranormal experiences.

Quite apart from psychic sensitivities per se, there is also the question whether NDErs and UFOErs are, as writers such as Hilary Evans and I have proposed,[15] especially susceptible to altered states of consciousness that would, in turn, disclose what have been called nonordinary realities. If, for the moment, we assume that NDEs and UFOs might have their origin in such a domain, then those persons who are particularly skilled at entering into those states of consciousness that afford perceptual access to that domain would obviously be most likely to report awareness of these extraordinary encounters (or EEs, for short). Therefore, a third objective of our study is to see to what extent persons who relate extraordinary encounters (EErs) were, again as children, sensitive to what we shall simply call for now *alternate realities.*

One factor that might theoretically account for such sensitivity, if indeed it proves characteristic of our experiencers, is *dissociation,* a form of psychological fragmentation in which one portion of the individual splits off, like an autonomous entity, from the conscious self. Since some theorists[16] hold that dissociation is the key that in effect unlocks the door into alternate realities, it is important to determine whether EErs are especially prone to dissociation, and so that, too, will be examined in *The Omega Project.*

It may, however, be asked why one should think that dissociation might be a part of the psychological profile of experiencers in the first place. The answer lies in the fact that one of the most common antecedents of dissociation, which is widely held to be a defensive reaction to stress, is *child abuse and trauma.* In this connection, there has been a persistent but tantalizing suggestion on the part of some abduction researchers and therapists[17] that perhaps various forms of childhood abuse and trauma may also play a significant role in abduction episodes where, as we have seen, the symbolic sexual overtones are already obvious. Similarly, in the area of near-death studies, there is some preliminary but mostly anecdotal evidence that NDErs may be more likely than others to have suffered such a childhood history.[18] In any case, since the possible link between child abuse and trauma, on the one hand, and the tendency to report extraordinary experiences, on the other, has never been carefully researched, this study represents the first effort to see whether such a connection can indeed be shown conclusively to exist.

These, then, are some of the childhood antecedents and psychological characteristics that are of focal concern to us here: fantasy proneness, childhood psychic sensitivities, susceptibility to nonordinary realities, tendencies toward psychological dissociation, and incidence of child abuse and trauma. However, these factors comprise only one aspect of our effort to delineate a *psychological profile* of extraordinary experiencers.

Earlier, when discussing CE IVs, I remarked that the study of the *effects* of these encounters would prove to be of crucial importance to us in our attempt to tease out the meaning of these most peculiar, and peculiarly consistent, episodes. And in my previous book, *Heading Toward Omega,* I had followed a research strategy for NDEs that also highlighted the long-term effects of these experiences. Therefore, it will not surprise you to learn that in addition to factors that may *predispose* persons to report extraordinary encounters, The Omega Project will also be concerned to document a wide range of *aftereffects* that appear to emerge following these experiences.

In general, however, the *types* of aftereffects that we shall examine in our experiencers divide themselves into two main categories: *psychophysical changes* and *shifts in beliefs and personal values*. Here, we need to say only a bit about each of these two types for you to understand the reasoning behind this second major goal of the research for the Omega Project.

As I have implied, the UFO literature is rich in anecdotal

lore about alleged physical and even physiological and apparent neurological changes that are said to have been triggered by UFO experiences. Despite the frequency of these claims and, if true, their obvious significance for understanding what may lie at the heart of UFO encounters, there has never been a careful survey of precisely what effects are reliably reported by UFOErs. The Omega Project, then, will attempt to break new ground here by providing this kind of information. Regarding NDEs in this respect, there is a similar lacuna in our knowledge. Again, we have the occasional self-report testimony of NDErs that they believe they have undergone significant psychophysical and psychoenergetic changes since their experience, but we have only the barest beginnings of any systematic research on the matter.[19] So here, too, the present research seeks to start sketching in the picture concerning what kinds of psychophysical changes follow NDEs.

We are clearly more advanced in our understanding of some of the value changes that tend to occur after NDEs, since a good deal of previous research has addressed this question.[20] However, even here, there is an obvious need for more systematic and statistically oriented work with larger samples of NDEs since even the best-known NDE studies are flawed or deficient in these respects. The Omega Project, in consequence, was designed to provide a more solid statistical basis for assessing NDE value changes. In UFO studies, on the other hand, we remain for the most part titillated by the pervasive unsubstantiated anecdote, but careful research on value shifts is regrettably notable only by its absence. And even the one study I know of that attempts to provide statistical information about UFOErs in this respect is marred by the lack of a control group and other methodological weaknesses.[21] Hence, here too, the Omega Project will afford much-needed information on this type of aftereffect.

In addition to our value surveys, we will also be able to draw on the findings from a new opinion inventory that will allow us to assess for the first time exactly how NDEs and UFOEs affect beliefs and worldviews, especially those having to do with ecological concerns and the possible evolutionary significance of extraordinary encounters. This information, of course, will have particular relevance to the themes of this book indicated by its subtitle.

This, then, in brief, is an overview of the principal purposes of the Omega Project, which I can sum up as an effort to arrive at a psychological portrait of the extraordinary experiencer, both in terms of antecedents *and* aftereffects. At bottom, it is simply an attempt to answer the question I raised at the end of the last chapter: Who exactly *are* these people who have described the astonishing encounters that have dominated our attention in the first part of this book?

How we came to delineate the portrait of the extraordinary experiencer—our NDErs and UFOErs—is what I will tell next.

THE RESEARCH STUDY[22]

In September 1988, my research assistant, Christopher J. Rosing, sent out the first of hundreds of letters of invitation to potential participants in the Omega Project. We had compiled our lists of possible respondents from various sources. For those in the NDE category, I had drawn on my extensive archives of letters from persons who had either had NDEs or were merely interested in them, taking care to eliminate from consideration any persons who had already been in one of my previous studies. I also obtained additional names from the archives of the International Association for Near-Death Studies, an organization formerly located at the University of Connecticut that has since moved its headquarters to Philadelphia. For the UFO category, I was able to obtain the names of many individuals who had either had UFO-related experiences or were interested in UFOs through the kind cooperation of various UFO researchers and others connected with the field. In some cases, I was given names of persons who had already been interviewed by UFO investigators; many other names came from lists of correspondents who had written about their experiences or persons who had attended UFO conferences.[23]

My letter of invitation was straightforward: It briefly described the Omega Project and requested the recipient to take part in it. All that would be required, I explained, would be filling out some questionnaires at home and returning them to me in the mail. No remuneration was offered for this participation; instead, however, I offered to send a summary of the findings of the study at its conclusion (which indeed I did, in January 1990). Accompanying the letter was a reply postcard with blanks for respondents to indicate: (1) their willingness to take part in the study and (2) their UFO encounter or NDE status (i.e., either experiencer or not).

Once their postcard was received, respondents were sent an Omega Project Battery (i.e., a booklet of questionnaires), along with a detailed letter instructing them how the battery was to be filled out. An informed-consent sheet was also enclosed and required to be signed to permit participation. All that was left for the respondents to do, of course, was to complete the questionnaires and send them back to me.

A brief description of each of the questionnaires that comprised the Omega Project Battery is given below.[24] The questionnaires are listed in the exact order in which they appeared in the booklet.

1. Background Information Sheet. Requests basic demographic information.

2. Experience and Interest Inventory. Determines experiential and interest history for respondents in both our NDE and UFO categories. Used for final assignment to appropriate experiential or control group (see below).

3. Childhood Experience Inventory. Assesses the incidence of unusual psychological and paranormal experiences in childhood, including fantasy proneness, psychic sensitivity, and susceptibility to alternate realities (29 items).

4. Home Environmental Inventory. Solicits information on factors related to child abuse and other childhood traumas (38 items).

5. Psychological Inventory. Provides a measure of tendencies toward psychological dissociation (40 items).

6. Psychophysical Changes Inventory. Covers a wide range of psychophysical changes (60 items).

7. Life Changes Inventory. Assesses changes in personal values and interests (50 items).

8. Religious Beliefs Inventory. Provides an overall measure of the extent to which respondents shift toward a generalized universalistic *spiritual* (rather than sectarian religious) perspective (12 items).

9. Opinion Inventory. Assesses respondents' understanding of their experience (or interest) and its impact on their beliefs and worldviews.

Of the seven principal instruments, four (numbers 3, 4, 6, and 9) were specifically constructed for use in the Omega Project while the remainder (i.e., numbers 5, 7, and 8) have already been successfully used in previous research.[25] Inventories 6, 7, and 9 had four slightly different forms, each one appropriate to one of the four principal groups in the study, as I will explain shortly.

Upon receipt of each respondent's completed questionnaire packet, it was first inspected to insure that all inventories had been properly filled out. Then the Experience and Interest Inventory was checked in order to make certain that the respondent was entitled to be assigned to one of the four basic groups that were to comprise the study. These groups were defined and are abbreviated as follows:

NDE: Persons who reported an NDE

NDC: Persons who were interested in NDEs but never had one themselves

UFOE: Persons who had reported some kind of UFO encounter[26]

UFOC: Persons who were interested in UFOs but had no significant UFO-related experience themselves

It is important to say just a word about these four basic groups and the reasons why each of them is integral to the study. The NDE and UFOE respondents define what I call the *experiential groups* of this research, made up naturally of those who have had some kind of extraordinary encounter. If I am right in suggesting that these two groups may have some heretofore unsuspected commonalities, comparison *between* these groups ought to reveal them. The remaining groups are of course our *control groups*. Obviously, in order to evaluate the effects of EEs, it is mandatory to have some basis of comparison with persons who have not had such experiences. For this purpose, it seemed appropriate to provide our NDE and UFO experiential groups with a corresponding control group formed of individuals who were *interested* either in NDEs or UFOs but *who had no significant experience along these lines*. Thus, the NDC and UFOC groups are also crucial to the design of this study and represent what are called "tight" controls since all four groups can be assumed to have a high level of interest and knowledge about either NDEs or UFOs, depending on their defining category.

The Omega Project, beginning with our first letters of invitation in September 1988, continued over the next fifteen months, during which time we received completed batteries from a total of 264 persons. Eventually, they were sorted into the four basic groups in the following numbers:

NDE = 74
NDC = 54
UFOE = 97
UFOC = 39

Of course, a good part of the second half of 1989 was taken up with the coding and computer analysis of the wealth of data that the Omega Project afforded us.[27]

Conducting a project like this, where one waits so long before the results of one's research can be known, is a little like cooking a meal in a sealed oven for a year or so and hoping that by the time one can open it, there will truly be a delectable meal as one's reward. So it was with our research team—we would collect, code, and enter our data on the university's computer system, a process taking many months and involving many tedious hours at our computer terminals; then, at the end, almost overnight it seemed, we would be swimming in computer printouts themselves swarming with masses of numbers! You can imagine we had some fair degree of apprehension as to what patterns these numbers would finally resolve themselves into and whether there would be—to revert to my previous analogy—even a digestible meal, if not a delicious one, after our many months of toil and doubt.

That we eventually feasted on what we saw in those computer printouts you will now come to see for yourself. Let's look—finally—at the results of the Omega Project.

CHAPTER 6

CHILDHOOD ANTECEDENTS OF EXTRAORDINARY ENCOUNTERS

Far and away the most important question we can ask is, why do some people have them and not others? The encounter experience would be a lot easier to understand if it could be shown that it happens only to a particular kind of person.

—Hilary Evans

Childhood! That's the key. Not the only key, but the first key to the mystery of the human creature.

—Robertson Davies

A REASSURING WORD TO THE RESEARCH-WARY

In the next three chapters, I am going to present the main findings from the Omega Project. Of course, I realize there is a fair chance that you may not be as enamored of computer printouts and statistical tables of data as I am, so I want to assure you at the onset that you will find none of that here in the text (virtually all of the statistical information from this study is located in Appendix II for the interested reader). What I shall do instead is to take you on a kind of walking tour of our results, pointing out the essential items of interest as straightforwardly as I can and with as little jargon as necessary. As we proceed, you will gradually see how the findings from the Omega Project form a coherent profile of the psychology of the person who is prone to extraordinary experiences such as NDEs and UFOEs. And to make this developing picture as clear as possible to you, I shall also pause from time to time in our tour to summarize or otherwise *highlight* the gist and significance of what we have seen before continuing.

Having said all this, I have one final suggestion for anyone who still feels a bit skittish or doubtful about this rendezvous with the data from the Omega Project.

Try skimming along with me, absorbing what you can in your own way, and concentrate on the summaries—they will be enough for you to follow the general trend of the argument and to see the outline, as it emerges, of the portrait of the extraordinary experiencer I mean to sketch in this and succeeding chapters.

Before beginning, however, I need to tarry a moment just to explain a little bit about how we classified our UFO respondents.

A CLASSIFIED MATTER

In getting our battery of questionnaires ready for the computer analysis, we were immediately confronted with a serious problem: How to categorize our UFO respondents?

From recalling the material of Chapters 2 and 3, you can easily appreciate that there are formidable complexities here. First of all, there is the sheer range of UFO encounters—from mere sightings of anomalous and apparently inexplicable lights in the sky all the way to episodes featuring claimed abductions by alien creatures. Then, there is the factor of variations in the *quality* of the experience, which covers a spectrum from dreamlike telepathic contact to apparent physicality. Finally, there is the thorny issue of the *number* of such experiences, regardless of type.

As our research team sorted through the pros and cons of several different classificatory possibilities, we eventually arrived at a scheme that allowed us to code each UFO respondent into one of *ten* comprehensive categories. Each written narrative was then independently scored by my four research assistants and me. A given narrative was assigned to one of the ten categories whenever at least three of us agreed on it; in a few cases when this wasn't initially the case, we reviewed the narrative in question and reached consensus through group discussion.

Next, for purposes of statistical analysis, each adjacent pair of categories was combined to form *five basic groups,* as follows:

1. Interest in UFOs only *or* a psychologically nonimpactful sighting ($n = 39$, i.e., 39 respondents fell into this group).
2. A psychologically impactful sighting *or* physical trace cases ($n = 20$).
3. Perception of *or* encounter with humanoid beings [without abduction] ($n = 21$).
4. Abduction episode with *or* without sighting ($n = 38$).
5. Dreamlike, telepathic encounters *or* multiple experiences[1] ($n = 18$).

In this final classification, group 1 represents the UFOC sample, while the remainder (i.e., groups 2–5) comprise the UFOE sample.

When we made our preliminary statistical comparisons among these groups,[2] we discovered the first of many surprises in this study. Virtually all comparisons showed that all four *experiential* groups did not reliably differ from one another (though, collectively, they did tend to differ from the control group on most measures). The importance of this finding for us is this: *Those reporting abduction episodes are* not *a psychologically distinctive group compared to others who had had different UFO-related experiences.* Even when we did a refined analysis using only the most clear-cut abduction episodes, the results did not change. In view of these unexpected findings, it was appropriate for us to combine *all* of our experiential groups into a single large group ($n = 97$) in order to contrast it with our UFO control group ($n = 39$).

It was in this way, then, that we arrived at the fourfold-classification scheme of all of our respondents in this study that was mentioned in the last chapter, which, for convenience, I shall reproduce here:

NDE: Persons who reported an NDE

NDC: Persons who were interested in NDEs, but never had one themselves

UFOE: Persons who had reported some kind of UFO encounter

UFOC: Persons who were interested in UFOs but had no significant UFO-related experience themselves

With the problem of the UFO respondents resolving itself so neatly, it was now possible to proceed with the analyses of real substantive interest. And of these, the first that naturally demands our attention concerns *childhood and developmental factors* associated with later encounter experiences. Since our results here were based on the Childhood Experience Inventory, it's time we took a closer look at it.

CHILDHOOD EXPERIENCE INVENTORY (CEI)

This questionnaire, presented in a true-false format, provided measures of three psychological factors that could possibly sensitize persons to the existence of anomalous phenomena, such as NDEs and UFOs, that may be said to have their locus outside of the normal range of ordinary sensory-based waking consciousness. The first of these factors is *fantasy proneness*, whose influence in shaping such perceptions was assessed by a ten-item scale that was embedded in the CEI.[3] Three items from this scale will give you a sense of it:

As a child, I had a very vivid imagination.

When I was young, I daydreamed a lot.

As a child, my fantasy world was very rich.

If fantasy proneness is a propensity that increases the likelihood of reports of extraordinary encounters, as some theorists have argued, then we should find our experiential respondents (i.e., those in the NDE and UFOE groups) scoring reliably higher than their controls on this factor.

Our findings, however, will disappoint the fantasy-proneness advocates. In fact, as you can see if you take the trouble to glance at the first row of Table I in Appendix II,[4] fantasy proneness is definitely *not* a trait that differentiates our experiential groups from the controls. Indeed, the average score on this measure is actually identical for the two UFO groups and nearly so for the ND groups. (The UFO groups score somewhat higher than the corresponding ND groups, but the difference is not statistically reliable.) Accordingly, there is no evidence from our study that either UFOErs or NDErs are distinctively characterized by tendencies toward fantasy proneness.

Nevertheless, further analyses soon revealed that although unusual proclivity for fantasy was not a feature of the psychological makeup of our experiential sample, other traits most decidedly were. For example, another of our measures derived from the CEI dealt with the extent to which our respondents had as children been sensitive to what we called *alternate realities*. Again, a few statements from this eight-item scale will give its flavor and also suggest how it differed from that concerned with fantasy proneness.

As a child, I was aware of nonphysical beings while I was awake.

As a child, I was able to see into "other realities" that others didn't seem to be aware of.

> When I was a child, I could see what some people call fairies or "the little people."

Here, as you can see, the items are not so much concerned with obvious immersion in fantasy worlds as they are indicative of subjectively *real* perceptions of nonordinary realms and of the unusual denizens of those domains. When we came to examine our data here, we found striking differences between our experiential and control groups. UFOErs, and to a somewhat lesser extent NDErs, were much more likely than respondents in our control groups to affirm that as children they were *already* sensitive to these alternate realities. Indeed, our statistical analysis revealed a huge difference in this respect between our experiential and control groups.[5] A close inspection of the actual means (i.e., statistical averages) for the four groups, as presented in the second row of Table I, however, will disclose a particular rank order that will be found to recur for several other comparisons in this chapter: The UFOErs are highest, followed by NDErs, then by the UFO control-group respondents, and finally the ND controls.

Precisely the same group rank order in fact was found to hold for our next comparison, the reported incidence of *childhood psychic experiences*, a result that is not altogether surprising in view of the high correlation between this measure and that for sensitivity to alternate realities.[6] Here we used a six-item scale whose flavor is suggested by statements like these:

> As a child, I seemed to know things that were going to happen in the future—and they did.

> During my childhood, I had out-of-body experiences.

> When I was a child, I was very psychic.

And again what we found was another huge effect favoring our experiential respondents[7] although, as before, the UFOE group was clearly highest of all.

What We Have Learned So Far

To summarize this first set of data, then, what we discovered from our analysis of the CEI is that persons who as adults report UFOEs or NDEs are not as children especially inclined toward a world of fantasy, but *they are apparently already sensitive to nonordinary realities*—and this is particulrly true of our UFOE respondents. As we shall later see, this is a finding that will prove to be of no small importance when it comes to interpreting the nature of encounters with UFO beings—as well as NDEs, which, as we know, also often involve contact with entities of various kinds.

The Childhood World of Extraordinary Experiencers

Although our statistical findings here are clear-cut, mere numbers alone can never convey the subjective realities they summarize as well as a few personal narratives can. So, if "a picture is worth a thousand words," a single story is easily worth a spate of figures—especially ones conveniently tucked away in an appendix. Let's take a moment, then, to enter the childhood world of some of those people who will later describe extraordinary UFO and near-death encounters. Understanding their psychological sensitivities as children and the special realities they seem to have been aware of will help us to see why they are natural recipients for extraordinary encounters of all sorts.

The most common kind of nonordinary perception during childhood reported by the respondents in our study involves the sighting of one or more nonphysical beings who are usually spotted at night when the child is roused from sleep. Most respondents say, and some even insist, that they were not dreaming at the time. Although I did not specifically request this kind of information from my respondents, their questionnaires, and sometimes their accompanying letters, provided ample instances of this kind of childhood encounter. Though I won't take the time here specifically to identify the respondents whose brief illustrative narratives are presented below, most of them are UFOErs, though some of them have also had NDEs. The emotions triggered by these encounters, however, vary. For example, some are apparently or clearly frightening:

[1] I was asleep in my own room [she was fifteen years old at the time of this particular incident but claims to have had previous experiences beginning when she was two!]. I woke— I do not know what time it was. I lay there thinking for a while—nothing serious or upsetting, and finally, rather disgusted at being awake, turned over to try to go back to sleep. There was a fully illuminated man standing beside the bed. My first thought was, "Oh, my God! There is a very live dead person standing there!"

He was humanoid, sandy hair, blue eyes, and dressed in a manner similar to but significantly different from the "Blue Boy" painting. Blue brocade, white lace, tailored coat, breeches.

I was terrified! He told me telepathically, "Turn on the light." I jumped out of bed and hit the light switch. He was still there! I just stared at him, terribly frightened. Then he slowly vanished, just faded away. When he disappeared, the fear vanished completely. I turned off the light, went back to bed and to sleep.

[2] I was nine or ten years old. I shared the bedroom on the third floor of our house. On this particular night, I was alone though, at least at this time. I had not yet fallen asleep when I looked into my brother's room and saw what seemed to be a thin and kind of shadowy figure sort of float over the bed, from one side of the room to the other, until it was out of sight. I pulled the covers over my head until I guess I fell asleep. I also had seen things in the wall of my room. These visions were white, and one seemed to glow.

[3] Woken from a sound sleep late at night [he was eight years old]. I felt that something was watching me closely and trying to communicate to me. I slowly opened my eyes to see two slightly glowing objects before me at the edge of my bed.(One in the foreground was seeming to communicate. One in the background not to do so.) I was unable to move or scream. I was able to think clearly. I felt that the objects were ghosts. I suddenly went to sleep. . . . I felt that the objects were trying to tell me of some kind of relationship between themselves and me.

[4] I lived with my mother, father, and brother in Reno, Nevada. I shared a room with my brother. During the night I thought I was having a nightmare [age not specified]. My mother had always told me, "If you have a nightmare, pinch yourself and you will wake up." A being appeared in the room. I started pinching my arm and screaming for my mother, so I knew it wasn't a nightmare. He didn't move, and my brother didn't awaken. When my mother entered my room, the being vanished. My mother tried to convince me it was a nightmare. I explained to her that he was wearing white "long-legged underwear." I am forty-nine years old, and the memory is as clear as it was then.

[5] I was three (or so). Asleep, I awoke in the night and looked around my room. I saw a light outside (blue/white)—it moved around. Very bright—a small blue light moved around my room. Across the walls and closet door. Little "white" men . . . came into my room. They looked like "Casper, the friendly ghost" to me. There were five or six of them. They had a teeter-totter . . .—they wanted me to come with them, to "play" with them. They spoke without voices—I heard them in my head. They tried to get me out of my bed. I was afraid, but I knew that my daddy and mommy would *not* help me. . . . I do not remember more. I blacked out . . . This kind of "dream" . . . happened many times as a child and an adult. Only as a child do I remember "seeing" them.

Such encounters need not be frightening, however, nor do they always occur at night. Case in point:

> In June 1968, at the age of thirteen, in the middle of intense prayer, a woman appeared to me in my bedroom. She told me she was not "from this place" and also told me that my prayers would be answered. She stayed and conversed with me for quite a while. I was not afraid of her. She was beautiful.

And in other cases, though the encounter apparently begins realistically enough, it soon takes on fantastic elements of the sort that one finds in the literature on "astral travel." Nevertheless, the experience may have and retain the quality of an actual event to the respondent. Here's an example:

> At age three I *remember* a *very* tall man appearing in my room in Cleveland. The next thing I knew, we were in a mountain in Egypt. Inside were many semi-clear containers with people in them. The man said these people were "sleeping" for a long time, but in the future would be awakened to complete their tasks. I was shown a book which I could understand at the time, but now do not remember. When I finished the book, I was returned to my room.
>
> I have had verification of this mountain and what is in it by an Egyptian man who has *seen* it as a child. . . . I've had this *memory* for almost forty-three years. It *was not* a dream!

With this example, we have obviously crossed the boundary from experiences that appear to represent what I have called alternate realities to those that begin clearly to shade into the psychic realm. And of course there are others that are inaugurated by a subjectively compelling paranormal event, such as an out-of-body experience, and then develop into full-blown perceptions of alternate realities. Consider, for instance, what happened to this woman when she was turning three:

On my third birthday my mother gave me a party and a diamond ring. While we were sitting around the table waiting for the cake, I was out of my body, hovering around the ceiling watching myself and the other children. When mother brought in the cake and I blew out the candles, I entered my body. That night I was too excited to sleep. My bed was under a window. I sat with my elbows on the sill, looking at the stars and my ring. As I looked up at the sky, three lights became bigger and brighter and closer. They came close to my window and hovered there. Then they turned into people shapes. Each one was a predominant color: gold, blue, and pink. They had brought me here to learn. They told me that Earth is a school, that I would experience many difficult things, that I would meet strange people, and that my task was to learn to love them regardless of what they did. They told me that no matter what happened, my true self would never be touched. Then they left.

The narrative fragments I have presented to illustrate these unusual childhood encounters serve to give us an impression of the experiential frame of reference that may be typical of the childhoods of many of our NDErs and UFOErs, but even collectively they fail to do justice to the lifelong personal context in which such experiences tend to be embedded. That is, for many of our experiential respondents, such events are not merely solitary or isolated incidents, but *recurrent motifs* in childhoods marked by anomalous occurrences of various kinds. Therefore, before concluding this section, it will be useful for us to see something of this overall pattern by examining at least one respondent's personal history at some length.

Gina Willoughby, a thirty-seven-year-old librarian, lives in a small town in Virginia and claims to have been aware of paranormal and other extraordinary experiences from virtually the beginning of her life:

It may have started as early as my birth [she writes in a letter to me], for I have had "visions" (for lack of a better label!) of my actual birth experience, but I viewed this from an out-of-body perspective, as if I were in the corner of the ceiling looking down on my infant body (it was a home birth, European style), and I have memories of pre-birth, that is, a womb memory. *My life has been a case history of paranormal potpourri* [my emphasis].

And as a child, she clearly continued to have out-of-body experiences:

. . . I would separate (after going to bed at night) from my physical body, sometimes hover over my bed and then walk around my house and around the outside of my house, passing through material objects, etc. This type of experience happened often.

Later on, Gina would find herself in other realms:

I began to experience a rush into a second stage realm. In this realm, I was in a beautiful lighted place aware of others around me—and I felt "love." Love for everyone, a special connected love. I felt at home in this place, I wanted to stay there—I loved it there.

When she was about eight years old, she began to encounter beings:

[When I was] around age eight, two beings, one male and one female, started appearing to me. This always happened outdoors and in particular areas of the farm I lived on. They would speak to me telepathically. They said they were from a place named Zenith (just like the TV) and that they were my "true parents." My relationship with them was quite extensive and went on for about three years. (They said they loved me and protected me.)

During this period, however, another, and stranger, being manifested to her:

[When I was] age ten, a new entity began to come to me. He (it was a *he*) was very tall and looked like a "big foot"— all hairy and apelike. There was telepathic communcation and he had a name, but I don't recall what it was. He claimed to be my protector and he said he loved me, just as my "Zenith parents" did. He was with me briefly, maybe a year or so at the most.

Gina also saw fairies as a child. To the item pertaining to this matter on the CEI, she wrote in the margin, "God, yes!" and then adds this intriguing comment, "My six year old daughter now sees and plays with them, too" (followed by a parenthetical aside: "I know it sounds crazy.") Later, she explains herself:

By fairies, I mean non-physical entities that one is *aware of* but may not necessarily actually see in a physical sense. My little girl speaks of "fairy friends" because it is a label she learned through reading about such creatures in fairy tales! But she does say that she can *only* actually see them when she goes to "fairyland." Fairyland is a dream state. She describes traveling to fairyland in her dreams in the same way one would describe an out-of-body experience—which was the same for *me* as a child.

Gina's Omega Project battery is virtually riddled with unsolicited descriptions (for which I am nonetheless grateful) of her unusual experiences, both in childhood and later on, and I have also received several letters from her that provide much additional information about her history of such encounters. However, I think I have quoted enough excerpts to suggest the accuracy of her own previously cited self-assessment: "My life has been a case history of paranormal potpourri," she says.

And Gina herself is hardly a rare specimen of this sort of psychic life tapestry among those who also have come to report a UFO encounter along the way. Other students of the UFO phenomenon have already noted the same distinctive and illuminating pattern. Jenny Randles, in her study of abductees, for instance:

> Abductees tend to be psychic. . . . [T]he extent of these claims about psychic phenomena in the history of a witness simply cannot be evaded . . . this correlation between abduction witnesses and their previous strange encounters does exist.[8]

Furthermore:

> I believe this superior imaging ability, coupled with the high ESP scores in other experiments, and the very clear incidence of paranormal experiences in abductees' lives, will prove to be the key to the entire mystery, for *these seem to be the only things that make them in any way different from everyone else* [my emphasis].[9]

Randles also cites the research of Ken Phillips, another English ufologist, who has carried out his own studies of the lives of close-encounter witnesses and has administered some personality tests as well. His findings show that

> . . . dream reportage of UFOs and flying (floating) is much greater . . . and even more significantly, there is a high level of ESP reportage.[10]

Meanwhile, another keen writer on UFO and other extraordinary encounters, Hilary Evans, after surveying a great deal of the literature pertaining to such persons, has ably, if informally, summarized the general view of investigators like himself:

> I suspect that most of us, off the record, would say we have a fairly good idea of the kind of person most likely to have an encounter experience. I suspect also it would be the kind of person we would—still discreetly off the record—vaguely describe as "psychic."[11]

In support of his position, for example, Evans elsewhere cites the work of Berthold Schwarz, who has written of close-encounter witnesses:

> A contact is not just an isolated event in an individual's life but something that must be viewed in the larger context of his past history and his postcontact experiences, attitudes and behavior . . . Many have dissociative personalities, in some cases even multiple personalities. They are susceptible to trance states . . . Another thing that happens is the unleashing of psi [i.e., psychic] phenomena around the percipient. Perhaps it's to be expected, since trance-like states are conducive to the production of ESP and psychokinesis.[12]

Schwarz's observations are not only most apposite to my main point here, but as we shall see before long are also quite prophetic of the direction and findings of our own inquiry.

However, before we follow Schwarz's lead, we mustn't let *the main point* of *this* discussion elude us. In one respect, the statistical findings and case history material we have already reviewed in this section also add something new and important to the picture that has just been summed up in the preceding quotations, and that's this: It isn't just that those who report EEs are psychic or otherwise unusually susceptible to altered states of consciousness—*It is that they are already oriented that way as children.*

The question that now confronts us, of course, is what factors might we suppose are at work in the developmental histories of our experiential respondents to make them so sensitive in the first place to these nonordinary realities?

This brings us to the second questionnaire in our Omega battery, which we labeled somewhat neutrally the Home Environment Inventory.

THE HOME ENVIRONMENT INVENTORY (HEI)

The HEI was actually intended to be a measure of various components of childhood abuse and trauma, since, as I indicated in the last chapter, in doing this study we sought to determine whether there might be any relationship between such childhood experiences and susceptibility to extraordinary encounters. Accordingly, we constructed this inventory of the following five factors[13] so as to yield measures of childhood abuse and trauma, each illustrated by a couple of sample HEI items:

1. Physical abuse and punishment
   Were you physically mistreated as a child or teenager?
   Did your parents ever hit or beat you when you did not expect it?

2. Psychological abuse
   Did your parents insult you or call you names?
   Did your parents blame you for things you didn't do?

3. Sexual abuse
   Did you have traumatic sexual experiences as a child or teenager?
   Did your relationship with your parents ever involve a sexual experience?

4. Neglect
   As a child, did you feel unwanted or emotionally neglected?
   How often were you left alone as a child?

5. Negative home atmosphere
   As a child, did you feel that your home was charged with the possibility of unpredictable violence?
   Did your parents verbally abuse each other?

Respondents were asked to answer these questions by using a five-point scale that ranged from never (0) to always (4).

The results—as shown in Table 2 of Appendix II—reveal a most intriguing, clear-cut, and disturbing pattern. *There is a consistent tendency for both UFOErs and NDErs to report a greater incidence of childhood abuse and trauma.* Indeed, such differences between our experiential and control respondents emerge on *all* five components here, and usually at highly significant statistical levels (as shown in the last column of Table 2). Because scores on these various components tended to be highly correlated, it made sense to us to devise an overall index of childhood abuse and trauma based on all these measures combined. When we did so, we found that this composite index of childhood abuse and trauma again demonstrated a significant effect: our extraordinary experiencers in *both* categories score much higher than the controls.[14] Thus, just as we have seen for measures based on the CEI, here, too, our UFOErs and NDErs turn out to be very *similar* to one another (and both differ markedly from the control groups), suggesting, obviously, that these two categories of experiential respondents may well have had similarly troubled childhoods.

Beyond the evidence from the HEI that our experiencers have more stressful childhoods than controls, there is some additional data from the CEI that points in the same direction. On that questionnaire, we had also inquired into the incidence of serious and even life-threatening illnesses when our respondents were children. In the light of our results from the HEI, our findings here are of no small interest: Experiential respondents (again in both categories) are much more likely to attest that they were seriously ill as children,[15] which clearly implies that in this way, too, their childhoods were a greater source of stress to them than were those of our control respondents.[16]

What We Have Now Learned About Childhood Abuse and Trauma in the Lives of Extraordinary Experiencers

The overall results of our analysis of both the HEI and CEI, then, strongly support our earlier inference that one significant predisposing factor in the developmental history of our extraordinary experiencers may well be *the presence of relatively high (compared to our control groups) levels of childhood abuse and trauma and possibly other forms of stress*. The possible etiological role such incidents may play in the genesis of NDEs and UFO reports is a matter that can be considered properly, however, only after a full presentation of our findings intended for this chapter is laid out. Therefore, I shall defer its discussion for just a few moments more.

And Some Important Qualifications

Still, because the factor of childhood abuse and trauma *will* prove to be a crucial link in the chain of our eventual interpretation and also because it is obviously such a sensitive issue in its own right, it would be imprudent not to offer at least some cautionary statements about it here—and what the data from the Omega Project can really disclose to us about it.

First, it goes without saying that like all studies based on self-reports and personal testimony, this one can actually tell us nothing for certain concerning the actual childhood histories of our respondents. For of course we know only what they *tell* us; from our data alone we can never learn what in truth occurred in the lives of our respondents.

Second, *what* they tell us is that those of them who report UFOEs or NDEs also say they experienced more abuse and trauma as children. Does that mean, even assuming these self-reports are valid, that many or all such persons must have such histories? Obviously not! Indeed, exactly what proportion of our experiential and control respondents may be said to have had a troubled childhood depends on arbitrary cutoff points for defining "significant abuse";[17] it cannot be answered definitively from our analyses. To repeat, all we can say here is that such reports are simply made *more frequently* by our extraordinary experiencers.

Finally, though obvious, it still needs to be said that of course abuse and trauma in childhood aren't the *only* factors that may make for heightened sensitivity to nonordinary realities. Doubtless there are others (and I shall mention some possibilities shortly)—but they were not assessed in our study. They remain to be identified in future research. Child abuse and trauma— and other stressors such as serious illness—may *contribute* to this kind of sensitivity, but this study doesn't establish that it has a primary, much less exclusive, role in this regard.

Right now, to conclude the data portion of this chapter, I must point out that *if* indeed it is true that our extraordinary experiencers have endured more child abuse and trauma than controls, then something else should follow. Exactly what that is, we attempted to measure with the third instrument in our battery, which received the somewhat misleadingly bland and general title of Psychological Inventory.

PSYCHOLOGICAL INVENTORY (PI)

This questionnaire, in fact, is far more specific in its focus than its innocuous label implies. Devised by a former university colleague of mine, Dr. Michael Wogan, now at Rutgers University, the PI is designed[18] to measure tendencies toward psychological dissociation, and in that regard it has previously been used in research by others.[19] In its format, the forty-item PI uses another five-point scale, with response alternatives ranging from strongly agree to strongly disagree, and affords a single overall score indicative of dissociation tendencies. Here are a few representative items from the PI that reflect these tendencies:

I feel as though I have always been able to hypnotize myself.

I feel as though I've been "absent" part of the time.

Sometimes I have blank spells when I do things without being aware of what I've done.

When I am tense or under a strain, I can relax by blocking everything out of my mind.

I have been hypnotized unintentionally, for example by looking at a lighted sign or listening to a recording.

We employed this questionnaire in the Omega Project for two reasons: (1) to provide an indirect check on our supposition that UFOErs and NDErs might have a history of child abuse and trauma; and (2) to explore the possible role of dissociation in *mediating* access to nonordinary realities.

As to the logic of the first point, since it is known that persons with reported histories of childhood abuse and trauma are more likely to score higher on measures of dissociation or even, with extreme abuse, to develop serious dissociative disorders such as multiple personality,[20] it follows that we should expect our extraordinary experiencers to show elevated dissociation scores, too. Such a finding would of course be entirely in keeping with the contention of Berthold Schwarz, previously mentioned (p. 137), that many close-encounter witnesses tend to have dissociative personalities. Regarding the second purpose, since theorists such as Hilary Evans[21] have persuasively argued that it is the ability to dissociate that governs access to alternate realities, and since we already know that our experiential respondents seem especially sensitive to these realms, it is reasonable to expect them to score relatively high on our measure of dissociation.

This, then, was the prediction that the PI was used to test.

And, as Table 3 makes clear, our expectations were on the whole borne out: Our EErs *do* score significantly higher than their corresponding controls on dissociation tendencies, with UFOE respondents scoring the highest of all and UFO respondents *in general* tending to exceed their counterparts in the ND categories.[22] Although the statistical effects here are somewhat weaker than before, I should point out that the *rank-order pattern* of the differences among our four basic groups is nevertheless exactly the same as that we have seen previously for the alternate realities and psychic sensitivity measures of the CEI— a finding that squares nicely with Evans's hypothesis that dissociation mediates access to nonordinary realities.

Furthermore, there is evidence from another study that the dissociation scores for *all* groups except the NDC, and particularly of the UFOE group, should be viewed as quite high compared to normal controls. Barbara Sanders and her colleagues[23] recently found that an unselected sample of 270 undergraduates at the University of Connecticut averaged only 91.90 on the PI. That score is not significantly different from that of the NDC group, but is markedly lower than that of all other groups in our study.[24]

What We Have Learned About Psychological Dissociation and Extraordinary Experiencers

To summarize the main findings here, there seems to be good support for the assumption that tendencies toward dissociation should indeed be considered a part of the psychological profile of our extraordinary experiencers, and especially so for our UFOErs, just as Schwarz has claimed. Now, just to forestall any misunderstanding here, I should be clear about one thing: It is normal to dissociate. We all dissociate to a degree and sometimes. Dissociation, except when it reaches an extreme, is not in itself pathological; in such cases, it is customary to speak of dissociative *disorders,* and not merely *tendencies* toward dissociation. Therefore, what I am saying here is merely and simply this: Overall, individuals who report UFO encounters and NDErs appear to have a greater likelihood of showing dissociative *tendencies* in their psychological functioning.

We have now completed our survey of the principal findings that give us information about the psychology of extraordinary experiencers, and especially of their unusual and indeed sometimes troubled childhoods. What we need to do before proceeding, however, is to strive to make sense of what we have seen. Let us take a few moments, then, to consider how to put all these data pieces together to form a coherent image of the development of extraordinary experiencers.

A DEVELOPMENTAL THEORY OF PROPENSITIES FOR EXTRAORDINARY ENCOUNTERS

Our initial findings dealing with possible childhood antecedents of EEs and the dissociative mode of psychological functioning typical of those reporting such experiences appear to me to hang together quite neatly from a theoretical point of view. I say this despite my awareness that, strictly speaking, the Omega Project does not in itself permit one to draw any causal inferences about how these factors are related. Nevertheless, it is permissible—and I think I would be remiss if I did not do so—to offer a *theory* about how the propensity to experience EEs might be understood to have its actual origins in the childhood history of the individual. Such a theory could then provide the basis for rigorous hypothesis testing in future research. Accordingly, what I would like to do next is to present a tentative formulation concerning how people who are sensitive to extraordinary encounters, such as NDEs and UFOEs, get that way. Doing so will help you to see more clearly how the data of this chapter form a plausible theoretical pattern.

My argument begins with the proposition that a history of child abuse and trauma plays a central etiological role in promoting sensitivity to UFOEs and NDEs. My second assumption, which reflects a now increasingly widespread understanding of some of the consequences of childhood abuse and trauma, is that growing up under such conditions tends to stimulate the development of a dissociative response style as a means of *psychological defense*. After all, a child who is exposed to either the threat or actuality of physical violence, sexual abuse, or other severe traumas, will be strongly motivated selectively to "tune out" those aspects of his physical and social world that are likely to harm him by splitting himself off from the sources of those threats, that is, by *dissociating*. By doing so—and this is my third assumption—he is more likely to "tune into" other realities where, by virtue of his dissociated state, he can temporarily feel safe regardless of what is happening to his body.[25] In this way, precisely as Evans has theorized,[26] dissociation would directly foster relatively easy access to alternate, nonordinary realities.

This kind of attunement, however, is not a gift of dissociation itself, which only makes it possible, but of a correlated capacity, that for what is called *psychological absorption*. This is the ability to concentrate and focus one's attention on the figures and features of one's inner reality to the exclusion of events taking place in the external environment. My assumption here is that it is precisely the person who can easily transcend the sensory world *and,* as the poet William Blake—himself a master of this form of awareness—put it, "attend the minute particulars" of his interior states, who is especially likely to register and recall extraordinary encounters. That is, once the shift to nonsensory realities has occurred, it seems to be the capacity for psychological absorption that is crucial.

Interestingly enough, childhood abuse and trauma, which tend to trigger dissociative reactions, may also promote psychological absorption. For example, a recent study of persons suffering from multiple-personality disorder, which is almost always associated with especially cruel forms of child abuse, has suggested that multiples may have truly extraordinary gifts for attuning themselves to inner realities and thus should score extremely highly on measures of psychological absorption.[27]

However this ability comes into being, though, its role in experiences kindred to NDEs and UFOEs seems clearly established. For example, a recent study of predictors of mystical and visionary experiences found that the trait of psychological absorption was the single most important personality variable implicated and was in fact linearly related to the frequency of such experiences.[28] This overall finding jibes well with other studies of the correlates of mystical experience[29] as well as with investigations of spontaneous and induced out-of-body experiences, facility for which also seems to be related to absorption tendencies.[30] Furthermore, in the specific context of NDEs, there is at least one study that clearly demonstrates a relationship between psychological absorption and NDEr status.[31] Finally, our own data from the Omega Project, especially those having to do with pronounced sensitivities to alternate and psychic realities, can easily be incorporated under the larger construct of psychological absorption. This quality, then, seems to be the hallmark of what we might call *"the encounter-prone personality."*

We have now in effect set the developmental stage for an extraordinary encounter—either an NDE or a UFOE. To summarize our theory to this point, we have as a prototype an individual who, coming from a history of childhood abuse and trauma, has developed dissociative tendencies as well as a capacity to become deeply absorbed in alternate realities. Indeed, we can assume that such an individual, by virtue of this kind of psychological conditioning, is well accustomed to such unusual states of consciousness since he has often had recourse to enter them.

When, therefore, in later life, such persons undergo the trauma or shock of either a near-death incident or one involving a UFO, they are more likely than others, because of their history of familiarity with these nonordinary realities, spontaneously to "flip" into that state of consciousness, which, like a special lens, affords a glimpse of these remarkable occurrences. As a result, they are likely to "see" and register what other persons may remain oblivious to.

What I am suggesting, then, is that these individuals are what we might call *psychological sensitives* with low stress thresholds, and that it is their traumatic childhoods that have helped to make them so. From my own personal point of view, however, these UFOErs and NDErs are actually the unwitting beneficiaries of a kind of compensatory gift in return for the wounds they have incurred in growing up. That is, through the exigencies of their difficult and in some cases even tormented childhoods, they also come to develop *an extended range of human perception beyond normally recognized limits*. Thus, they may experience directly what the rest of us with unexceptional childhoods may only wonder at.

Now in laying out these assumptions having to do with the development of the encounter-prone personality, I have—in view of the findings presented in this chapter—naturally given the factor of child abuse and trauma a primary and presumably causative role. However, it is of course important to keep in mind that childhood abuse and trauma are only *one* route—and the only one we happened to investigate in this study—that leads in time to the propensity to undergo the extraordinary encounters that access to alternate realities makes possible. Certainly, it can be assumed that some people are simply *born* more psychologically sensitive than others while still others may be nurtured through positive means, such as their parents encouraging imaginative involvement in childhood, to cultivate their sensitivity to nonordinary realities. In short, there are likely to be many different pathways associated with the emergence of the encounter-prone personality.

Let me now attempt to recapitulate the major components of this theoretical framework for you in the form of the chart shown in Figure 1. The factors listed in the first column of the chart are obviously those that facilitate the development of the encounter-prone personality, while those in the second column summarize the psychological characteristics necessary for sensitivity to extraordinary encounters. Both sets of factors then establish the conditions for actual detection of such an encounter when the appropriate situational stimulus is present as the remainder of the chart makes clear. Of course, like all models, the one schematized in Figure 1 is a simplification. For example, it may be that, as Rogo has suggested at least for abduction episodes,[32] conditions of heightened personal stress increase the likelihood of sensitivity to extraordinary encounters—something that isn't indicated in the chart. Yet this model is, I believe, a *useful* simplification since it does at least account for the pattern of relationships of concern to us in this chapter that appears to link child abuse and trauma, psychological dissociation, and sensitivity to nonordinary realities to one another in meaningful ways. In any case, in offering this formulation here, I am hoping that it will serve as a spur to others to carry out the careful and in-depth psychological studies necessary to establish its validity and utility for understanding the encounter-prone personality.

CONCLUSIONS—AND A PERSONAL QUALIFICATION

Throughout this chapter, we have been concerned with a puzzle: Why is it that some people, and not others, register, remember, and report extraordinary encounters? Our search for

FIGURE 1
A DEVELOPMENTAL/SITUATIONAL MODEL FOR EXTRAORDINARY ENCOUNTERS

Childhood Antecedents	Mediating Psychological Processes	Situational Stressor or Stimulus	State of Consciousness	Perceived Event in Alternate Reality
Native sensitivity to alternate realities	Dissociation + Absorption	Near-death incident	Altered, nonordinary	NDE
Abuse and trauma		Anomalous lights		UFOE
Cultivation of imaginative potential				

the answer has led us back into the childhoods of our experiential respondents as well as to study their characteristic modes of psychological functioning. The data from this inquiry, and the theory that seems to make sense of it, have brought us to the notion just presented of a distinctive personality type—the encounter-prone personality—a concept I wish to propose as an answer to the epigraphic question raised by Hilary Evans at the beginning of this chapter.

In delineating this kind of person, however, and especially by dwelling as I have on the unhappy childhood circumstances that seem to foster his particular development, I run a risk of being misunderstood about one important matter. Lest this point be overlooked, I want to address it now. By discovering the role that child abuse and trauma apparently play in promoting sensitivity to extraordinary encounters, I do not intend to serve the interests of those who would "pathologize" these experiences or denigrate the individuals who report them. Anyone who is already familiar with my previous work on NDEs will know that I personally have long endorsed the spiritual authenticity of NDEs and have been supportive of NDErs and the organizations that serve them, one of which, the International Association for Near-Death Studies, now with branches in a half-dozen countries of the world, I helped to found. Nothing that I have said here alters my stance toward NDErs, or, by implication, UFOErs. By focusing on some of the childhood antecedents that predict who will experience these extraordinary encounters, I have only tried to answer some persisting questions about the psychological profile of those who relate them. The mystery and numinous power of NDEs and UFO encounters themselves remain intact, and though I will eventually come to deal with questions of their ultimate meaning, it is my judgment that they are unlikely ever to be fully explained in terms of psychological or scientific concepts alone.

Of more immediate concern to us, however, is this consideration: If one concentrates on the antecedents of extraordinary encounters, as we have done so far, one naturally tends to look at the development of the encounter-prone personality. But when one recalls that this study was also concerned with the *aftereffects* of NDEs and UFOEs, one needs to be prepared for something else. And indeed, from here on, we shall no longer be fixated on just how the encounter-prone personality may have been fashioned from a complex matrix of genetic and social influences, but rather with what has been created directly out of the crucible of these extraordinary encounters.

And what we shall find is that what leads up to these experiences may be very different from what they lead *to*. Hardship may precede these encounters, and trauma accompany them, but, judging from our research, human transformation is often the final fruit harvested from their seemingly unpromising vines.

CHAPTER 7

PSYCHOPHYSICAL CHANGES FOLLOWING EXTRAORDINARY ENCOUNTERS

*Because the phenomenon fits none of the usual categories
. . . UFOs cannot be analyzed through the standard research techniques. . . . All we can do is trace their effects
on humans . . .*

—Jacques Vallee

*The final feature that is sometimes noted as an aftereffect of
the NDE . . . is a psychophysiological transformation . . .*

—Margot Grey

We come now to an entirely new vantage point from which to
view the landscape of extraordinary encounters. From here, we
look *back* on them in order to take note of the changes they
have wrought in the psyches and bodies of those whose lives
they have touched. And as we take this survey, we shall find
that our understanding of the nature and significance of these
experiences is radically altered in quite unexpected ways as a
result of gaining this kind of distance from them. In short, to
gain temporal perspective will allow us to see *a dimension of
meaning* in these encounters that up to now has been almost
completely obscured.

Now in this regard, the most striking findings of the Omega

Project, and perhaps the most thought-provoking, are those that point to a pervasive pattern of wide-ranging and powerful *psychophysical* changes following either a UFOE or NDE. To be clear about the nature of these changes, however, it is necessary at the outset to be specific about what I mean by the term *psychophysical*. So before I tell you about some of the remarkable effects that seem reliably to ensue following these extraordinary encounters, let me take a moment here to explain this term.

As you might readily infer, a psychophysical change refers to an alteration that involves both mind and body. In some cases, it makes sense to suppose that a psychological state may bring about a modification in one's bodily state. For example, in hypnosis, it is well known that a suggestion can sometimes cause physical symptoms, such as warts, to disappear, or, to take another context, that strongly identifying with the crucifixion of Christ may result in signs of stigmata. In other cases, of course, it is true that somatic changes can induce profound alterations in consciousness, such as, for instance, those that women experience during pregnancy or premenstrual conditions. Regardless of the direction of "the causal arrow," or even whether it is possible to specify one, it is clear that a broad range of cognitive, emotional, physical, physiological, and behavioral changes may be systemically linked together in such a way that these components form one integrated whole.

In this study, I use the term *psychophysical changes* in a generic sense to refer to changes of this kind. In most instances, however, the focus is on one or another specific component, for example, a physiological factor, but the implied *context* is always the larger psychophysical system.

Exactly what psychophysical factors did we think might be affected by extraordinary encounters? The answers will be found by taking a moment to examine the items comprising another of our questionnaires, the Psychophysical Changes Inventory,[1] whose contents I shall summarize and illustrate next.

PSYCHOPHYSICAL CHANGES INVENTORY (PCI)

Since we were interested in assessing *changes,* of course, respondents were asked to indicate on the PCI in effect how, if at all, they had changed (i.e., either increased, decreased, or noted no difference) on a variety of psychophysical factors since their experience or, for the control groups, since becoming *interested* in that type of experience. This sixty-item instrument was in fact designed to survey six principal domains of psychophysical changes. The main areas covered, as well as some of the specific issues addressed, are presented below.

1. Physical sensitivities—for example, sensitivities to light, sound, humidity, alcohol, etc.

2. Physiological and neurological functioning—for example, body temperature, blood pressure, nervous system, etc.

3. Psychoenergetic functioning—for example, overall energy level, sleep patterns, unusual energetic sensations in body, etc.

4. Emotional functioning—for example, mood fluctuation, emotionality, etc.

5. Expanded mental awareness—for example, increased information-processing capacity, sense of mind expansion, awareness of alternate realities, etc.

6. Paranormal functioning—for example, telepathy, precognition, psychokinesis, etc.

When we looked at the results from the PCI, we were astonished at the magnitude and consistency of the differences we found between our experiential and control groups. Both NDErs and UFOErs are *much* more likely than their controls to report that they underwent many psychophysical changes following their experience, and, furthermore, these differences are obvious across the board, on each of our principal psychophysical domains, as can be seen if you take a moment to peruse Table 4 in Appendix II. In fact, from a purely statistical point of view, the differences here are huge and highly significant, and are the most impressive of the entire study in this respect.[2] Finally, the extraordinary similarity between the two experiential groups, NDErs and UFOErs, as well as in their corresponding controls, in overall level of reported psychophysical changes is unmistakable, as Table 5 makes evident.

When we begin to look at the specifics of the psychophysical shifts attested to by our experiential respondents, we again see evidence of a coherent *pattern* of change. It begins with suggestions of heightened physical sensitivities to various environmental conditions, such as light, sound, and humidity, and, though not shown in Table 4, our extraordinary experiencers also state that they became more sensitive to such substances as alcohol, pharmaceutical drugs, and various foods afterward. Thus, there appears to be a *generalized sensitivity effect* stemming from extraordinary encounters.

The pattern continues with a cluster of consistent effects having to do with decreases in various physiological indices, such as metabolic rate, body temperature, and blood pressure. Although so far as I know, this is the first study to document these self-reported physiological state changes in a large sample, it is *not* the first time such changes have been anecdotally reported by extraordinary experiencers. For example, one of Margot Grey's NDErs provides this congruent testimony concerning some of the aftereffects of her experience:

> After recovery from my near-death crisis I went through a very strange period of convalescence which at first I put down to being the aftereffects of my illness. I became very cold and my temperature was discovered to be subnormal. It was also found that my pulse rate was abnormally slow and at the same time my blood pressure was abnormally low. . . . This condition became so acute that at one stage I was sent to hospital for two weeks and put under obser-

vation, during which time I underwent a number of tests. But the result of all this was that nothing organically wrong could be found and I was sent home still suffering from the same malady.[3]

In view of our findings, it appears that such changes may in fact be part of an overall pattern of psychophysical transformation following extraordinary encounters and not, just as was apparently the case for Grey's respondent, a medically worrisome condition as such.

More evidence along these lines is provided by our experiential respondents' statements concerning neurological changes they believe took place following their encounters. Almost one half of them (compared to about 15 percent of the control groups), for example, claim that their nervous system now functions differently than it did before, and not quite a third of them (compared to about 7–8 percent of the control groups) also assert that their brains are "structurally different" than before. In regard to this latter contention, it is doubtless true. Our brains are changing all the time. However, it is obvious that most of us are not at all *aware* of such changes. What is it that has happened to our extraordinary experiencers to make almost a *third* of them report that they have become aware of structural brain changes? Perhaps some of the other psychophysical data summarized in Table 4 will at least give us some hints as to the answer here.

Continuing our overview of the pattern of psychophysical changes, however, we next see that experientials are also more likely than controls to indicate that their energetic and emotional levels have shifted. Many of them, for instance, say that they are now aware of something like currents of energy flowing through their bodies, that they need less sleep for optimal functioning, and that their emotionality and mood fluctuations have increased.

Finally, there is a clear tendency for experiential respondents to describe that they have undergone a kind of mind expansion. More than half of them (compared to less than a fifth of the control groups), for example, say that they are now flooded with more information than they can absorb. However, they also claim to be able to process new information better than before and are as well now sensitive to information from "other dimensions." Perhaps correlated with this is the fact that well over half of them (compared to less than one quarter of the control groups) report that their psychic abilities increased after their encounters.

What the PCI Tells Us About Psychophysical Changes

In summary, our findings from the PCI reveal that our experiential respondents reliably describe a wide spectrum of psychophysical changes following their encounters. These include increases in a variety of physical sensitivities, suggestions of mutually consistent differences in physiological functioning, alterations of neurological and brain states, as well as a miscellany of unusual psychoenergetic, psychological, and paranormal experiences. As a totality, these changes in the aftermath of extraordinary encounters seem indicative of a more subtle level of psychophysical functioning and expanded states of mental awareness. If these self-report data are valid, it is clear that at face value they suggest that there may be something about these encounters that may actually *reprogram* an experiencer's physiological and nervous system so as to make that individual inwardly and environmentally more sensitive. To be sure, the *interpretation* of our data here is open to many possibilities, some of which I shall comment on later, but for now it is enough to note that the data themselves imply that there are reliable, dramatic, and in many cases tantalizingly intriguing effects that appear to emerge following UFOEs and NDEs.

THE ELECTRICAL SENSITIVITY SYNDROME

To illustrate just one of the provocative implications of this set of results now, let me call your attention to a curious, but in the end most telling, anomaly whose existence is disclosed by the last row of findings in Table 4. The odd effect I am referring to comes from responses to this statement:

> I found that electric or electronic devices (e.g., car batteries or electrical systems, lights, watches, tape recorders, computers, etc.) more often malfunctioned in my presence than I remember being the case before.

Interestingly enough, experiential respondents are more than three times as likely to endorse this item as are controls, with almost a third of them doing so—a highly significant difference. Significant of what, exactly?

The search for the answer to this question took me on a most unexpected but ultimately enlightening detour. However, in fairly short order I found that it had in fact led me precisely to where I could clearly see the real significance of the anomaly I had almost inadvertently discovered.

Now in all likelihood you are already aware that claims of this sort are not rare. Certainly in my own research on NDEs, I have heard quite a few experiencers complain about such things as causing electric lights inexplicably to blow, having persisting problems with their computers, wristwatches failing to work properly, and so on. And it's equally apparent that other UFO researchers have come across them in their investigations, too. Jenny Randles, for instance, comments:

> One of the most fruitful areas of research is into the surprising number of people who have major problems working electronic equipment such as computers. It seems as if some folk just scramble the electrical signals. [This makes] life very difficult, with visual display screens going haywire, telephones crackling with static and electrical appliances burning out far too often. In our study of cases we have seen this happen and it turns up quite frequently among witnesses.[4]

Whitley Strieber in his work with experiencers has also encountered cases of electrical sensitivity. He gives this example:

I also seem to have bad luck with electrical appliances. Vacuum cleaners will work for other members of my family, but not for me. It has been a long standing joke in our family, when I am in the car, to watch out for street lights going out when I drive under them. My friend's son Jeff always asks to accompany me to the store or across town, so that he can have a laugh when the lights go out. I even have a few favorites that I can make blink on and off at will. I've never given it much thought; it's just another of my mechanical mishaps.[5]

Noting the statistical prevalence of such claims among my own sample, however, I was forced to think about this issue more than casually. Deciding to look into it further, I first thought to go back to our Omega Project batteries to see whether any of our respondents might have provided more than just a checkmark indication that they had experienced such electrical anomalies in their own lives. Though none of our questionnaires had specifically requested such accounts, I nevertheless found quite a few of them spontaneously offered as illustrative examples.

A brief and somewhat amusing instance comes from Hazel Underwood, the fifty-three-year-old radio station manager whose UFO sighting I described in Chapter 2. She actually ended her account with this statement:

After the "incident" I was able to literally "cut off" a 1000 watt radio transmitter. By touching the side of the case and [sic] control the TV at home—and broke my stereo. Needless to say, now when I do commercials, I don't touch the equipment!

In some cases, however, these effects are seemingly so pervasive that they appear to cause a veritable epidemic of electrical mishaps. The following two respondents, both women, will illustrate how extensive these problems can become. First, from a forty-three-year-old college-educated administrator who has had repeated "dreams" of "space beings" visiting her since early childhood:

> I am extremely sensitive to high frequencies; I cannot wear watches that wind up. They don't work while on my body. Watches with batteries—the batteries have to be charged frequently. I have continual problems with cars and the electrical systems (like trunk releases automatically popping open, radios full of static, electric door locks/seat adjustments malfunctioning—in all my cars). Electric anomalies within the home—using dozens of light bulbs; power surges, etc.

The second woman, a thirty-six-year-old NDEr with a high school diploma, writes in a similar vein:

> Dr. Ring, I have a difficult time as many computers malfunction and lights will blow when I walk under them. This has happened for years, and I tried to ignore that this was happening. I simply cannot wear a watch for long before it breaks down. I went to . . . a department store and walked in front of their brand new computer and it quit working . . . When I [held a fluorescent light in my hands], the entire bulb lit up, like it was turned on. It seemed like there was a lot of static electricity.

In other cases, the electrical effects are just as obvious, but episodic. A thirty-seven-year-old college-educated registered nurse, who had had both an NDE and a UFO encounter, told me:

> Immediately following my 1971 [UFO-related] event and 1980 NDE, every time I'd turn an electrical switch, the bulb would explode or stop working or burn out. These episodes would last a few weeks, then phase out. I have had 5–8 such episodes in the last 10 years.

Hannah Markham, whose NDE in 1971 was related in Chapter 4, subsequently had a UFO encounter whose aftermath she described as follows:

> I didn't notice I affected things electronically until after my UFO incident with the ball of light in 1984. I still have the problem every now and then with affecting street lights, tape recorders, irons, TV, etc. The incident with the street light was every time I would pass, it would go out, then I'd pass it again, going the other way, and it would go back on. But this has not happened since 1987.

In my sample, women were more likely to provide such written amplification of their electrical misadventures, but men apparently have them, too. One thirty-nine-year-old high school graduate who had an NDE when he was twenty-two simply said:

> When upset lights blow; electrical components malfunction when new.

My curiosity about these strange electrical problems encountered by some of my experiencers having been raised still further by the kind of anecdotal testimony I've just shared with you here, I next sought to learn whether any systematic research had ever been carried out on such persons.

I was somewhat surprised, but definitely delighted, to find out there had indeed. Michael Shallis, a lecturer at Oxford University and an astrophysicist by training, had in fact recently published a book[6] dealing in large measure with persons who had come to his attention precisely because they had chronic complaints about their electrical sensitivity. Eventually, he studied more than two hundred of these cases personally, using a combination of questionnaires and interviews, and what he discovered by doing so ties in neatly here and helps to provide something of a larger framework for the interpretation of our own findings from the Omega Project.

In addition to quickly establishing that this condition was by no means a rare statistical oddity, Shallis was able to show that such persons—whom he calls *electrical sensitives*—tend to have certain traits in common. That is, it appears as if there is a coherent *syndrome* of electrical sensitivity. Its components, as delineated by Shallis, are most interesting.

To begin with, consistent with our preliminary findings, most electrical sensitives—about 80 percent—are women. For another, electrical sensitives often have many allergies. According to Shallis, about 70 percent of his sample had allergy problems, compared to about 15 percent in the normal population. They have other sensitivities as well, claiming to be abnormally sensitive to bright lights and sound (70 percent) and to approaching thunderstorms (60 percent). Emotionality and emotional lability also seem to be associated with this condition, and, just as our own last example implied, emotional stress appears to be a trigger for seemingly personally generated electrical disturbances.

Intriguingly enough, electrical sensitives usually have had at least one surgical operation (70 percent), usually major, says Shallis. And, finally, a similarly high percentage of these persons (69 percent) claim to have had psychic experiences, and some of them feel that they have been enabled to heal others through paranormal means.

Even though Shallis's work is only suggestive (for one thing, he doesn't have a proper control group), I could of course see plainly that the relevance of his electrical sensitivity syndrome to our findings was undeniable. My discovery of Shallis's book in fact again forced me to reexamine some of our PCI data, for in reading his book, I had realized that for quite different reasons we had assessed most of the traits that he finds implicated in his electrical sensitivity syndrome. Table 6 presents the results of our analysis here, but, as usual, I shall simply summarize them for you now.

When we compared our experiential respondents to our controls on such factors as (1) allergies, (2) sensitivity to light, (3) hearing acuity, (4) mood fluctuation, (5) psychic abilities, and (6) healing gifts, we found that our extraordinary experiencers were anywhere from *twice to four times* as likely to assert that they are now characterized by such qualities.

In a phrase, there appears to be something about these encounters that tends to move our experiencers in the direction of *becoming an electrical sensitive.* This trait, too, is thus now revealed to be a definite part of the psychophysical transformation that such experiencers report following their UFOEs or NDEs.

Why should this be? One can only speculate, of course, but for starters, we might recall that NDEs often involve powerful episodes "in the light." And light is, after all, an electromagnetic phenomenon. Likewise, the UFO literature is replete with instances of apparent electromagnetic effects (e.g., automobile engines stopping in the presence of a UFO, but afterward inexplicably starting up again). One therefore begins to wonder to what extent the pattern of psychophysical changes we have found to be characteristic of our experiencers might be mediated by subtle electromagnetic effects, possibly causing a direct change in the respondent's electrical field.

Other researchers and investigators have found themselves sniffing out the same electromagnetically charged trail, albeit sometimes (though not always!) for reasons largely unrelated to our concerns in this book. For example, Edgar Wilson, a physician, writing in the inaugural newsletter of the International Society for the Study of Subtle Energies and Energy Medicine, states:

> The molecular substrate of the nervous system and energy system of the body has been characterized by the development of increasingly complex molecular structures capable of electromagnetic excitability. . . . Humans seem to possess an extremely complex biomagnetic energy field that operates outside of the confines of the nervous system alone.[7]

Another physician, Robert O. Becker, who is widely known for his important and highly regarded work on the biological effects of electromagnetism,[8] takes a similar stand and eventually extends it to subsume psychic phenomena in general:

> . . . scientific discoveries of the past three decades have gradually resulted in a new paradigm of the nature of life.

> Living things now may be viewed as basically electromag-
> netic in nature, possessing an internal, organized, analog type,
> DC electrical system that regulates the basic functions of
> growth and healing, provides the basic operational level for
> brain activity, and produces magnetic fields of a specific na-
> ture that are detectable outside of the body . . . All living
> things are intimately tied to the natural geomagnetic fields
> of the earth. . . .

> This intimate relationship between the earth's geomagnetic
> field and living organisms stimulated a re-evaluation of the
> relationship between electromagnetic fields and psychic
> phenomena . . . [and showed that] a firm link has been es-
> tablished between (them).[9]

With respect specifically to electrical sensitives, Shallis is
also inclined to attribute their reactivity and electrical difficulties to fluctuations in or undue sensitivities to electromagnetic
fields. Such sensitivities may also, he conjectures, be affected
by the hormonal state of the individual, a factor that could, he
thinks, be responsible for the apparent sex difference in electrical sensitivity.[10]

And, finally, several researchers interested in UFO encounters and abduction experiences, most notably neuro-
psychologist Michael Persinger, and others such as Jenny Randles
and David Gotlib, a physician, have all argued that a variety of
UFO experiences are causally affected by electromagnetic fields
and personal sensitivity to those fields.[11]

What this body of research, theory, and speculation suggests to me is that if the psychophysical changes reported in
conjunction with UFOEs and NDEs reflect some sort of *psy-
chobiological* transformation, as our data certainly strongly hint,
it may in fact ultimately be rooted in some kind of "electrical"
transmission that has the effect of permanently increasing one's
sensitivity to electromagnetic fields. This is itself admittedly an
extravagant speculation, but personal electrical fields *can* be
measured in the laboratory[12] and some researchers, such as
Wilson, have already indicated their interest in conducting careful

studies of exceptional human beings, such as healers, psychics, and mystics, to determine whether such persons do indeed have distinctive patterns of electromagnetic activity. If such investigations could be undertaken with a sample of UFOErs and NDErs as well, it would be extremely worthwhile to see whether these two categories of persons would have similar electrical field patterns that are furthermore clearly distinguishable from those of normal controls.

Descending now from the thin air of these conjectural—though testable—musings to the hard ground of our findings on psychophysical changes, we next need to consider one further set of data from the PCI here since it, too, like the electrical sensitivity syndrome, appears to underlie many of the psychophysical effects of extraordinary encounters.

THE KUNDALINI SYNDROME

You may be aware that some of the changes listed in Table 4 also appear to match another syndrome that Western psychology has come increasingly to recognize as being implicated in certain forms of mystical experience and is often associated with deep psychophysical perturbations. I am speaking of course of *the kundalini syndrome,* whose energetic manifestations have already been linked to NDEs, if not yet to UFO encounters.[13]

To elucidate just a bit on the basic concept of kundalini, as it is discussed in the tradition of tantric yoga, it is said to be a subtle form of bioenergy that, though it usually lies dormant "at the base of the spine," can be activated by various kinds of spiritual disciplines or experiences. The arousal of this potent energy may be extremely destabilizing, both physically and psychologically, however it is brought about. Symptoms are variable, but include, at the physical level, spontaneous changes in body postures and breathing patterns, sensations of tingling, tickling, and itching, orgasmic sensations in the absence of any sexual arousal, sensations of extreme heat or cold, sensations of "energy currents" in the body, and severe headaches, among others. Psychologically, the awakening of kundalini can lead to

experiences of the most profound ecstasy and cosmic awareness, or in some cases it can trigger tremendous anxiety and
dreadful fears of impending madness; in many instances, of
course, the psychological concomitants of kundalini activation
fall between these two extremes. Whatever the nature of its
physical and psychological manifestations, those who experience its energies tend to be deeply affected by its occurrence.[14]

Although kundalini, which literally means "coiled up" (like
a serpent), is a term that derives from the ancient tradition of
yoga, it has gradually found a place in modern Western thera-
peutics as more and more people here have become interested
in the process of psychospiritual transformation. The seeking
or cultivation of powerful spiritual experiences, or their spontaneous emergence, as in involuntary NDEs, often generates
what are now understood to be kundalini reactions. Because
most people who have such reactions may be utterly unpre-
pared for them and fail to understand their nature and significance, they can precipitate a form of personal crisis called
spiritual emergencies.[15] As a consequence of many persons
undergoing such crises, increasing numbers of therapists and
researchers interested in spiritual experiences are now familiar
with kundalini and its manifestations, and the concept itself is
finally finding a home in Western psychology.

Returning now to the Omega Project, we were interested to
see whether kundalini might raise its serpent's head in the
aftermath of the extraordinary experiences we were concerned
to study. As I have indicated, there was already some evidence
from other studies, including one of my own, that NDEs may
stimulate kundalini arousal, and more has turned up since.[16]
However, because most of this evidence was fragmentary and
purely anecdotal, and there had not yet been any investigations
at all into this kind of experience in the wake of UFO encounters, we decided to embed a nine-item kundalini scale in the
PCI. The items comprising this scale, which inquire mostly about
the physical or energetic manifestations typical of kundalini activation, are listed in Table 7, along with the percentages of
respondents indicating their presence.

If you take a moment to glance over our findings here, you

will see that there is a clear-cut and consistent kundalini effect across all nine items of the scale demonstrating that experiential respondents are roughly three times more likely to report these symptoms afterward than our controls, with more than one third of the former doing so, on the average. Furthermore, when we examined the *overall* kundalini scores for our four basic groups, as shown in Table 8, we not only again found an enormous statistical difference between the experiential and control groups,[17] but once more, our UFOE respondents were very similar to our NDErs. Both groups display substantial evidence of kundalini activation following their encounters, which of course reinforces our earlier findings pointing to their essential functional equivalence.

What the significance of our findings regarding kundalini may be, as well as what kind of connection may exist between this syndrome and electrical sensitivity, are questions that will occupy our attention at the conclusion of this chapter. For now, however, it is enough to note that the kundalini syndrome, too, must be regarded as a part of, and possibly underlying, the pattern of psychophysical changes brought about by UFOEs and NDEs.

SOME INTERPRETIVE CAUTIONS

Before we consider how our data here may contribute to our understanding of the nature and meaning of extraordinary encounters, we need to take a moment to enter some cautionary provisos. Of course it is obvious that, according to their self-reports on the PCI, subjectively at least our experiencers believe that they have been profoundly affected—physiologically, psychologically, and presumably spiritually—by the encounters they have undergone. The thorny interpretative question we face here, however, is just what factors may be responsible for this undeniably provocative pattern of self-report data.

One could argue, of course, that it is something in the nature of these experiences themselves—and we do seem to have to discuss UFOEs and NDEs together here since the reported aftereffects are so similar for each—that induces these changes directly. I have already speculated, for example, about the possible role of electromagnetism in triggering some of these effects. However, it is equally reasonable and indeed perhaps even more plausible to surmise that these changes are more likely to be traceable merely to differences in life-style afterward: changes in diet, meditation, or other spiritual practices or, perhaps more indirectly, the kinds of groups people join or the reading they do. Without controlling for such factors, it is obviously impossible to draw any definitive inferences concerning *what* may mediate these changes. At this stage in our research, we must admit that we know only that they are reliably reported to occur; we don't yet know why.

In this connection, I must point out another limitation of this research, though, like the last, it is certainly one that future investigations could and should overcome. You will readily agree, I think, that however intriguing our findings on apparent psychophysical changes may be, the fact of their subjectivity renders them less than certifiably true. As such, these self-reports, though valuable and certainly suggestive, are no substitute for the kinds of objective measurements that could be made using instruments in the laboratory. Our data as well as my previous interpretive comments do, of course, strongly imply that the step from survey research to laboratory investigation of persons who have had NDEs and UFO encounters would be well warranted. Indeed, another NDE researcher, Bruce Greyson, has recently persuasively advocated precisely the same approach.[18] In any event, it is my hope that our own findings on the psychophysical changes reported after extraordinary encounters—as well as some of the testable interpretations they have spawned—will stimulate qualified researchers to continue the search to document these effects in the laboratory. Without such research, our self-report data must remain beguilingly suggestive but ultimately inconclusive; with it, we may one day know for certain whether the extraordinary claims made by our experiencers are in fact corroborated by independent and objective investigations.

There is one more concern about our findings on psychophysical changes that needs to be aired here. You will remember that the format of the PCI simply asks respondents to indicate how, if at all, their experience (or interest in extraordinary encounters) changed them. But of course one wishes to know if such changes *last*. In short, how stable are they, and how long do they endure?

To explore this matter in a preliminary way at least, we performed an analysis in which, to permit meaningful statistical comparisons, we divided our total experiential sample into four groups according to how much time had elapsed since their encounter. The first group had had their experience within the past five years; the second, between six and fifteen years ago; the third, sixteen to thirty years; and the fourth, more than thirty years ago. Using this classification, we determined the average index of overall psychophysical changes (the same one that was presented in Table 5) for each group separately. The results of our comparison were unequivocal: There were no differences among the groups, indicating that the psychophysical aftereffects tend to be maximal within five years and stable over time. Thus, our findings here are congruent with the inference that these aftereffects are by no means transient changes but represent enduring traits.

And on this result, as will soon be seen, I shall now begin to build my thesis concerning just what implications may be discerned from the study of the long-term effects of extraordinary encounters.

EVOLUTIONARY INTIMATIONS: THE OMEGA PROTOTYPE

If for the moment we assume that the changes described by our experiential sample are indeed valid, then the general implication is as clear as it is unavoidable: *Extraordinary encounters appear to be the gateway to a radical, biologically based transformation of the human personality.*

The idea that the NDE itself is a transformative experience is of course hardly new; indeed by now it has nearly the status of a received truth in the literature on NDEs. But here we are talking about, and finally have some empirical evidence for, a kind of transformation that goes beyond a mere change in values and outlook. Our data suggest that this transformation is in fact *psychophysical,* that NDErs—and by implication, UFOErs, too, of course—through their experiences undergo certain changes that affect their physiological functioning, nervous system, brain, and mental processes so as to permit a higher level of human nature to manifest. The emergence of what appears to be a more highly evolved human being out of the chrysalis of extraordinary encounters has led Bruce Greyson to coin a new term, *the Omega Prototype,* by which to designate this particular kind of individual.

What is it about these experiences that helps to shape such individuals into the form of an Omega Prototype? I have already said that we need to have more research done on such persons before we can be certain that they have changed in the way they describe, but, again, assuming our preliminary findings here are supported by subsequent investigations, my candidate for the driving force behind these psychophysical transformations would be kundalini. In this supposition, of course, I am hardly alone, for the most common assumption about the nature of kundalini is that, to quote perhaps the leading authority on kundalini in modern times, Gopi Krishna,[19] it is "the evolutionary energy in man." That is, according to kundalini theorists, it is this latent energy that, once released, transforms the nervous system and promotes the psychospiritual evolution of humanity. A succinct and representative expression of this position is provided by John White, in the introduction to his anthology, *Kundalini, Evolution and Enlightenment:*

The kundalini experience, then, considered from the viewpoint of individual transformation, is said to be a path toward enlightenment. But if a large number of enlightened people were to appear in society at the same time, the result could well transform society itself. So the kundalini experience, in its broadest aspect, is evolutionary—a path for the advancement of the entire human race to a higher state.[20]

What I am proposing of course is that, consistent with our findings, extraordinary encounters tend to activate this transformative energy, and that it, in ways we still do not but need to understand, permanently alters the biological system of the individual, probably (in my opinion) by acting upon the autonomic nervous system.

The assumption that it is the arousal of kundalini that kindles the changes NDEs lead to is neither new nor unique to me. Although I did suggest this as a hypothesis in my last book on NDEs, *Heading Toward Omega,* since then other NDE researchers have come to identical conclusions and attributed similar evolutionary import to them. For example, Margot Grey's studies were done entirely independently of mine, and she had no idea what conclusions I had reached when she was working on the manuscript of her own book, *Return from Death.*[21] Yet her words are an unmistakable echo of mine in *Heading Toward Omega:*

> It would seem that similar physiological mechanisms are operating in both the NDE and kundalini phenomena and that they are both aspects of the same evolutionary force. Taken together, these spectacular instances of transformation add up to a surprisingly large and increasing percentage of the population and might therefore be expected to have a growing influence on the collective awareness of the rest of the species, at both a conscious and subconscious level. . . . It would appear that a new breed of mankind may be about to be born, and that in order for this to happen our consciousness and biological structure are undergoing a radical transformation.[22]

Bruce Greyson is another NDE researcher who has recently provided a preliminary report on his own findings concerning NDEs and kundalini activation. He, too, devised a questionnaire to detect kundalini arousal in his respondents and, like me, found that NDErs were about twice as likely to report such symptoms as were his control-group respondents. He concludes:

> Here, then, we have near-death experiencers reporting precisely the kind of physiological changes that are associated in Eastern traditions with the bio-energy that drives evolution. . . It is possible that future [laboratory] work in this area could lead to vital new insights into the evolution of humanity toward a different level of consciousness.[23]

What *is* new about the interpretation I am offering here is that I now mean to *extend* it to persons who have undergone UFO encounters as well, *and by implication to others who have had other varieties of extraordinary encounters.* You may remember that in the preface to this book, I mentioned that when I first read Whitley Strieber's *Communion,* I was led to wonder whether UFO encounters might turn out to be an alternative pathway to the same kind of spiritual transformation NDEs seemed to bring about. Of course, our findings on psychophysical changes suggest precisely that, and that being so, one is now naturally drawn to speculate whether there are *other* types of extraordinary encounters, such as those that occur in shamanistic or meditative visions, that might represent still other avenues leading to the same psychophysical destination. Needless to say, I hope that future research will furnish the answer to this question that must be left tantalizingly open for now.

Finally, where does the electrical sensitivity syndrome fit into this matrix of interpretation and speculation? Since we know so little about this syndrome—much less in fact than we do about kundalini—it would be reckless to offer anything more than an unalloyed guess here. But if even a guess is worth considering at this point, then my own would be that electrical sensitivity is still another, heretofore neglected, manifestation of kundalini activation. Our own data, at any rate, suggest that at the very least electrical sensitivity and kundalini activation are likely to be *correlated effects* associated with extraordinary encounters. Therefore, it seems reasonable at this juncture to

suppose that they tend to arise together as part of the psycho-
biological alchemy of these experiences. Some, like Shallis, may
choose to focus on the electrical properties of sensitives, while
other researchers, more familiar with the concept of kundalini,
may be observing similar or related phenomena but will tend to
describe them in different terms. In the end, they may find that
they have followed different routes to the same dynamic energy
vortex, and it may be only a matter of preference which label
to give to it. Since kundalini is an ancient concept, and one
that, as indicated, is gaining increasing acceptance in the West,
I am inclined to see it as basic to the electrical sensitivity effects we have discussed. But on this issue, too, we must leave
it to future research to resolve the question definitively.

However these conceptual and theoretical matters are ultimately sorted out, we are still left with the hypothesis that *the
real significance of extraordinary encounters such as NDEs and
UFOEs may lie in their evolutionary implications for humanity.*
Of course, the postulation of something like an Omega Prototype is based on inferences mostly from our PCI data, and though
similar findings from the work of other researchers may have
led them also to embrace the idea, that is obviously far from
sufficient to conclude that anything like a substantial case has
been made for it. As it stands, it is best regarded as a re-
searcher-generated hypothesis still in need of more empirical
support before it can be properly evaluated.

But of course researchers aren't the only ones who have
ideas about these issues, and they aren't even necessarily always in the best position to evaluate them, either. What about
the experiencers themselves, then? Surely, they must have given
these matters considerable thought in the aftermath of their own
encounters. What do *they* think? It is time to give them a chance
to speak for themselves.

CHAPTER 8

BELIEFS AND VALUE SHIFTS
FOLLOWING EXTRAORDINARY
ENCOUNTERS

*We should go on analyzing landing traces, interviewing wit-
nesses and "abductees," feeding computers with sighting
details, and scrutinizing the heavens with cameras and radio
telescopes. But this activity will be completely useless if it is
not related to an investigation of the secondary impact, the
shift in our worldview that the phenomenon produces.*

—Jacques Vallee

We have seen that the extraordinary encounters visited upon
our respondents left a deep psychophysical imprint on many of
them. But in continuing to trace the further effects of EEs in
this chapter, we shall shortly come to appreciate that such experiences tend to initiate some profound alterations in one's
personal values and belief system as well. In many instances,
these changes are tantamount to an entirely new worldview (or,
perhaps better said, *view of the cosmos*) and appear to lead to
a distinctive pattern of behavior that serves to express and
communicate to others the essential insights that such sojourns
have seemingly implanted in these travelers to unearthly realms.

In this last phase of our report of the findings from the Omega
Project, it will be useful first to review the results of our assessment of changes in *personal values* since these will furnish
a helpful context of understanding for the belief and worldview
shifts to follow. To evaluate such changes, we used two sepa-

rate instruments. The Life Changes Inventory was constructed so as to provide an index of change for a number of personal value domains. The Religious Beliefs Inventory, as its label implies, has a more limited focus; specifically, it was designed to measure the extent to which individuals shift toward a more universalistic spiritual, rather than a narrowly sectarian religious, orientation.[1] We shall begin by looking at the pattern of findings stemming from the more general Life Changes Inventory, but, as usual, in order to increase your understanding of the meaning of the findings to be presented, we should first spend a moment or two getting familiar with the structure and specific content of this questionnaire.

LIFE CHANGES INVENTORY (LCI)

The LCI, an enlargement of a similar questionnaire I had previously used in my *Heading Toward Omega* study of NDErs, consists of fifty items, all of which relate to a specific type of value. Altogether, there are nine principal *value clusters* that comprise the LCI, all but one being composed of at least three items. These value clusters are:

1. Appreciation for life
2. Self-acceptance
3. Concern for others
4. Concern for *impressing* others
5. Materialism
6. Concern with social/planetary issues
7. Quest for meaning
8. Spirituality
9. Religiousness

Participants were required to respond to each item of the LCI in terms of a five-point scale indicating whether and to what degree they felt they had changed after their extraordinary encounter (or, again for the control-group respondents, after becoming *interested in* such experiences). Let me use a specific example now to illustrate this procedure, taking the first item in the questionnaire, "My desire to help others," as the statement at issue. The set of alternatives for this item (and of course for all others) was in effect as follows:

Strongly increased (assigned a value of $+2$)

Increased somewhat (assigned a value of $+1$)

Didn't change (assigned a value of 0)

Decreased somewhat (assigned a value of -1)

Strongly decreased (assigned a value of -2)

Thus, if a respondent felt that his desire to help others had strongly increased following, say, his NDE, he would be credited with a score of $+2$ for that item.

These scoring protocols should be kept in mind when perusing the data from this questionnaire in Table 9 in Appendix II since they are indispensable for a proper interpretation of the figures presented there. However, as always, regardless of whether you take the trouble to examine these statistical data for yourself, I shall give a brief verbal summary of them here.

What the LCI Tells Us About Value Changes

Essentially, three separate statements will serve to encapsulate the main trends to be discerned in the LCI table:

1. In general, *all* groups report becoming more altruistic, having greater social concern, and increasing in spirituality.

2. In general, these changes are somewhat more evident for our experiential respondents and are *significantly* greater[2] for the following value clusters: appreciation for

life, self-acceptance, concern for others, materialism (decrease), quest for meaning and spirituality.

3. In general, the ND sample shows a greater shift than the UFO sample on altruistic (increase) and materialistic (decrease) values. Specifically, the changes are statistically significant for concern for others, impressing others (decrease), and materialism (decrease).

Readers already familiar with my own previous research on the aftereffects of NDEs, as reported in *Heading Toward Omega,* will be quick to realize that the data on the NDEr sample in the Omega Project arrayed in Table 9 essentially duplicate all my prior major findings on this point. Since those earlier results were also broadly supported by work of several subsequent NDE researchers,[3] this new independent replication—with a fresh sample of respondents—appears to indicate that this pattern of aftereffects among NDErs is, at least in this country and England, a very robust and consistent aspect of the NDE phenomenon itself.

Value Changes Illustrated

Since I have, however, spent many pages elsewhere providing abundant qualitative material from NDErs to illustrate these changes, I hope I shall be forgiven if I forgo such treatment here. Instead, perhaps it will suffice if I simply cite a portion of one Omega Project NDEr's musings on what his experience taught him. As will be readily apparent to anyone conversant with the general literature on NDEs, this man's reflections are typical of such experiencers. In any case, they certainly well exemplify the kinds of value changes that many NDErs in this study imply by their LCI responses took place for them, too. The man I quote is one whose NDE itself was partially presented in Chapter 4 (page 90). He writes:

It's been a year now and in this year I have learned more about what life is about than in all my other years together.

Before my [cardiac] arrest, I had my priorities mixed up.
The list flipped completely over; everything that was on the
top belonged on the bottom. I learned that life was to be
lived one day at a time. Like the song says, "Stop and smell
the roses." Well, I not only smell them, but I embrace them.
I've learned that the candle of life can go out at any time
and I have too much to do before it goes out. . . . Life is
now, not yesterday, not tomorrow, but right now. And right
now, this minute, I'm in love with life. I know now that we
take nothing out of this life except what is in our hearts.

Still other aspects of commonly reported NDE aftereffects
are not only implied by the statistical data for our *UFO sample,*
of course, but directly suggested by the spontaneous comments
of some of those respondents. Here a couple of such testimon-
ies will be sufficient, I think, to underscore our mass of quan-
titative material for these experiencers. In the first instance, I
draw again on the account furnished to me by Hazel Underwood, the fifty-three-year-old station manager from Georgia
whose UFO sighting I quoted in Chapter 2 (pages 50–51). In
her case, I need merely continue her narrative from where I
had broken it off:

It changed my outlook on life. I was raised in a Baptist family, grew up in the Baptist church and have a brother who
is a Baptist minister. But I have read more of the Bible since
July 1987 than I have read in my entire life before. I understand the Bible now. Before I was reading words. Now I
understand everything I read. I am not more religious. I do
not go to church regularly. I do not feel that I have to—or
have ever had to. But my compassion for other people and
my understanding of other people and events have led me
to greater peace within myself.[4]

Gina Willoughby, the thirty-seven-year-old librarian whose
extensive childhood history of encounters in alternate realities
we examined in Chapter 6 (pages 133–135), provides a second
example—and a particularly richly textured one—of the weave

of value changes seemingly wrought by EEs. In one of her letters to me, Gina, in considering these matters, summed up her
insights in this passage:

> I have one answer to the big question: "What is the mean-
> ing of life?" The answer has come through loud and clear
> in many of my experiences:
> "LOVE"
> Love is very important. It is the main reason for our exis-
> tence as human beings in our physical bodies. We must un-
> derstand love—and we must understand love in a wholistic
> sense, altruistic love, etc. We can never fully experience
> love or give love unless we also know compassion. To un-
> derstand compassion, we must know pain, and loss—not just
> our own pain and loss, but the ability to feel the pain and
> loss of others. Love is a complex and powerful force. We
> must become part of the consciousness of love, for it is an
> entity in itself. Yet it is part of us, and we are part of it.
> When we are separated from this force we are not total, we
> are not whole.

In this brief paragraph, Gina has once again allowed us to
see the *larger patterning* of the values that typically emerge
out of the matrix of extraordinary encounters and, as our quan-
titative findings suggest, does so for both NDErs and UFOErs
and, to a somewhat lesser but still significant extent, for those
who have become *interested* in these experiences as well. Her
emphasis on love (agape), compassion, and wholeness reflects
some of the most essential and widespread trends in our data
on value shifts following EEs and points toward still other
changes that we shall soon have cause to consider.

In any case, certainly the overall thrust of our LCI results—
and this, I think, is the main point to be grasped here—is that
individuals who have become involved in the world of NDEs
or UFOs, whether through personal experience or simply personal interest, tend to state that on the whole it has made a
positive difference in their lives, if one is willing to grant that
having a greater appreciation for life, oneself, others and the

world at large, and so on, are positive changes. That this is so despite the traumatic nature of the circumstances often associated with the onset of NDEs and UFO encounters appears to be persuasive testimony to the transformative power of these experiences. However these changes are to be interpreted—a matter to which we shall return—they must be acknowledged as important aftereffects of immersion in *both* of our domains of extraordinary encounters whose similar repercussions here will once again be evident.

Before turning to the aspect of our LCI findings for which Gina's comments are prologue, I should add just a word about the *persistence* of the value changes I have been describing. As with the psychophysical changes we examined in the last chapter, we want to know here whether the value shifts indicated on the LCI are transient or relatively enduring. To address this question, we again performed a statistical analysis in which we divided our experiential respondents into four groups on the basis of how much time had elapsed since their encounter. We thus formed the same four groups I mentioned in the last chapter, but this time determined the stability of the changes for two representative value clusters: concern for others and spirituality. Our findings were likewise the same as before: The changes reported do not diminish over time but remain stable. Therefore, as with the psychophysical changes described by our experientials, the kind of value shifts that occur following EEs seem to persist over many years.

ECOLOGICAL SENSITIVITY AND PLANETARY CONCERN

When I read Strieber's book *Communion,* one of the first hints I found that suggested there might be a connection between NDEs and UFOEs had to do with the "ecological message" that seemed to inform not only his own experiences but those of others he alluded to. Now, it is well known that in a previous era of UFO history—that of the so-called "contactees"[5]—one of the prevailing themes in the experiences reported in those days dealt with the dangers of humanity's development and stockpiling of nuclear weapons. At the time, of course, that issue had just become the basis for a worldwide peace movement, so it was already a leading motif in the "ecological consciousness" (if I can use that phrase here) of the world of the fifties. But Strieber's account suggested that these days, the intelligence behind UFO encounters (what that intelligence may be will be the subject of our last chapter) has a much broader and more *au courant* ecological concern. Now, for example, it isn't only the threat of nuclear annihilation but such dangers as, for example, ozone depletion and deforestation, that UFO encounters seem to sensitize some of their subjects to.

Here is a big clue to the mystery.

Reading Strieber's commentary and then other UFO literature, I couldn't help seeing that there appeared to be a fairly obvious connection between the moral injunctions of these experiences and the dominant social issues of the times. And likewise, from my background research on NDEs, it was impossible for me not to notice that today's ecological and planetary concerns were also matters to which many NDErs were at pains to stress that *their own encounters with death* had led them to become more sensitized. Indeed, a small subset of NDErs have even described to me (and other researchers have reported similar findings) that as a part of their experience or in its immediate aftermath, they have had a terrifying vision of global cataclysm.[6] Likewise, Strieber himself comments that his encounters with other abductees have hinted at such possibilities and also avers, I think correctly, that "throughout the literature of abduction, there is a frequent message of apocalypse."[7]

In the light of these reflections, it seemed important to make a special attempt to assess changes in these sensitivities in the aftermath of extraordinary encounters. Accordingly, I incorporated into the revised version of the LCI a new value cluster, concern with social/planetary issues. The general findings for this cluster have already been presented in Table 9 and show an overall increase in such concern for all groups. However, this overall effect obscures the *strength* of the tendencies toward increased concern for ecological and planetary welfare per se.

The group averages pertaining to these two items in particular are therefore shown separately in Table 10 and reveal very marked positive shifts; indeed, the value for the UFOE group on the planetary welfare item is higher than *any* other of the thirty-six averages that make up the whole of Table 9.

The magnitude of these shifts can perhaps be even more clearly appreciated if we take a moment to examine the percentage of respondents who say they have shifted positively on such matters. For example, fully 85 percent of UFOErs report an increase in their concern for planetary welfare following their UFO encounter, and of these, nearly 60 percent state that it has *strongly* increased. NDErs are similar, with almost 80 percent also indicating a positive shift on this item, and not quite half that number similarly saying that it represents a strong increase. Indeed, the degree of these shifts is especially marked for the experiential groups, who are almost twice as likely as the controls to claim a strong increase for all item comparisons. The data here are reported in full in Table 11.

Thus, the heightened sensitivity to ecological matters and to the condition of our earth generally seems, statistically at least, to be among the most important value changes that follow extraordinary experiences. And here it is also evident that although interest in such experiences is itself sufficient to explain part of this shift, *the experience* seems to give a very significant impetus to it, for it is among the experiencers themselves that the strongest surge of interest in these issues is expressed.

This is also revealed in some of the spontaneous comments that experiencers made regarding these planetary or ecological perspectives. For example, one woman who has had a UFO sighting said that she felt she received a telepathic transmission concerning "a joint cooperative mission in service to the planet." Another woman, who has had both an NDE and a UFO sighting, remarked:

These experiences made me cherish all life as I had never done before. I really began to be aware of everything in my experience on a deeper level. I even began to "salute" animals I would meet, recognizing their individual worth, and of course, my recognition of human individual worth began to grow.

And finally one man who has had multiple encounters with what he regards as extraterrestrials offered this observation:

> I was told that because of our violent nature toward each other and a disrespect for all living things in the environment, we are evolving against the naturalness of the Universal Flow . . . The ETs avoid "overt" contact because they are not allowed to interfere in one's free will, but can on subtle levels if it preserves life and helps the evolutionary process spiritually or the species to survive.

These ecological motifs and the sense of a shared mission between humanity and other forms of intelligence to preserve and protect life on the planet will prove to be critical markings on the trail of our inquiry into the meaning of extraordinary encounters. Here, however, it is simply enough to note them, but we shall certainly return to them later on in order to explore their significance in much greater depth.

RELIGIOUS BELIEFS INVENTORY (RBI)

You will recall that in addition to the LCI, we used another measure of value changes in the Omega Project that was directed to assessing the nature of the changes in one's spiritual or religious orientation following an extraordinary encounter. The RBI, another instrument I had used previously in my research on NDEs,[8] provides a measure of the degree to which an individual shifts toward a universalistic spiritual or a more sectarian religious position in the aftermath of an EE. It is composed of just twelve items, and the respondent is simply asked to indicate whether he now agrees more or less with the item in question or has experienced no change. Sample items indicating a universalistic orientation are:

The essential core of all religions is the same.

More and more, I feel at home in any church.

Those reflecting a more conventional religious orientation are:

I believe there is a heaven and hell.

In order to live a truly religious life, the Church or some such other organized religious body is an essential.

The way that the RBI is scored, a net *positive* score reveals a shift toward universalism, while a net *negative* score means a shift toward religious sectarianism, and no change of course means no shift in either direction.

Before we look at the findings based on the RBI, however, let us consider certain hints that I have already dropped or that are implicated in the data I have previously presented in this chapter that give us a sense of what we might expect here. If, for example, you've taken the trouble to inspect the LCI table (Table 9), you may remember that whereas there is a strong increase in spirituality for all groups, there is essentially no change in overall religiousness following EEs. A driblet of qualitative data, offered earlier in another context, also suggests what we shall find writ in large figures in the RBI: Hazel Underwood's remarks on pages 50–51 will turn out to be representative of many respondents, as my note (number 4) in that connection implied.

What the RBI Tells Us About Religious Changes

In any event, the RBI data themselves, presented in Table 12, are as straightforward as they can be: *All* groups show a very marked movement (and it is highly significant statistically[9]) toward religious universalism. Thus, *following extraordinary encounters, respondents, on the average, don't become more religious, they become more spiritual.* This is precisely what I had previously found for NDErs, by the way, and now we see that the same thing holds for our UFO sample as a whole.

Religious and Spiritual Changes Illustrated

Again, the qualitative data amply reinforce the numerical findings here. For instance, one woman who, like Hazel Underwood, was reared a Southern Baptist, almost echoes some of Hazel's own words when she writes, "I can no longer follow any organized religion," and describes herself now as a "closet Buddhist." Another respondent enclosed with her questionnaire a copy of a pamphlet she had written, significantly entitled, *The Diamond Symbol of Religious Unity*. It is indeed a paean to religious unity, as the following excerpts will attest:

> . . . at the heart of each religion is the White Center of God, which is Absolute Purity . . . It is this mystic knowledge which unifies all [religions]. The White Center resolves all differences. It is a symbol of spiritual convergence, drawing all souls to God . . .

> This understanding takes nothing away from any religion, except their prejudice of each other. It should only intensify and unite them all. In time, they should grow closer together with an emphasis on their basic unity, and respect for their differences. . . .

> I have felt a day when there were no religious barriers between men—a profoundly beautiful feeling of love for all. I have heard a great hymn of all religions singing together, praising God in mutual holy love.

OPINION INVENTORY (OI)

The RBI really marks something of a transition from the realm of personal values to that of beliefs, but with the OI, the last questionnaire in our battery, we are clearly in the domain of the belief systems and worldviews of our Omega respondents. In this instance, our participants were merely asked to express their agreement or disagreement with a set of thirty statements (or register no opinion). Thus, they were not required as such to indicate whether their opinions had changed in the light of their experiences or interests regarding UFOs or NDEs. Nevertheless, since this questionnaire was filled out only after such experiences had occurred or such interests had developed, the OI may safely be regarded as a kind of post-test without the pre-.

In any case, the OI assessed three principal domains of beliefs and worldviews: (1) the possible evolutionary significance of these experiences; (2) their possible purposive nature; and (3) possible extraterrestrial influence in human affairs. Rather than presenting a list of sample items here to illustrate these three categories, however, I shall cite them specifically in connection with our findings from this questionnaire, to which we shall turn in just a moment.

1. First, a prelude of sorts regarding the domain of the OI concerned with determining what, if any, evolutionary meaning EEs are given by our respondents. You will recall that in my preface, I alluded to the speculation I offered in my last book on NDEs that such experiences, in their collective aspect, may be serving as a catalyst for human evolution and that Whitley Strieber seemed to imply that something similar might hold for UFO encounters. Now, having just reviewed in the previous chapter the nature of the psychophysical changes reported by our experiential participants, we were able to see that there is at least some empirical evidence that is consistent with such notions. However, toward the close of that chapter, I cautioned that such a claim was one that had been asserted so far only by some researchers and writers, and that it would be useful to hear from the experiencers themselves on this point. Therefore, the OI was designed to provide exactly this kind of information: What in fact do our Omega respondents think about this evolutionary hypothesis and the possible role of EEs in furthering it?

We constructed several items to assess the matter, and here
are some of them:

I believe that the changes I've undergone since my UFO
experience[10] are part of an evolutionary unfolding of humanity.

In my opinion, the widespread occurrence of UFO experiences is part of a larger plan to promote the evolution of
consciousness on a species-wide scale.

We are already on the verge of a New Age.

Evolutionary forces are already at work which will transform humanity at large into a more self-aware, spiritually
sensitive species.

From the results of our analysis, the answer to the question
I posed above is unambiguously clear, as Table 13 demonstrates: There is widespread agreement across *all* groups with
statements implying that we are in the midst of an evolutionary
spurt toward greater spiritual awareness and higher consciousness—and that the occurrence of UFOEs and NDEs is an integral part of that progression. For example, with respect to the
second statement listed above, not only do a majority of our
respondents in all conditions endorse it, but among those expressing a definite opinion, it is favored by a margin of anywhere from roughly 4 up to 7 to 1, depending on the group. In
other words, it receives an overwhelming affirmation from our
respondents.[11] Thus, the evolutionary hypothesis that I proposed in *Heading Toward Omega* receives, in effect, a strong
vote of confidence from the respondents in *The Omega Project*.

2. Turning to the second, and certainly related, question
on the OI of a possible larger purpose behind the emergence of
NDEs and UFOs in our time, Table 14 provides a sampling of
our respondents' opinions on this matter. To follow the ensuing
discussion, however, it will be necessary to bear in mind a few
of the items composing this cluster. They are:

I believe that my UFO experience was "arranged" or "designed" by a higher agency or by my higher self.

I believe that my UFO experience occurred so as to awaken me to the existence of larger cosmic forces which are affecting our lives.

I feel I have a mission to use what I have learned from my UFO experience to spread God's love to all.

Here we see a different pattern begin to emerge. To begin with, analysis of the first two items makes it evident that our respondents are inclined to agree that there are "higher forces" orchestrating these experiences and that they are meant to awaken individuals to the existence of a cosmic plan for life on earth. Not surprisingly, those who actually have had these experiences are somewhat more likely to endorse these statements than persons who have only an interest in them, but the overall trend of support for items of this kind is strong even for the control groups. Second, it is equally clear from the analysis of the last item that though purpose is ascribed to the occurrence of these experiences, what *kind* of purpose is discerned differs radically for our two categories of experiences. Those who have had or become interested in NDEs are inclined to see a spiritual meaning to NDEs, specifically, "to spread God's love." [12] Our UFO sample, on the other hand, is much less likely to endorse this opinion, and this is true for experiencers and controls alike, who split 50–50 on this interpretation. Here, for one of the few times in this study, we finally have a *difference* to note between our UFO and ND sample.

Something of the contrast in the substance, if not the form, of these missionary tendencies is suggested in some of the spontaneous comments of our respondents. For example, Sandra Gibson, a thirty-six-year-old NDEr, not previously quoted, gives this characteristic statement concerning the meaning she attributes to her NDE and how she needs to express what it has taught her in her relations with others:

. . . I have no doubt that this personal experience was part of a collective planetary evolution. My ideas about God have changed drastically and are basically that God is a life force of light, love and truth that exists in all things. I know I am a core of love and the lessons I seem to be learning now are how to express/share this love on the physical plane in my daily affairs.

Now, there is nothing in this declaration that Gina Willoughby would take exception to; indeed, as we have seen, she, too, is an apostle of love. But she has also expressed a sense of mission that captures other facets of this need to communicate what one has learned from these experiences. Her exigent tone may also be typical of some NDErs, but the content of the following passage suggests, I think, how the UFOErs' sense of purpose may be somewhat different from that of NDErs:

I never thought of myself as one of those people who ended up with a "sense of mission" as a result of their paranormal experiences. I never had an urgency of mission. That is, until now, for suddenly I do feel driven to talk about "these things." I want to just go up to people and say, "Listen, there is a whole other reality out there that is just as real, just as valid as what you think is the only reality. Open your minds. Look into this. It's important to you, too!" I feel foolish and afraid to do this, but the drive is there. Somehow I feel as if time is running out, as if something big is about to happen. Don't ask me to explain it any better, for I can't. All I know is that this is important—it's a feeling I have, that's all!

3. The difference between our two categories of experiencers that began to emerge when we considered their sense of purpose seems to grow even more evident in the last opinion domain, that of possible extraterrestrial influence in earthly activities. Representative of these differences are the responses to the two following statements:

I believe that humanity may be the object of biological experimentation by extraterrestrial life forms.

I believe alien beings are likely to exert increasing control over human life in years to come.

In Table 15, we see the clearest evidence in the entire study of a divergence between our UFO and ND samples, and in the end it is not a divergence either in developmental history or, strictly speaking, in aftereffects. Instead, it is literally a *difference of opinion* over the possible role of extraterrestrial influence in human life. In broad terms, it's easy to state this difference: Our UFO respondents tend to be more convinced that extraterrestrial forces are at work on earth than are ND respondents who consistently reject such claims. Specifically, the UFO sample on the whole is quite open to the possibility that aliens are engaged in biological experimentation with humans and to a lesser but still significant extent that they may continue to increase their control over human life. A seemingly ominous prospect.

And yet this would be a fallacious reading of the matter, for there are still other data from this portion of the questionnaire that give a much more hopeful hue to this picture of possible intervention by otherworldly beings. Consider, for instance, these two items:

There are higher order intelligences that are bent on exploiting our planet in some way.

There are higher order intelligences that have a concern with the welfare of our planet.

Here, as the last two rows of Table 15 disclose, we see that UFO respondents not only fail to endorse the statement that higher intelligences are exploiting the planet, as does our ND sample, but *even more* than their ND brethren, they overwhelmingly concur with the assertion that higher intelligences are concerned with the earth's *welfare*. Thus, it appears that whereas there is plainly a difference between our UFO and ND samples regarding belief in the *existence* of alien intelligence per se, both groups seem to agree that however these "higher forces" are conceived, they represent essentially beneficent influences. Indeed, only by making some such assumption is it possible to reconcile the common avowal of both the UFO and ND groups that these experiences are serving a positive evolutionary purpose for humanity (see Table 13) with their superficially discrepant opinions concerning the role of extraterrestrial influence. What we are saying, then, is that in *this* final analysis, the difference in beliefs we described earlier tends to dissolve when seen in the context of a *larger evolutionary worldview* that both groups are known to share.

What the OI Tells Us About Beliefs

In summary, in the sphere of beliefs and worldviews, all groups tend to agree that these experiences reflect a purposive intelligence and that they are part of an accelerating evolutionary current that is propelling the human race toward higher consciousness and heightened spirituality. These opinions are of course generally compatible with the pattern of psychophysical and value changes we have already observed. Indeed, we can easily suppose that the aftereffects of extraordinary encounters would actually tend to give rise to these very convictions. Finally, without wishing to deny that there are some differences between our UFO and ND samples (for example, on *how* they see the purpose of their experiences), even their answers to our opinion inventory seem to point once again to their essential kinship.

A SUMMING UP—AND A LOOK AHEAD

As my concluding comments on the OI implied, we find that in the realm of aftereffects, just as it was with our constellation of psychological and developmental factors, our results generally conform to a highly coherent pattern. Certainly, with respect to the personal values, beliefs, and worldviews of our respondents, there is an impressive consistency in their assertions of how their experiences of or concerns with NDEs or UFOs have changed them, often quite fundamentally, and largely in positive ways. In the last two chapters, we have seen, then, how through their involvement with the world of UFOs and NDEs our Omega participants have been *expanded*—in their psychophysiological functioning, cognitive processes, and social values—and made *more hopeful* concerning the outcome of humanity's spiritual evolution.

You will remember, though, that when we considered the results based on the PCI, we were confronted with enormous statistical differences between our experiential and control respondents. In this chapter, however, we find, on the whole, a pattern of unmistakable *similarity* between them. On the LCI and RBI, for example, commonalities in responses among the four groups are the rule, not the exception. But this finding, too, is nonetheless remarkable because our control groups, it will be recalled, are made up of persons who have a very different kind of developmental history than our experiential respondents; furthermore, they show no particular affinity for states of consciousness disclosing alternate realities or propensities for dissociative thinking, and they plainly don't report anything like the profound psychophysical changes that characterize our experientials. Yet, when it comes to the expression of personal values and religious beliefs, these individuals seem to view the world in much the same way as do our experiential respondents, as though they are seeing it essentially through the same eyes. This of course implies that whereas having UFOEs or NDEs may in themselves promote the kind of shifts our questionnaires reveal, merely becoming *interested* in these phenomena may also accomplish the same end. To sort out the relative influence here of personal experience versus social contagion is not possible from our data alone, but our findings do suggest that this would be a most worthwhile task for the social psychologist or the sociologist interested in social movements.

Although the overall similarity between our experiential and control groups was perhaps the most important finding deriving from the LCI and RBI, there were of course some differences, too. As I noted earlier, though both experientials and controls tend to move toward more prosocial values, this trend was on the whole somewhat stronger for our experiential respondents, suggesting that the personal experience factor may indeed give a boost to such changes. Moreover, our finding that on certain values NDErs shifted more than UFOErs replicates the work of the only other researcher I know of who has taken the trouble to make this specific comparison.[13]

Finally, to return once more to the OI, here again it was the similarity between all of our groups that was most noteworthy. Our sample as a whole appears to regard UFOs and NDEs positively and believes that they hold out potential benefits for humanity that we can hardly conceive of today. In interpreting these findings, we face the same problem we have encountered before: It is impossible to know how much these opinions are shaped by direct personal experience, how much through social influence processes within the UFO and NDE communities, and how much through the operation of the Zeitgeist with its apocalyptic imagery and expectations. All we can say here is that the general belief system represented by the body of our findings on the OI is entirely in keeping with our pattern of aftereffects and might therefore simply be regarded as their cognitive aspect. At any rate, only further research can hope to clarify how these opinions come to be formed and how they are maintained. Here we must rest content merely with our preliminary assessment of the *nature* of these beliefs. And that, fortunately, will be enough for our purposes, which only require that we know *what* they are, regardless of how they came to be.

In the last three chapters, I have presented a complex array of findings from the Omega Project having to do with the precursors and consequences of two varieties of extraordinary encounters. You have, I hope, learned quite a bit about what kind of people are likely to undergo NDEs and UFO encounters, and what changes follow in their wake. We have also seen how astonishingly similar these experiences are, if not in their content, at least in their antecedents and aftereffects. But we have now reached the end of our empirical trail, as it were, and must look up to the challenge that lies before us—to climb the mountain that will afford us a clear view of the interpretation and meaning of the data that are now all laid out for us to see.

Along the way of our travels, we have, of course, already come across some hints and portents, but the job of connecting these scattered pieces of a puzzle whose boundaries can scarcely be guessed at still remains to be done. And here, finally, we come to all those inescapable questions long deferred but certainly not forgotten: What is the nature of the reality of these experiences? For UFO encounters, can it be that there are actually alien beings who are orchestrating the strange encounters whose effects we have been considering here? What, at bottom, *is* the intelligence that is the governing force behind the manifestation of NDEs and UFOEs—and could it be the *same* force for experiences whose phenomenology is so radically different? And, finally, what more can be said concerning the apparent connection between the "lessons" of these experiences and the social issues that dominate your consciousness and mine today?

Make no mistake: These are not merely questions of academic interest but potentially have deep consequences for the future of humanity. Let us hasten, therefore, to begin the last stage of our journey. The mountain awaits.

CHAPTER 9

HEADING TOWARD OZ:

Demystifying Extraordinary Encounters

Between living and dreaming there is a third thing.
Guess it.

Antonio Machado

Extraordinary encounters such as UFO abductions and NDEs have the power to exert an almost hypnotic fascination over us. It is easy to find ourselves entranced with a sense of their beguiling, tantalizing mystery as we are caused to wonder what unknown forces may generate such strange experiences into human consciousness. There is in many of us perhaps even a desire not so much to *solve* the mystery as to *savor* it, for the appeal of a mystery is precisely that it calls forth our own imaginative and creative potentials. Further, in the case of seemingly miraculous mysteries, there is an obvious temptation to allow one's imagination to soar along the course charted by its ardent yearnings for the truly fabulous and to entertain possibilities that mundane considerations normally banish from view. Concerning UFO encounters, for example, most persons would probably agree that it is a thrilling notion that visitors from other star systems may actually be here and have established contact with us. Similarly, the idea, strongly suggested by NDEs, that there is a realm of absolute love and peace permeated with the presence of God that awaits us after death is a deep and perennial longing of humanity that even a skeptical age like ours has failed to quell. Such beliefs may surely, without blushing, be called "soul-stirring," and whether we adhere to them or not, we must admit that even the thought that they may be true excites and moves us in an almost primordial way. And now, the very fact that scientific inquiry into UFOs and NDEs seems to provide a kind of empirical support for these beliefs has only served to quicken our hopes still further.

For these reasons, then, there is an understandable tendency for many of us to accept reports of UFO encounters and NDEs at face value. Since we have compelling motives to want to believe them and to take them literally, we are naturally reluctant to look at them with a critical eye or perhaps to ask too many probing questions about them. We would sometimes rather simply believe than to know, or to imagine we know when we know only what we imagine.

Now, even though I have so far taken a psychological approach toward the extraordinary encounters we have been concerned with in this book, I must concede at this point that of course it is conceivable that these UFO reports and NDEs may very well have the extraterrestrial and otherworldly implications that many people, and certainly most of those who have experienced them directly, would impute to them. That is, there may really be "aliens among us" and a "heavenly hereafter" in store for us. No findings that I have so far presented and nothing that I have said here in this chapter preclude those possibilities. And yet I hope you would agree that without further inquiry it would be rash and unwarranted to assume that what *might* be true, or certainly what we might hope to be true, is necessarily so.

You can see that this preamble is intended to identify and dislodge some of our sources of resistance to a closer and critical examination of the remarkable experiences on whose psychological roots and behavioral consequences we have already lavished so much attention. Acknowledging that we may be reluctant to probe into the whys and wherefores of these experiences too fully, at the same time, it is, I think, obvious that there is also a part of us that wants to make the attempt to penetrate the mystery further and to follow the trail of that inquiry regardless of where it leads. Let us, then, in the spirit of demystifying these encounters, follow our own version of the Yellow Brick Road in search of Oz. But, be prepared, it may be that we will find an even deeper mystery awaiting us at the end of our journey.

SOME PRELIMINARY CONSIDERATIONS

At the outset, it is important to keep certain considerations in mind. For one thing, you remember that we have found that although the nature of UFO encounters and NDEs is very different, the kind of person who is susceptible to them is much the same. Therefore, any theory that we devise has to account for these commonalities among UFOErs and NDErs.

For another, we need to specify the types of factors that such a theory will need to include if it wishes to explain satisfactorily the various features and consequences of these experiences. In particular, there are three types of factors that will concern us.

To begin with, there is the question of the condition that triggers the experience in the first place. In the case of the NDE, of course, the cause, at least in general terms, is obvious: It is a near-death crisis of some kind resulting in a cardiac or respiratory arrest that initiates the occurrence of the experience. In UFO encounters, as we have seen, the precipitating agents are both more variable and more ambiguous than in NDEs. Often it is an anomalous light of some kind, but of course it could actually be a spacecraft or even the perception of an apparent extraterrestrial being that sets it off. Plainly, this is a matter that will require some closer scrutiny before we can hope to clarify just what these originating conditions may be.

Second, there is the issue of just who will be sensitive to such triggers, whatever they turn out to be. We have already seen of course that not everyone who undergoes a near-death crisis or is a potential witness to a UFO actually has, or remembers having had, an extraordinary encounter. Only *some* people do, and we have labeled such individuals *encounter-prone personalities* and have indicated some of the childhood factors that seem to foster the development of such sensitivity. But there are still unanswered questions here having to do with what neurological conditions may underlie such receptivity to these events in the first place. Indeed, such a link will prove to play a crucial role in our understanding of the biological basis underlying the encounter-prone personality.

Finally, we shall have to deal with the ineluctable and unassailable fact that there is a distinctive *patterning* to these experiences and to their aftereffects. In other words, we must account for why these experiences have a relatively constant form and just why they take the form they do. In the case of NDEs, it is precisely this kind of thematic unity that has intrigued both researchers and the lay public ever since these episodes gained widespread attention in the mid-1970s. With respect to UFO encounters, of course the most striking parallel with the NDE is found in the abduction narrative, where again a reliable sequence of events is normally described—and one that, as I have often noted, is at the same time very different from those characteristic of NDEs. Of course, the obvious solution to the problem of the form of UFO abductions would be to argue that they are literally taking place and thus abductees are simply recalling what has actually happened to them. But since appearance may not be reality, it is arguable that there may well be other answers to this conundrum. In any case, with respect to this matter of what causes these encounters to have the shape that they do, we shall have to conduct a most searching inquiry before we can arrive at a formulation that holds out hope of making good sense of the whole phenomenon of extraordinary encounters.

In our search for answers to the questions I have raised, it will prove both useful and expedient to begin with some recent attempts to understand the nature of UFO encounters in general and abduction episodes in particular. And since many reports of UFOs are normally triggered by the appearance of a strange light, let us start with that.

EARTH LIGHTS, EXTRAORDINARY
ENCOUNTERS, AND THE TEMPORAL LOBE

It has long been known that natural processes of the earth and its atmosphere produce unusual displays of light. A Welsh researcher and writer, Paul Devereux, has provided a useful generic term for these strangely fascinating luminous phenomena; he calls them *earth lights*.[1] A familiar, if still not well-understood, example of earth lights would be what is usually called "ball lightning." Typically, though not always, associated with stormy, thunderous weather, balls of light have been observed in various forms and colors, and are sometimes as large as beach balls, or larger. They may be either translucent or opaque, and their motion is likewise variable: According to Devereux, they can hover, float languidly, fall to the ground, remain stationary, or move as if purposefully.[2] Interestingly, Whitley Strieber has described some incidents that he witnessed as a child that appear to have involved ball lightning and makes it clear that they can be terrifying indeed.[3]

Another manifestation of terrestrial luminosity is earthquake lights. These displays, which may occur before, during, or after quakes, also evince a variety of forms, such as auroralike discharges, meteoric lights, and other kinds of atmospheric glows, including, once again, balls of light.[4] Earth lights are also known to occur in conjunction with volcanic activity, and other seemingly inexplicable lights have been reliably reported by witnesses at sea.

In many instances, these unusual lights seem to emerge from the ground (or water) and either swiftly dissolve or merely hover in the air. Less often, they are observed to be "flying" over a considerable distance and sometimes are reported to reach a height of several thousand feet, occasionally touching down and then ascending again. In daylight, the lights may even sometimes appear to be metallic in nature.[5]

Most intriguingly of all, Devereux has found that recurrent earth-light phenomena have been observed in certain regions in many countries for generations—so much so that they have been incorporated into local folklore, superstitions, and place names. Devereux and his colleagues have in fact made a special study of a number of these areas in the British Isles in order to determine what, if any, commonalities may be associated with these consistently reported and locally familiar anomalous light patterns.[6]

And what emerges from these studies is indeed, as Devereux implies, quite a revelation. There is, first of all, a clear connection between these light displays and the presence of fault lines. But more than that, other consistencies have been noted: Earth lights often appear near bodies of water, especially lakes and reservoirs, but also rivers and waterfalls. Significantly:

> Lights are regularly reported near power lines, transmitter towers, mountain peaks, isolated buildings, roads and railway lines. The lights like to haunt quarries, rocky ridges, mines and caves.[7]

In short, there appears to be a definite and unmistakable relationship between the occurrence of earth-light features, on the one hand, and certain specific geological sites and electrical devices, on the other.

What could be the basis for these earth lights, which, according to Devereux, strongly suggest an electromagnetic nature? Here, the work of another researcher, Michael Persinger, a Canadian professor of psychology and a clinical neurophysiologist by training, will prove to be most germane. Extensive empirical and statistical studies by Persinger and his colleagues have convinced him that the underlying energy basis for earth lights is tectonic stress. Persinger has in fact elaborated a general theory for this position that is known as the Tectonic Strain Theory (TST), and it will be helpful if we now examine some of its principal assumptions—as well as some supportive data for the theory he has put forward.[8]

The first postulate of the theory is that most UFO phenomena are natural occurrences that are direct products of the stresses and strains of the earth's crust. In other words, UFOs are ultimately geologically derived events that are then, of course, misinterpreted according to the currently widespread belief in the existence and proximity of extraterrestrial craft. Although the exact mechanisms by which these earth lights are generated are either poorly understood or unknown, Persinger, in agreement with Devereux, has found that they do and would be expected to take place close to fault lines, rifts, rivers and other water systems, towers, electrical installations, and the like. Statistical studies have shown that seismic events are also clearly related to UFO reports in the affected area, with the correlations ranging from .50 to .70, which are very substantial indeed given the unreliability of UFO reports.[9]

Persinger goes on to assume that the earth lights that are generated by these natural geological processes—and that provide the basis, but not in themselves the complete explanation, for UFO perceptions—are transformations of the energy associated with mechanical deformation of the earth's crust, and that they have electrical, magnetic, sonic, or sometimes even chemical properties, in addition to photic ones. A further derivation from Persinger's theory, and a crucial one for the understanding of certain features of UFO phenomena, he states as follows:

> . . . one would predict that most UFOs generate substantial electromagnetic fields that include the entire spectra of light (and color), biologically hazardous ionizing radiation, and even quasistatic magnetic field components that are sufficient to affect lighting and ignition systems.[10]

Now, let's see if we can translate this rather formidable-seeming technical language of Persinger's into an understandable scenario for what may happen during UFO encounters.

Suppose there is first of all some sort of manifestation of an earth light some distance away from where a witness is standing. If that person is sufficiently far from the presumed electromagnetic field in which the light form is embedded, he will probably just note an anomalous, perhaps inexplicable-seeming light that may also be moving in a strange, possibly erratic manner. If the individual is drawn to approach the light, or it comes closer to him, he may then find himself within the ambit of its electromagnetic field and, significantly, begin to feel its effects. Initially, these might be experienced as tingling sensations, goose bumps, hair raising, or other signs of nervous excitation. A deeper immersion in the field, however, could produce stronger reactions, both somatically and in terms of psychological disturbances, for at close range the brain is likely to be affected by this field. In particular, as Persinger points out, the temporal lobe of the brain is especially susceptible to such influences, which in turn would tend to kindle certain characteristic impressions.

It is here, of course, that Persinger's training in neuroscience is brought to bear on his argument, which is as follows: Stimulation of the temporal lobe, and specifically of two structures within the limbic system, the hippocampus and amygdala, is known to generate intense hallucinatory activity that may nevertheless seem distinctly real to the individual in the manner of a waking dream. Among the impressions that can be produced in this way are the sense of a presence, apparitions, floating and spinning sensations, out-of-body experiences, hearing inner voices, powerful convictions of deep meaningfulness, and, afterward, amnesia or a sense of time loss. If this stimulation occurs as a result of the individual's being exposed to an electromagnetic field associated with an anomalous light display and to an individual already predisposed or conditioned to believe in UFOs, it is easy to see how, during the influence of this altered state, the definite impression that one has actually had such contact could be convincingly created.[11]

In short, what Persinger is asserting is that UFO encounters of the kind we have been considering in this book are brought about by electromagnetic phenomena and are likely to induce an unusual transient state of activity in the temporal lobe of the brain that might be thought of as something like a microseizure. It is precisely this type of temporal-lobe instability, says Persinger, that sets the stage for the perception of an apparent UFO event. The distinctive state of consciousness that results, *in combination with the preexisting definition of the situation,* causes, as it were, a kind of perceptual hallucination, the events of which are later recalled as actual memories—as indeed they are, but not necessarily of the kind that the individual thinks they are.

At this point, it is necessary to make a momentary, but vital, reference to the second type of extraordinary encounter we have been concerned with, i.e., NDEs. From what I have just said about the possible role of temporal-lobe activity in UFO encounters, you should now easily be able to see how in principle a similar case could be developed for its relevance to the NDE. Clearly, in the circumstances in which NDEs occur, the "definition of the situation" is very different from that prevailing in UFO-encounter settings, yet if the temporal lobe can be shown to be sensitive to the trauma of near death, it is apparent how its stimulation in *that context* could give rise to many, if not all, of the features that define classic NDEs.

This neurological extrapolation to the NDE is, I sadly concede, far from being original with me. Indeed, it has already been made, in one form or another, not only by NDE researchers themselves,[12] but also by those whose primary interest is in UFO phenomena—or in events that have, in their view wrongly, sometimes been *interpreted* in UFO terms. For example, Paul Devereux himself was quick to point out this possible neurological linchpin between UFOEs and NDEs:

> It is certainly the case that many abductees report floating to the alien "craft," floating being a typical sensation produced by temporal lobe stimulation. In near-death experiences, people feel themselves floating along or up a tunnel towards a light. Abductees sometimes experience being drawn up a lightbeam towards the "craft." The imagery and sense of motion are very similar. There are many facets shared by abduction, out-of-body and near-death experiences. It is similarity that should not go unnoticed.[13]

And it hasn't. Not surprisingly, Persinger, with his special interest in the role of the temporal lobe in various altered states of consciousness, has been insistent on its role in NDEs, too.

In a paper specifically directed to this issue, he not only claims that this is strongly indicated theoretically, but that he has some experimental data that support this contention as well:

> There is little doubt that the class of experiences that comprise mystical experiences in general, and NDEs in particular, is strongly correlated with temporal lobe activity. . . . Kate Makarec and I have found that all of the major components of the NDE, including out-of-body experiences, floating, being pulled towards a light, hearing strange music, and profound meaningful experiences can occur in experimental settings during minimal electrical current induction to the temporal region due to exogenous spike-and-wave magnetic field sources.[14]

Whether this approach of Persinger's provides a *complete* explanation for the features and form of the NDE experience is another matter and one that even he appears hesitant to insist upon. But that *some* reference must be made to the connection between the temporal lobe and the NDE is now an increasingly common position among neuroscientists and physicians concerned with explanatory models for this phenomenon. That being so, it is now at last possible for us to understand something that has been a puzzle throughout this book—namely, why there should be such undeniable commonalities between NDEs and UFOEs with respect to their antecedents, structural form, and consequences. In the light of the preceding argument, the answer is obvious: There is a common neurological mechanism that underlies them both.

Returning now to our hypothetical individual who finds himself caught up in the electromagnetic field engendered by an apparent UFO, we can both trace the whole progression of the consequences of such an encounter and summarize the gist of Persinger's general neurological interpretation with one final citation from him here:

> Because most UFO phenomena are assumed to be energetic natural sources, close proximity to them would preferen-

tially evoke electrical instability within the observer's brain. The types of symptoms and their intensity would vary as a function of the current induction within the brain. As the current density increases, the consequences would change from tingling sensations or sense of a presence, to odd smells or sounds and then to the release of dream-like images. At very intense currents, partial amnesia might occur and severe hypertonus or convulsions would ensue. Very intense currents would be lethal; unless precise postmortems were completed, the symptoms would simulate a heart attack. If the body was associated with burns, death would probably be attributed to a lightning strike.[15]

Obviously, the theories of Devereux and Persinger—which have received a measure of factual support—are designed to provide a naturalistic interpretation for both UFOEs and NDEs. For that reason, both of these investigators are at pains to show how many of the characteristic features and aftereffects of these EEs may in principle be explained by their theories. Although it goes without saying that a case can be made for many different interpretations of EEs, I see some special reasons in view of the findings of the Omega Project to accord the Devereux-Persinger explanation pride of place in the hierarchy of possibilities. For one thing, it helps us to understand, as most other theories do not, the intriguing and unmistakable pattern of psychophysical changes we have already noted in Chapter 7. Persinger's ideas especially also enable us to make sense of the electrical-sensitivity syndrome that tends to crop up in the lives of a significant number of our experiential respondents, a matter that I shall try to elucidate briefly in a moment. Moreover, and perhaps most compelling of all, in the views of these men we discover just why we should actually expect there to be generalized similarities between UFOEs and NDEs, which is certainly a stumbling block for more conventional, and especially literalistic, interpretations of UFOEs. And, as we shall shortly see, there are still other facets of the Devereux-Persinger model that fit, like Cinderella's slipper, perfectly onto the pattern of some of our other findings, adding yet again to the cogency of their position.

Still, there remain a number of elements for which we have to account before we have anything approaching a comprehensive theory even for the data of the Omega Project. One, alluded to earlier, is the undeniable fact that not everyone who survives a near-death incident has an NDE, or, similarly, not everyone present at a UFO event registers it. I have, of course, already commented on this point in my discussion of the encounter-prone personality. The issue now, however, is what *additional* insights can the Devereux-Persinger perspective bring to this question of differential sensitivity to extraordinary encounters?

THE ENCOUNTER-PRONE PERSONALITY REVISITED

In Chapter 6, we noted that some persons are especially susceptible to perceptions that seem to have their origin in what I called *an alternate reality*. These are our encounter-prone personalities, found, as we know, disproportionately among our experiential respondents. Returning to a consideration of such persons in the light of some of Persinger's neurological formulations, however, leads us to ask a new question about them: Are they perhaps different from normals with respect to their temporal-lobe functioning? Specifically, is there any evidence that they have a greater degree of temporal lability?

Paul Devereux, with his usual prescience, has already been hot on the trail of these speculations and offers his own succinct conclusion on the matter:

Some people are more liable to electrical "microseizures" within the temporal lobe area than others, and are consequently more sensitive to appropriate stimuli. This is, no doubt, reflected in the findings of Keul and Phillips [an Australian and English UFO researcher, respectively] whose close encounter witnesses exhibit profiles similar to ESP percipients. It is possible, therefore, that such a person entering electromagnetic fields associated with earth light appearance might be "triggered" more readily than someone less electrically sensitive.[16]

This paragraph reads as if Devereux is describing individuals similar to those I have labeled encounter-prone persons, but it is impossible to be sure of this. Besides, since we obviously have no direct measure of the temporal-lobe lability of our respondents, we have no way of asserting that our sample of encounter-prone persons is necessarily more sensitive with respect to stimuli triggering temporal-lobe activity. Still, we do have, it turns out, a good deal of circumstantial data that point to the tenability of the temporal-lobe hypothesis. Here again we turn to Persinger, who has conveniently provided us with a clinical portrait of persons with temporal-lobe lability. See to what extent his rendering of their psychological profile seems to overlap with the qualities we know or might infer to be characteristic of encounter-prone persons.

> The personalities of normal people who display enhanced temporal lobe activity . . . usually display enhanced creativity, suggestibility, memory capacity and intuitive processing. Most of them experience a rich fantasy or subjective world that fosters their adaptability. These people have more frequent experiences of a sense of presence during which time "an entity is felt and sometimes seen;" exotic beliefs rather than traditional religious concepts are endorsed.[17]

Elaborating on this last point elsewhere, Persinger goes on to say that not only is temporal-lobe lability associated with "exotic" beliefs, but it is also strongly correlated with psychic experiences such as telepathy, clairvoyance, and precognition. Furthermore, persons displaying such temporal-lobe characteristics are also prone to generate and remember vivid visual imagery, especially concerning childhood events. Finally, such persons tend to be hypnotically suggestible and to be dissociative.[18]

Commenting specifically on abduction cases, Persinger also makes specific mention of the strong correlations that exist between early histories of sexual, physical, and psychological trauma (especially between the ages of four and six) and enduring tendencies to dissociate under stress. Such childhood trauma, he implies, can itself increase temporal lability.[19] And consistent with this contention is his observation that there are indeed moderate intercorrelations between temporal-lobe epilepsy, multiple personality, and early child abuse.[20]

The foregoing descriptions do not pretend to cover all of the traits said to be typical of individuals who score high on temporal-lobe lability, but I think I have provided enough of a list to suggest the point I wish to make: From a correlational standpoint, *there appears to be considerable evidence that our encounter-prone persons are likely to be characterized by greater than average temporal-lobe sensitivity.* More research on this matter is obviously needed, but it does seem that here, too, the Devereux-Persinger model makes an important contribution to our understanding of individual differences in susceptibility to EEs in the first place. Again, heightened temporal-lobe sensitivity appears to be the key.

ALIEN ENCOUNTERS: FORM FOLLOWS FICTION

So far, we have considered some of the conditions that may give rise to extraordinary encounters as well as a neurological hypothesis that helps us to understand why certain people should be especially susceptible to them. All this finally makes it clear why experiences as different in content as abductions and NDEs should nevertheless have essentially the same underlying *structure.* But nothing we have considered to this point provides an explanation for the *specific thematic motifs* of the two types of EEs we are examining in this book. That is, just why should UFO encounters assume one highly characteristic form, as represented by abduction narratives, for example, and NDEs, a very different one? Let's begin to examine this issue with a consideration of the distinctive form of the UFO encounter in our own time, the abduction episode.

To introduce some of my basic assumptions here by reference to a specific case, ponder the larger implications of this instance, as summarized by Paul Devereux:

> The woman [in question] was in her forties, clearly distraught by her experience. She felt she had been awakened in her bedroom by two strange beings with "leathery skin" who "floated" her to a nearby field where she was taken inside a large spaceship. She underwent the sort of intrusive physical examination widely reported by abductees. She described the craft as being illuminated "like a fairground," she showed the investigators faint marks on her arm where she said a tube had been inserted, and mentioned a smell like that of cinnamon[21] while events were taking place on the spaceship. She eventually found herself back in her room, and the next day showed physical symptoms she ascribed to the event.
>
> The investigators spoke to the woman only two days after the abduction had supposedly taken place. They were convinced that her emotional distress was genuine. However [Jenny] Randles felt the case might be suspect as the reported abduction had happened on the same night as the British TV showing of an episode of the American soap opera *Dynasty* in which Fallon, a character in the series, was depicted as being abducted by a UFO. The investigators raised this with the woman, who freely admitted she had watched the program but strongly denied that it had influenced her experience. Nevertheless [the investigators] noted that the detailed description of the woman's UFO closely matched that of the TV version, and that the smell of cinnamon and the leathery skin of the aliens were components of the soap opera as well. The investigators felt "the chances of someone being genuinely abducted on the same night as the *Dynasty* abduction *and* having an almost identical experience are pretty slim."[22]

Now, of course, a single instance like this, while it *proves* nothing, is sufficient to raise a whole host of dark suspicions concerning the origins of and influences upon abduction narratives. In any event, this apparent pseudo-abduction forces us to open our minds to certain possibilities that can no longer be ignored.

Many, and I would suppose most, students of the history of UFO phenomena appear to agree that its manifestations tend to be viewed and interpreted in terms of the prevailing belief and conceptual systems of the times.[23] During the medieval period, for example, unexplained celestial events might be seen as "dragons flying through the sky" or some other kind of fiery supernatural object or portent. If apparitional beings were sighted, they were likely to be thought of as angels, witches, demons, or perhaps merely sylphs of the air. In later times, UFOs might be mystery airships, secret weapons such as experimental rockets, or high-flying spy planes. In short, whatever the existing or anticipated technology of the epoch makes it possible to conceive, that, in conjunction with the dominant worldview, appears to dictate the identity and purpose ascribed to UFOs. The extraterrestrial-spacecraft interpretation, though it is occasionally mentioned in earlier periods, is simply the most recent and popular of these projections onto the Rorschach of the UFO blob in the sky. Interestingly enough, this particular reading of the UFO started to gain ascendency in the late 1940s, in the immediate aftermath of the beginning of the nuclear era, and, perhaps even more significantly in the present context, with the rise of a new and distinct literary genre, *science fiction*.

In my opinion, it is not possible to understand the form of modern-day UFO encounters without reference to the role that science fiction has played in helping to establish their plausibility. The collective dream of life elsewhere in the universe is one that has been given to popular culture not so much by the astronomers and astrophysicists as by the creative writers and artists who, in countless stories, films, and television programs during our lifetime, have implanted their visions and made them ours. According to polls, we live in an age where now most people believe that "UFOs are real" and that "people like us live on other planets."[24] In that context, since angels and demons are out of style, they now dress in the costume of our own epoch's archetypal figure—the extraterrestrial alien—whom we can see precisely because we can now *conceive* of him; he both conforms to and expresses our current ideas of imaginative possibility.

The formative influence of science fiction on UFO encounters is no mere speculative theory. It has been the object of serious research by UFO scholars. The French writer Bertrand Méheust, for example, in a book that deserves to be better known than it is,[25] has shown in case after case the connection between early science fiction stories and contemporary UFO reports. Here's just one representative example, which has been brought to the attention of English readers by another distinguished UFO scholar of French extraction, Jacques Vallee:

Typical of his case material is the following abduction report, involving Mr. Belans, a Belgian who suffered missing time and amnesia following an encounter with a flying craft. The incident occurred at dusk, as he was walking in an isolated area of Brabant where suspicious traces—notably crushed vegetation—had been noticed by farmers in their wheat fields. At the site, he saw a man dressed in black waiting for something under a tree. Intrigued, Belans stopped and watched. Soon a strange feeling of tiredness came over him, as if another entity had taken control of his actions. He heard a buzzing sound, soon followed by a very bright light, as an elongated craft landed near him. A door opened over a faintly luminous rectangle, and the man in black climbed into the object. A force impelled Belans to follow. He found himself in a room that was evenly lit but without any observable source of light. A faint vibration was felt and the craft took off. An opening then became visible in the wall of the room and a very tall man entered. He seemed to "guess" Belan's every thought and was able to answer him in French. He revealed that he came from a faraway star.

"Why don't you establish open contact?" asked Belans.

"Because we do not wish to force the rapid evolution of elements that are foreign to our own civilization," the tall ufonaut responded.

Belans was eventually returned to earth, with a significant period of missing time.

The most interesting fact about the Belans abduction case is that it is a science fiction story written in 1930 by Ege Tilms. Entitled "Hodomur, Man of Infinity," it was first published four years later.[26]

Vallee goes on to comment that abduction by alien beings is in fact a recurrent and central motif in the science fiction of the early twentieth century—which is precisely what Méheust's own exhaustive research has amply demonstrated.

Other writers, such as Hilary Evans, have come to similar conclusions,[27] and so, with specific reference to cases of the abduction type, have some American investigators, notably Martin Kottmeyer.[28] The latter, who seems to know his way around the arcana of science fiction in comic strips, books, and film as no other American student of the UFO phenomenon I am familiar with, has even dug up an old Buck Rogers cartoon strip (circa 1930) that shows unmistakable anticipations of modern abduction narratives. But more than that, Kottmeyer has analyzed certain classic cases of UFO abductions, including the granddaddy of them all, the Betty and Barney Hill incident,[29] and made a very convincing argument that many of the events of their story can be traced to the film *Invaders from Mars,* and to a popular UFO book of the time that Betty had read. After considering a number of such cases from the standpoint of their likely origin in science fiction, especially of the filmic variety, Kottmeyer arrives at the landmark studies of abductions that America's best-known researcher into this domain, Budd Hopkins, has offered as evidence for their literal occurrence. Kottmeyer is not impressed:

Ufology in the eighties is dominated by Budd Hopkins and his abduction studies, *Missing Time* and *Intruders.* The latter is a straight-faced advocacy of the proposition that aliens are conducting interbreeding and hybridization experiments on humankind. This fascination is less amazing for its biological perversity[30] than its claim to novelty. Hopkins seems to believe that there was never any fiction with the theme of aliens taking women and impregnating them for their own mysterious purposes. Barbara Eden's 1974 TV movie, *The Stranger Within,* is one obvious precursor as would be the 1953 story which spawned it, *Mother by Protest,* by Richard Matheson. Then there are such movies as *Night Caller from Outer Space* (1966), *Mars Needs Women* (1966), *Village of the Damned* (1960), and *The Mysterians* (1957). One could go back even to 1939 and Eric Frank Russell's *Sinister Barrier* to find speculations about aliens indulging in artificial insemination, virgin births, and the creation of odd hybrid humans offered up in a Fortean [a reference to the American student of anomalies, Charles Fort] vein.[31]

Likewise, Eddie Bullard, the reigning scholarly authority on abductions, though not necessarily a partisan of this view, has nevertheless made a cogent argument in its behalf. Writing in a more detached and certainly less sardonic mode than Kottmeyer, Bullard, in his presentation on the matter, serves ably to sum up my own thoughts on the possible role of science fiction as a prime shaper of the form of the abduction narrative. I shall therefore quote him at some length in order to drive home the main points of this thesis, as well as to give some further illustrations of it.

Aliens have become a fixture in popular culture, described and depicted countless times in pulp literature, comic books, cartoons, television series, and movies. The image of the alien has only occasionally squared with the humanoids of abduction reports, but [H.G.] Wells [in *The War of the Worlds* (1897)] made a pertinent contribution when he added an evolutionary perspective to his Martians and enlarged their brains at the expense of their bodies. A large head, browless eyes, and hairless skin combined with a small frail body match the aliens of abduction stories with the evolutionarily advanced aliens of imaginative fiction. Wells also speculated that the Martians' digestive systems had so atrophied that they took nutrients directly from the blood of lower animals, recalling the more lurid rumors of what abductions are really all about.

Many 1950s science fiction movies lent visual immediacy to themes and images later to appear in abduction reports. In *This Island Earth* (1955) humans captured by aliens assist in a project to save a besieged and devastated planet. The invaders in *Earth Versus the Flying Saucers* (1956) are frail humanoids who have already lost their planet and seek a new home on Earth. They bring captives into a large circular and domed room inside the craft and steal their thoughts by means of a device suspended from the ceiling. The *Invaders from Mars* (1953) tunnel underground and insert an electrode into the back of the neck of each captive, who then obeys Martian commands. Perhaps the most parallels appear in *Killers from Space* (1953). Here a pilot killed in a jet crash finds himself in an underground operating room with his heart dangling above him as strange beings bring him back to life with surgery that leaves no scar. They have bulging eyes and wear dark, tight-fitting uniforms. Communicating by mental telepathy, the leader shows the pilot scenes of the destruction of the aliens' home planet and reveals how they will emerge from their tunnels to take over the Earth, but then blocks the human's memory by means of hypnosis and plants orders for him to perform an act of sabotage. These few examples demonstrate that "abduction" motifs circulated widely in popular culture years before abduction reports surfaced.[32]

A final and important caveat is necessary in order to forestall a possible misunderstanding of the position I am advocating here. In suggesting that there is a clear-cut link between the tradition of science fiction and the form of modern abduction narratives, I feel I am only stating a conclusion that is both intuitively obvious to many people as well as one that is supported by an abundance of scholarship. From this statement alone, it might appear self-evident why the neurological skeleton of these experiences has come to be outfitted in the garments of science fiction. However, I do not want to be construed as saying or implying that this connection is itself *the entire explanation* for abduction cases. That it is part of the explanation is, I think, unquestionable, but that it is sufficient to explain them *away* is, in my opinion, dubious. There is more to abduction stories than their science fiction parentage. What more that is, we shall presently have cause to ponder. In the meantime, however, we need to turn our attention to our other category of extraordinary encounter, the NDE, in order to inquire into the sources of its singular patterning.

NEAR-DEATH EXPERIENCES: THE PROTOTYPE OF THE SHAMANIC JOURNEY

Although the NDE is certainly known to be influenced by external cultural factors to a degree,[33] on the whole it appears to be a phenomenon of remarkable stability over geographical space and historical time. Of course, it has only been in our own era that the NDE has been named and studied intensively, and that it has received an enormous amount of publicity through the media. Such considerations might easily lead one to think that it, too, like the abduction story, must have been shaped to a great extent by these modern influences. This inference, however, does not appear to be correct; rather, it is the view of most NDE researchers that the publicity given today to these encounters has mostly had the effect of *creating* a climate for their emergence, but not of creating them per se.[34] From whence, then, do these experiences originate?

Students of shamanism—the ancient and virtually universal cultural tradition whose initiations and techniques are said to provide access to a nonsensory world beyond death—claim to know. They find the basic elements of the NDE to be inherent in the shaman's journey and in principle available to anyone who finds himself in the kind of altered state that shamanic practice seeks to induce. A representative statement of this position is found in the work of a German writer on shamanism, Holger Kalweit:

> Recent findings show that this is a universal human experience, ultimately accessible to anyone and relatively easy to trigger—namely by placing oneself in a situation that could easily prove to be fatal. Whenever we are involved in a serious accident . . . or when we become severely ill, have a fainting fit, or enter a state of trance of ecstasy, our consciousness can become independent and live through a characteristic sequence of near-death motifs. The prerequisite for such death experiences is the deconditioning and annihilation of our customary modes of perception, the interruption of biophysic functions. In the near-death state, the out-of-body experience, and during the journey to the Beyond [that is, in shamanic journeys], we are confronted by real phenomena of consciousness and not just by symbols of the unconscious.[35]

The shaman, whom Carol Zaleksi aptly characterizes as "the prototypical otherworld traveler,"[36] is thus an individual who has learned consciously and voluntarily to enter into the same realm that the NDE is thrust into, without warning or preparation, by virtue of falling victim to a life-threatening crisis. Or to put it the other way around, the NDEr has been inadvertently initiated into the first stages of the shaman's journey. In any event, the commonalities between these two categories of experience are unmistakable, as students of both have been quick to point out.[37]

The implication of the foregoing argument—and certainly clearly indicated in Kalweit's statement—is that the features that define the NDE are not merely the experiential by-products of a distinctive pattern of neuronal discharges in the temporal lobe, but reflect a direct encounter with self-existing properties of an alternative domain of reality. In short, NDErs, and shamans, too, are tapping into a realm that in some sense *truly exists* outside time and space.

This of course is a huge assumption, and one furthermore that would seem to violate the entire reductionistic tone of this chapter. You may even think that on our way toward the Emerald City, we have suddenly been beglamoured by the illusions of the resident wizard there. Therefore, at this point, I should perhaps remind you that early in this chapter I dropped a hint that our journey of demystification might, in the end, hold out some surprises for us. This, clearly, would seem to be a major one, but is it, after all, so unreasonable a position to entertain? Let's linger over it for a moment to consider the matter more closely.

THE STATUS OF EXTRAORDINARY ENCOUNTERS AND THE PROBLEM OF REDUCTIONISM

Before we reached the path veering off into shamanism, we had been following a course that seemed to explain extraordinary encounters in terms of a combination of the effects of natural phenomena on the body and brain and a form of cultural conditioning. However, does it follow logically that because there are, for example, neurological correlates of these experiences, they are *caused by* such neurological factors? Just as a television set is not in itself the source of the images we see on its screen, the brain may not *generate* our experiences either. Instead, it may serve to *transmit* them. Taking that stand, it may be *necessary* that a certain neurological state occur before certain images and information can be received, but that state then would be more like a window (even if it distorts the input somewhat) than a signal station in its own right.

Even someone who is as temperamentally inclined to a reductionistic interpretation of extraordinary experiences as Persinger is willing to concede this point. On this matter, he allows that he himself does not

. . . perceive a conflict with those researchers who believe that NDEs are real rather than artifacts of the brain's construction. . . . If indeed structure dictates function, then the type of microstructural changes correlated with the NDE could forever alter the NDErs' detection of what comprises reality. Even the transient changes that occur during an NDE might allow the brief detection of information that has been traditionally considered as parapsychological.[38]

Interestingly enough, Devereux, at the end of his own inquiry into anomalous experiences, comes to a position very similar to Persinger's and virtually identical to mine. He writes:

There is a strong tendency to think of consciousness as resulting purely from complex interactions within the human brain, and that when the brain dies, consciousness ceases. This is the mechanistic view, which could be entirely mistaken. While there is evidence . . . that parts of the brain can be identified with certain functions of consciousness, this is not the same as saying it produces consciousness. If we can identify brain regions that are involved with the function of memory, for instance, it is not the same as understanding or locating memory itself. The brain is more likely to be a wonderfully complex processing organ. . . . In my opinion, we need to start thinking of consciousness as a *field effect,* an all-pervading element in the universe, perhaps associated with space-time in ways not currently apparent to us, and affected by the presence of electromagnetism and mass. Such a field would allow the operation of ESP phenomena to be constructed in fresh ways.[39]

Obviously, the ramifications of this position are going to require more elaboration later on, but with both Persinger and Devereux, perhaps surprisingly, remaining open to or even endorsing a nonreductionistic view of the brain and, by implication, extraordinary encounters themselves, we can now see that their views fit very well with the claim that NDEs may, after all, be windows into an alternate reality.

But for all that, there would still seem to be a problem with this formulation. Where does it leave UFO encounters and abductions? Are they somehow a "lesser" or lower-order type of extraordinary encounter compared to NDEs? Do we now have two different *kinds* of EEs, then—one (NDEs) with some sort of possible ontological validity, while the other (UFOEs) is merely a cultural artifact of purely human construction?

My answer would be no. Although the cultural overlay on UFO encounters may be more transparent, as I suggested earlier, I believe it would be a mistake to regard them as lacking any intrinsic elements of their own. In fact, I believe that a good case can be made, especially for abduction episodes, that they also have the structure of *initiatory journeys,* just as NDEs do. (Indeed, you may remember that I articulated exactly this position earlier in Chapters 3 and 4.) In some ways, one is even tempted to argue, with Carol Zaleski, that abductions may represent a particularly contemporary form of shamanic journey—one that fits and is phrased in terms of a highly technological society that has already turned its imaginative attention to star flight. As Zaleski puts it:

> Perhaps the otherworld journey motif is "camouflaged" in the modern lore of space travel which, like the fantastic voyage legends of the past, exemplifies what might be called the lure of the edge.[40]

Functionally, then, as well as structurally, abductions and NDEs seem to be equivalent experiences. Granting that, it may also be that abductions and UFO encounters generally, like NDEs, partake of an alternate reality, too. Perhaps the *same* alternate reality.

THE ALTERNATE REALITY OF EXTRAORDINARY ENCOUNTERS: A THIRD REALM

To many persons who have given some casual consideration to phenomena such as UFOs or NDEs, it may seem obvious that there are just two basic possibilities concerning what to make of them: Either they are products of fantasy, delusion, hoax, or hallucination—or they are real. Such thinking, though it may appeal to our "common sense," may nevertheless end by fostering a facile form of reductionism. This is especially clear in the case of UFOs, for example, where, following this brand of logic, one has a choice of declaring oneself either a debunker or a believer in the literal existence of UFOs as extraterrestrial spacecraft. Yet we have already glimpsed other explanatory possibilities that seem to fall between—or outside of—these narrow either/or confines, and, before proceeding, we must strive to make at least one of them clear and plausible. And that is the nature of the *alternate* reality that both NDErs and UFOErs are held to enter during the time of their extraordinary encounters.

The key to such entrance is surprisingly simple to state in words, although certainly not always easy to effect in practice. It all turns out to hinge on the *imagination*—though what I mean by this term is *not* what is commonly understood by it. Accordingly, let's take a moment to look at this familiar concept, the imagination, more closely in order to see how it actually holds the key to the door of the alternate reality whose properties we seek to know.

In the West, with the notable exception of certain champions of the imagination such as Samuel Taylor Coleridge, the English poet and critic, we have tended to use this term in a somewhat pejorative way to signify something "made up," or, in short, a *fantasy* of some kind. Certainly, there is usually the implication that the realm of the imagination is not truly real, as in the common phrase "That's just your imagination."

But perhaps there is after all a *third realm* of the imagination in its own right, not as something unreal, but as something *objectively self-existent,* the cumulative product of imaginative thought itself. Indeed, this is exactly the point of view that has been advanced within the past twenty years by many scholars representing such diverse fields as religious studies, mythology, psychology, shamanic studies, ufology, and NDE research.[41] Much of this work has been predicated on a now-classic distinction between the imaginary and *the imaginal,* originally proposed by a renowned French Islamic scholar named Henry Corbin in 1972.[42] This distinction is not only important; it is, I believe, absolutely fundamental to any formulation that hopes to shed light on the nature of the alternate reality gleaned during extraordinary encounters. To follow Corbin's argument, we need to start with his concept of the imaginal.

First of all, in dealing with the things of the imaginal realm, I must emphasize that we are *not* talking about the stuff of fantasy or even of "imagination," as these terms are generally used today. Specifically, we are not concerned here with fictive matters or with what is "made up" through creative invention. Instead, the imaginal realm refers to a *third kingdom,* access to which is dependent neither on sensory perception nor on normal waking cognition (including fantasy). Because it lies hidden from common view, it can usually be apprehended only in what we now call certain *altered states of consciousness* that have the effect of undermining ordinary perception and conceptual thinking. When these are sufficiently disturbed, the imaginal realm, like the starry night sky that can be discerned only when sunlight is absent, stands revealed.

The most important attribute of the imaginal realm, however, is that it is ontologically real. According to Corbin, who was a deep student of mystical and especially visionary experience:

> . . . it must be understood that the world into which these [visionaries] probed is perfectly *real*. Its reality is more irrefutable and more coherent than that of the empirical world where *reality* is perceived by the senses. Upon returning, the beholders of this world are perfectly aware of having been "elsewhere"; they are not mere schizophrenics. This world is hidden behind the very act of sense perception and has to be sought underneath its apparent objective certainty. For this reason we definitely cannot qualify it as being *imaginary* in the current sense of the word, i.e., unreal or nonexistent. [The imaginal] world . . . is ontologically as real as the world of the senses and that of the intellect. . . . We must be careful not to confuse it with the imagination identified by so-called modern man with "fantasy."[43]

Not only is the imaginal realm ontologically real, it is also a world that has form, dimension, and most important for us, *persons or entities*. Corbin suggests this when he writes:

> [This is] a world possessing extension and dimension, figures and colors, but these features cannot be perceived by the senses in the same manner as if they were properties of physical bodies. No, these dimensions, figures and colors are the object of imaginative [i.e., imaginal] perception, or of the "psychospiritual senses."[44]

In summary, imagination in Corbin's sense is actually, as Coleridge claimed, a creative power, and functions in altered states of consciousness as a kind of "organ of perception"—what the alchemists of old called *imaginatio vera* (true imagination). And the world that it discloses is, as another English poet, William Blake, knew, a supersensible reality that can be directly apprehended.

The relevance of Corbin's ideas for us is of course that they suggest that our extraordinary experiencers, because of their susceptibility to altered states, which as we remember is evident even in childhood, have learned to see with *imaginal vision*. In doing so, they have thus been able to enter into a realm that lies beyond both fantasy as such and the physical world, yet that is as real in its own way as the latter is real to our senses.

This conception of the domain to which extraordinary experiencers have become sensitized not only helps us to understand the subjective reality of these encounters but is also being recognized by other students of anomalies. For example, the English ufologist Jenny Randles, whose books regrettably are not yet well known in this country, has through her own extensive research come to a conclusion very similar to that we have reached. She, too, has found that persons who are subject to extraordinary encounters are highly imaginative, visually creative persons whose lives have generally been marked by a succession of unusual and paranormal events. But rather than writing them off as merely "fantasy prone" (which our data also refute, it will be recalled), she comments:

> I shall add that by calling these experiences "imaginative" or "subjective," and noting that most of us reject them from our lives during childhood, does not mean they are worthless or unreal. We adopt these words merely out of prejudice. It could be that these creatively visual people are not gullible and hyperimaginative, but open and receptive. . . . It could be that these experiences represent a form of reality which only the creatively visual people are able to perceive. . . . More and more psychologists, sociologists and folklore researchers are treating these phenomena not as mere illusions but as alternative potential realities.[45]

If we now take this hypothesis of a true alternate reality as a working model for these extraordinary encounters, we are led inevitably to still another, and even deeper, mystery, and the last one we shall try to unveil in this book. The mystery is this: What is the creative force that gives rise to the imaginal realm in the first place? Is it in some sense ultimately a purely human construction akin to a kind of planetary thought field created and sustained by the power of the human imagination itself? Or is there behind it still some sort of extramundane agency, an Oz of cosmic proportions, that is helping to orchestrate the sometimes peculiar, often transcendent, and always mind-boggling events that make up the continuum of extraordinary encounters? And, finally, if there is—but of this we can of course by no means be certain—some purposive design behind the form of these contemporary encounters, some message perhaps to be decoded from their arcana, what conceivably might it be?

These are, to be sure, formidable, and possibly unanswerable, questions. Yet without grappling with them, we forgo any hope, however slim, of unlocking the meaning of the mysteries we have been pondering throughout this book. Like a dream uninterpreted, the experience would be ours but we would forever remain ignorant of its significance. A sizable segment of modern humanity with imaginal vision has been dreaming a similar dream of late. Why?

CHAPTER 10

OMEGA REVELATION:

Ecological and Evolutionary Implications of Extraordinary Encounters

The image of being visited by a majestic power from the sky and lifted out of this world has been incubating in our collective psyche for close to two thousand years. Given the structural analogies between UFO contact . . . and near-death contact, I . . . believe we are dealing with a single mass reorientation in the global mind.

—Michael Grosso

Of course you know what Hesiod calls daimons: spirits of the Golden Age, who act as guardians to mortals.

—Robertson Davies

Let us assume the abduction experience is an extraordinary type of dream. The coherence of the experience shows it's not a private but a collective dream. A dream, perhaps, of the species mind. Produced by the species mind, like any dream, it is about the dreamer. Perhaps about the dreamer's future.[1]

So speculates Michael Grosso, a contemporary philosopher who has had a long-standing interest in the study of extraordinary encounters, and who has written extensively on the possible meaning of NDEs, UFOEs, and a wide range of other anomalous experiences. Perhaps more than any other commentator on these mysteries, Grosso has succeeded in formulating a conception of extraordinary encounters that permits a set of highly cogent and persuasive answers to the questions I posed at the end of the last chapter—questions that have to do ultimately with the source and significance of the types of EEs with which we have been concerned throughout this book. Accordingly, I want to begin this chapter by taking a few moments to expound some of Grosso's leading ideas, which will then also serve to frame my own interpretation of the meaning and message of EEs. In laying out this exposition for you now, I shall be drawing first on the line of argument that Grosso brilliantly develops in his book *The Final Choice*.

MIND AT LARGE AND THE ECOLOGICAL IMPERATIVE

His thesis is beguilingly simple. The threat of mass death from nuclear warfare, global ecological catastrophe, or both, is evoking a new level of consciousness from humanity at large. It is a consciousness that is aimed at lifting humanity above its usual sensate and materialistic concerns into the realm of the transcendent. This emergent level of consciousness is serving an adaptive evolutionary end, for evolution is teleological. Specifically, it is one that can foster our creative adaptation to the unprecedented requirements of living in an age when technological man now has the power to poison or otherwise murder the earth. And behind this evolutionary imperative operates a kind of planetary Overmind that Grosso characterizes as a ''helping intelligence'': Mind at Large.

This bald statement of Grosso's fundamental ideas may well make them seem naively simplistic, even Panglossian, and you may initially be tempted to view them as almost a caricature of a kind of fanciful New Age vision of some sweet Utopia that could truly exist *only* as a dream. Such an impression, however, would be quickly dispelled if you were to look closely and in detail at the thread of the argument that Grosso weaves so artfully in his book. In fact, he spends about two hundred pages thoughtfully sifting through some very perplexing problems in the fields of parapsychology, near-death and survival research, thanatology, and evolutionary biology, among others, as he slowly amasses the evidence he uses to make at least a plausible case for his thesis.

Similarly, his key concept of Mind at Large may seem something like a *deus ex machina* in the evolutionary drama Grosso sees unfolding. Here again, however, first impressions are misleading. Mind at Large, he insists, is not just a more acceptable contemporary euphemism for God. Rather, Grosso follows English biologist John Randall in postulating that Mind at Large is a benign transpersonal aspect of mind that is conscious, purposive, intelligent—and capable of interacting with matter. Again drawing on some of Randall's ideas, Grosso assumes that in critical times in the earth's evolution and history—for example, at the origin of life, the development of higher species, or at points of *extreme peril*—Mind at Large may intervene in earthly affairs in an effort to help bring about certain effects. In our own singularly dangerous ecocidal era, as we are confronted with our possible extinction as a species and with the specter of an irremediably polluted mother planet, Mind at Large has lately been attempting to broadcast its message concerning the kind of evolutionary change necessary for survival.

"Broadcast?" you ask. "How?" To understand Grosso's conception here (and of course he is far from alone in postulating the existence of some kind of guiding planetary intelligence), you must assume that Mind at Large is the apparent source of "signals" that are redolent with symbolic meaning for humanity, and that must be decoded before they can be understood. Imagine, that is, that humanity—or, more precisely, an especially psychologically sensitive segment of humanity—is now susceptible to something like a set of common images of a universal dream churned out by, as it were, its own collective unconscious, Mind at Large.

To apply this concept now, and to begin to decode the message of this conceivable collective dream, let us return to the opening quote of this chapter where Grosso posits that the abduction experience may itself be a dream of this kind. If so, how may its common images be interpreted? Here we follow Grosso as he provides a kind of Jungian dream analysis of the collective soul of humanity.

To start with, consider the major event of the abduction drama, the examination. We (humanity) are being examined. What is the symbolic meaning of this action? Grosso suggests that we are a sick species, we have gone off the mark (i.e., sinned). He writes:

> . . . I cannot help thinking it is we who are in need of dire examination; it is we who have to place ourselves on an "operating table." It looks to me as if something—some intelligence—is "examining" and "operating on" us. Medical operation implies a need for healing. The latest development in UFO symbolism [i.e., the abduction narrative] contains a message about healing ourselves.[2]

What is it in ourselves that needs healing? Even the commonly reported description of "the alien" gives us a hint. Think about his appearance. He is small, gray, sickly looking, with a head that, because it is disproportionately large in relation to his body, suggests an almost fetus-like character. Intuitively, we are reminded of Stanley Kubrick's conception of the "cosmic child" at the end of Arthur C. Clarke's *2001*—except that *this* child is frail and tortured-looking, his enormous black eyes reminding us, as Grosso observes, of the images we have all seen on our television screens and news weeklies of children dying of starvation in drought-plagued Africa. What is the message that is conveyed by this haunting image of the alien? The future of the human race—symbolized by the archetype of the child— is menaced as never before. We need to heal ourselves of all those tendencies—unthinking greed, mindless development, ruthless exploitation—that threaten our native habitat so severely as to make us fear that our progeny will be replicas of the stunted and deformed aliens that now infiltrate the collective nightmare that portions of humanity are dreaming.

Not just the appearance but the manner of these entities as they conduct their examinations gives us a further insight into the symbolic meaning of the abduction dream-drama, and one consistent with the general interpretation Grosso is advancing here. Abductees report that the entities who perform these procedures are cool, almost disinterested, and go about their business in a briskly efficient fashion. They are usually not so much malevolent as coldly professional, though if the abductee protests, the entities, as we have seen, can act harshly so as to subjugate the individual to the examination in a forceful manner. When ufologists discuss the way in which these creatures carry out their actions, they often make an analogy to how scientists may tranquilize and "tag" animals in their natural settings in order to monitor their behavior. From the Jungian perspective that Grosso invokes, however, there is a much more sinister level of meaning to this seemingly apt comparison: It is of course a perfect reflection of how we treat not merely animals but one another and the earth itself in our relentless and calculating efforts to gain control over life.

A leading motif of the UFO abduction scenario is of course that of the hybrid baby, the product of human and alien coupling. What is one to make of this recurrent fetal imagery and the implication that the creation of this new form of life is the principal reason underlying supposed alien intervention in human affairs? Grosso again offers a very different interpretation from that found in conventional ufological thought on the matter:

> Taken literally, the reason perhaps is to revitalize *their* ailing stock. Taken symbolically, the idea of hybrids would be about *our* need to be revitalized; the need to enhance our gene pool. It certainly makes sense to say that we need to embark on evolutionary experiments, to mutate *ourselves*. In other words, if we interpret the symbolism of the abduction experience as a strange kind of species dream, the message is that our world, symbolized by the otherworld, is a dying wasteland and that we have to evolve into a higher (and hence much more adaptable) species.[3]

Thus, we see that if we adopt Grosso's Jungian-inspired analysis of the abduction narrative, the entire episode may be understood as holding up a mirror in which we may view ourselves and our own environment—in symbolic guise. The alien, of course, turns out to be ourselves, his actions our own, his bleak world in need of regeneration our home planet's possible future unless . . . This collective dream, spawned by the benevolently guided intelligence of Mind at Large, itself in part a reflection of humanity's own deepest forebodings and intuitions, is a sort of diagnostic warning dream, a kind of prophecy, which, correctly interpreted, spurs us on to right action. Coded in images and symbols that reflect our contemporary space age's fascination with life elsewhere in the universe and using one of the dominant archetypal figures of our era, the extraterrestrial alien, as the metaphysical symbol of our own alienation, the abduction story is a call, sounded by humanity itself and in turn reflected through the agency of Mind at Large, to awaken to the earth's plight before it is too late.

There are only two related significant pieces missing from the puzzle that Grosso's analysis is helping us to put together, but they are absolutely basic to our understanding of the whole phenomenon of UFO abductions. Why now, and why abductions as a motif in the first place? Here again, Grosso has seen the importance of these questions and given, in my opinion at least, a thoughtful and compelling answer to them:

> UFO abductions begin in the late sixties with the classic Betty and Barney Hill story. They come to a focus in the 1980s. Why now at the end of the second millennium? Millennial thinking is quite strong in other quarters, and Christian fundamentalists yearn for the Second Coming and the Rapture. In I Thessalonians, Paul writes: "Then we which are alive and remain shall be caught up together with them in the clouds, to meet the Lord in the air." Significant portions of the American populace, brooding or at least vaguely worried about the coming of Armageddon, nourish, somewhere in their minds, the vision, the hope, possibly the expectation of *divine abduction*. This fact needs at least to be

noted in any attempt to assess the condition of the collective mind nowadays, especially the American mind. (Most
abductions seem to be taking place in America.)[4]

Now, as is well known, these ecological and and millennial
themes have been a part of the canon of the UFO world and its
literature for a long time, and many persons have already commented on their quasi-religious character. Indeed, in an age where
secular thinking has come to be the standard but from which
the religious impulse has never disappeared, it is psychologically very understandable why traditional religious images of
salvation have come to be projected onto the screen of a universe where, for some, it is easier to believe in ETs than in
God. Grosso, of course, is going well beyond these common-
places in arguing that there is a kind of helping intelligence, a
planetary mind that reflects our collective concerns as a species
and then feeds them back to us symbolically in the form of an
archetypal abduction drama that is orchestrating these experiences in *imaginal space*. This, ultimately, is the reason, if there
is any validity to Grosso's formulation, why abductions take
the form that they do, and why they are so widespread, particularly among persons who are susceptible to alternate realities
in the first place.

So far, of course, we have focused our attention on just an
aspect of UFO encounters, but naturally we haven't forgotten
about our other, momentarily neglected, category of extraordinary encounters, the NDE. And, fortunately, neither has Grosso.
For him, these experiences, too, as well as a variety of other
unusual encounters with religious or prophetic overtones,[5] can
easily be understood as still other, but consonant, signals from
Mind at Large. Not only does he consider this matter at length
in his book *The Final Choice*, but he has recently also written
an article[6] where, following a line of argument similar to that
which I used earlier in this book, he points to an array of common thematic motifs and structural similarities between NDEs
and UFOEs (not just abductions). From Grosso's perspective,
NDEs, too, are intimations from Mind at Large pointing to a
transcendent imaginal order and, like UFOEs, function as evo-

lutionary catalysts during a time of a possible *planetary near-death* crisis.

In his analysis of NDEs, Grosso draws on some of my work on possible prophetic aspects of these experiences. Specifically, as I noted in Chapter 8, I had discovered during the course of my research for my previous book, *Heading Toward Omega,* that a small subset of NDErs[7] have visionary experiences during or in the immediate aftermath of their NDEs that purport to show them what the short-term future of the earth will be.[8] These visions invariably include images of widespread, indeed global, geophysical cataclysm, including possible nuclear warfare, followed eventually by an emerging planetary order marked by human brotherhood and universal love in which a new type of human being apparently comes into manifestation. Other NDE researchers[9] have also discovered the presence of seemingly identical prophetic visions among their respondents, even down to the particular year in which these global catastrophes were said to be slated to reach their peak of destructiveness. Grosso uses these findings to reveal still another thread of connection beyond those I have already indicated in this book between NDEs and UFOEs—the idea that such extraordinary encounters are part of a *warning system* that has arisen to alert us to the danger of a kind of near-death experience for the earth itself:[10]

> The idea of a planetary near-death experience makes sense once you put together James Lovelock's Gaia hypothesis,[11] Jung's collective unconscious, and the fact that the ecosystems of planet earth are in peril as never before in human history. The clue—if the NDE is a clue to the UFO mystery—has led to the hypothesis that the whole spectrum of increasing contact experiences is part of a feedback mechanism produced by a source of intelligence interested in the fate of the earth. UFOs, on this theory, are part of an S.O.S. being sent out by some unknown Mind at Large. If so, we'd better wake up and do something.[12]

Grosso's analysis of the significance of and linkage between NDEs and UFOs (as well as other extraordinary encounters indicative of contact with a higher imaginal order) helps to make sense of the quality of apocalyptic expectation and messianic urgency that marks much of the recent literature concerned with these experiences. This tone, for example, is evident in Whitley Strieber's two books on his own personal experiences in nonordinary realities, *Communion* and *Transformation*. The latter book, for example, is full of references to possible ecological catastrophe, especially with respect to the ozone layer, while the former includes a reference to Strieber's own vision, in connection with a "visitor experience," of a planetary explosion akin to the prophetic visions of NDErs. In *Communion*, Strieber also shows that he is familiar with eschatological themes that permeate accounts of UFO experiences. Summarizing the sense of a discussion in one abductee support group he attended, Strieber wrote:

> A striking fact of the colloquy was the general expectation of catastrophe, a possibility that I also fear. Throughout the literature of abduction, there is a frequent message of apocalypse.[13]

Of course, it is well known that even before reporting his own extraordinary encounters in these books, Strieber had long been deeply concerned with the problems of planetary ecological disaster and nuclear warfare. He even coauthored two highly regarded works of fiction on these subjects, *Nature's End* and *Warday*.

Probably the most recent experientially based book that easily lends itself to a Grossian interpretation is *The Watchers* by Raymond E. Fowler. This book is mostly concerned with the continuing abduction and otherworldly experiences of Betty Andreasson Luca, whose personal narration in my seminar of some of her earlier experiences, you will recall, was one of the important stepping stones onto "UFO Avenue" for me. Even before the release of this most recent book about her, Betty was one of the most famous and referenced abductees in the UFO literature. Significantly, we now learn from *The Watchers* that Betty's most recent experiences are filled with portents of global ecological horror and intimations that the UFO entities have intervened because of these fated events. Indeed, the aliens, when asked by Betty, tell her that they are the ancient and true stewards of the earth:

> He says that they are the *caretakers* of nature and natural forms—*The Watchers*. They love mankind. They love the planet earth and *they have been caring for it and man since man's beginning. . . . Man is destroying much of nature.*[14]

Toward the end of the book, in a chapter significantly entitled The Message, Fowler sums up the meaning of Betty's encounters in this respect:

> Her abductors again told her that they were caretakers of the forms that life had taken on our planet. They assured her that their abductions of men and women were for good reasons. It was being done to monitor environmental effects on the body and to achieve restoration of the human form. Again, they stressed, perhaps for the very last time, that the balance of nature on earth was in jeopardy.[15]

The book ends with a revelation and an injunction:

> The acceleration of UFO activity is directly related to Man's increasing destruction of earth's life-supporting environment. . . . Man must engage in an immediate all-inclusive program to repair and protect the environment.[16]

Of course, these are precisely the same inferences for action that one draws from the symbolic Jungian interpretation that Grosso gives us based on his Mind at Large theory. Fowler himself prefers a literalistic interpretation of Betty's experiences. In the end, perhaps it doesn't matter—as long as "the message" gets across. Interestingly enough, however, Fowler—though he would take issue with Grosso's views—makes a major effort in his book to point out, as Grosso does, the connections between NDEs and UFOEs, and arrives at similar conclusions concerning the importance of considering the implications of both phenomena together. In this respect, at least, their views—and mine, too—tend to converge.

Some findings from the Omega Project serve to strengthen the argument that the tendencies evident in Strieber's books and in Fowler's may well be representative of today's extraordinary experiencers, too, at least in the United States. For example, you will perhaps recall that in Chapter 8 I have already presented evidence (see page 179) that Omega Project respondents show a heightened ecological sensitivity and concern with planetary welfare following their encounters or after developing an interest in such phenomena. Moreover, there is substantial evidence that many of them share the conviction that widespread global destruction is indeed in the offing before the end of the century unless humanity changes for the better. This opinion is in fact held by a majority of the participants in our study; furthermore, roughly a third of our respondents believe these changes are *inevitable*—that they will occur regardless of humanity's collective behavior. Overall, it's obvious that those who are drawn to an interest in NDEs or UFOs, for whatever reasons, are persons who tend to develop a heightened ecological consciousness against the backdrop of the possible devastation of our planet.

All this suggests, then, that extraordinary experiencers—as well as those deeply interested in EEs—have come to find themselves among the special votaries of what the historian Thomas Berry calls in his book *The Dream of the Earth* the coming "ecological age."[17] To inquire more fully into the reasons they have seemingly been led to play this role in the earth's drama during these last years prior to the dawning of the new millennium, it will serve us to look for a moment at Berry's own reading of the ecological situation in which we all find ourselves today.

To begin with, we have Berry's own unsparing assessment of the damage we have done and continue to do to our environment:

> We are changing the chemistry of the planet. We are altering the great hydrological cycles. We are weakening the ozone layer that shields us from cosmic rays. We are saturating

the air, the water, and the soil with toxic substances so that we can never bring them back to their original purity. We are upsetting the entire earth system that has, over some billions of years and through an endless sequence of experiments, produced such a magnificent array of living forms, forms capable of seasonal self-renewal over an indefinite period of time. . . .

These consequences are now becoming manifest. The day of reckoning has come. In this disintegrating phase of our industrial society, we now see ourselves not as the splendor of creation, but as the most pernicious mode of earthly being. We are the termination, not the fulfillment of the earth process. If there were a parliament of creatures, its first decision might well be to vote humans out of the community, too deadly a presence to tolerate any further. We are the affliction of the world, its demonic presence. We are the violation of the earth's most sacred aspects.[18]

We are, in short, the alien on our own planet, and a greater threat to it than any imagined invasion from another star-based civilization.

Yet despite Berry's censorious indictment, even he holds out the hope that it may not be too late to change course and to begin to restore what we have nearly killed. Intriguingly enough, since Berry is writing as a historian and certainly not one who traffics in such exotica as NDEs and UFOs, he, too, arrives at some conclusions that I have already suggested are implied by the findings from the Omega Project. Specifically, he also sees the reemergence of a "shamanic personality" in our time who, because he has journeyed "into the far regions of cosmic mystery," can return to the human community with precisely the kind of vision to bring about "a healing of the earth."[19]

In his book, Berry, whose evocative essays sometimes give the undeniable impression he writes not merely as the earth's advocate but almost as if he were its true voice, makes it clear what the earth requires and seems to be producing is its own form of shamanically oriented steward. The real caretakers of the planet, from this perspective, are not Betty Luca's aliens, but the Betty Lucas themselves, who have come to sojourn in a domain where they can detect the warning signals emanating from Mind at Large. This, of course, is precisely what those attuned to the world of extraordinary encounters—these often inconscient shamans—are enabled to do, and already, from what we have previously discussed, in fact seem to be doing.

A study of history and millennial movements shows that prophets tend to arise during times of cultural disintegration.[20] In our own historically unprecedented era, however, it is no longer merely that a single, isolated culture is threatened. The whole earth, culture itself, and our entire habitat, are under siege. The planet is imperiled as never before since the emergence of humankind in its midst. It is under these circumstance, if Grosso is right, that Mind at Large responds with increasing urgency. It releases the seeds of earthly salvation into the psyches of receptive and sensitive human beings by opening them up to the transcendental order and implanting within them the gifts of prophecy.

We are all familiar with the idea that certain great souls— artists or poets or religious personages—can serve a prophetic function for their contemporaries. However, what is true about our own time, I submit, is that this prophetic function is becoming democratized; ordinary men and women in increasing numbers are having bestowed upon them profound soul-opening experiences that carry the charge of prophetic revelation. I am speaking of course of NDErs and UFOErs, among others, those millions of persons who have been "tapped" by higher energies to be the carriers of this message of renewal, this ecological imperative, to the planet as a whole.

These persons, our extraordinary experiencers, are, I believe, the true visionaries of our time, the bearers of the emerging myth of the twenty-first century calling us to a cosmic-centered view of our place in creation, a myth that has the power to ignite the fires of a worldwide planetary regeneration and thus to save us from the icy blasts of Thanatos's nuclear winter.

Omega revelation. A new heaven and a new earth. We are experiencing the first bursts of a new self-renewing power for the healing of the earth, with millennial energies that have been liberated through direct contact with the transcendental order. It is these energies that may be producing the shamanic personality that Thomas Berry has spoken of so eloquently. These are the energies propelling human evolution. And they give rise to the possibility that not only our earth but we ourselves will be transformed if we have the wisdom to use them aright.

THE OMEGA PROJECT AS HUMAN EVOLUTION

In *The Final Choice,* Michael Grosso observes that the key to our continued survival as a species lies in our being able to develop deeper awareness of our transcendental nature. We are physical beings evolving toward spirit—or rather, we are in fact spiritual beings who are gradually becoming aware of our spiritual essence—and in this evolution, NDEs, UFOEs, and other similar experiences may be understood as catalysts, courtesy of Mind at Large, which promote the necessary insight into our true being.

As we have already seen, however, extraordinary encounters do more than provide us with a living, undeniable sense of our essential selves. They lead as well to a fundamental reorientation in personal values and worldviews, but most important in this context, they also appear to accelerate a *psychophysical* transformation. This, certainly, is the dominant impression that the data presented in Chapter 7 is meant to etch in the reader. The changes EEs bring about, then, may perhaps be said to be in both soul *and* body.

Those who have reflected on the possible significance of such changes in the aftermath of extraordinary encounters have discerned in them not merely the evidence of transformation, but conceivably of human evolution itself. For my part, I have speculated about the role of NDEs as providing a spur to psychophysical evolution and higher states of consciousness in my previous book, *Heading Toward Omega.*[21] John White, the author and editor of many books dealing with higher consciousness, and someone who has made a deep study of both NDEs and UFOEs, has stated this position as boldly as anyone in a recent book of essays, and his version of this thesis may be used here to bring out the issues I mean to discuss next. The term he favors to describe this emergent type of human being is *Homo noeticus*.

> Higher human development—evolution—has been accelerating in the last few centuries. The pace of change is now unprecedented for our species, and what is to come is, I believe, a new species. We are witnessing the final phase of *Homo sapiens* and the simultaneous emergence, still quite tentative because of the nuclear and environmental threats to life, of what I have named *Homo noeticus*, a more advanced form of humanity. . . .

> But the forerunners of *Homo noeticus* are here *now*, in increasing numbers, making their presence felt, crowding *Homo sapiens*, creating their own niche in the eco-psychosystem and pointing out to him his own potential to change consciousness and thereby evolve, directing his own evolution and accelerating the process.[22]

While I believe it is overstating the case to claim that an actual new human *species* is in the process of mutating itself into existence (and for this reason prefer to use the less inflated term *Omega Prototype*, as a label for the "new breed" of humanity John White speaks of), there are other students of EEs who tend to concur with this formulation. One of them, for example, is Whitley Strieber himself, who, in a recent interview, averred:

> I think it's rather obvious that . . . what we're dealing with is an exponential leap from one species to another. These beings that I have observed have properties and powers that I would suggest are far beyond what is present in normal human being, and I would suspect that what we're looking

at is the process of evolution in action. . . . This . . . process that is going on . . . will materially alter the nature of the human species to the extent that it will be, in effect, a new species.[23]

Of course, although writers like White and Strieber may themselves be out on the leading edge of these evolutionary speculations, their comments, when held up to the mirror of Mind at Large, do help us to see new contours of possible evolutionary significance in the study I have reported in this book. Even the very phrase, The Omega Project, receives another, and larger, shade of meaning. If Mind at Large is both the source and the reflection of these evolutionary energies, *and* if it not only generates mere signals and symbols but also helps to transmit inputs that alter the body and nervous system (as Grosso does in fact suggest), then perhaps the world itself could be said to be undergoing its own Omega Project. That is to say, one could regard Mind at Large as orchestrating the "production" of more highly evolved human beings, Omega Prototypes, as if it were conducting an Omega Project in its own right. It is in this sense that one might, with at least some justification, see the Omega Project *as* human evolution, and not merely as a research study of experiences with possible evolutionary implications.

We are of course already in the rarefied and intoxicating air of evolutionary speculation and have seemingly left far below the hard, firm ground of our findings on extraordinary encounters. But having soared into human evolutionary potentials this high, perhaps we may for just another moment continue our ascent and try to imagine what kind of alterations in the human experience might ultimately derive from long-term exposure to the world of extraordinary encounters. In other words, if we are really "heading toward Omega," what might we conceivably encounter during the course of our journey?

If, as I said earlier, extraordinary encounters imply both an evolution of body and soul, we now need to inquire into the latter. Evolution—that is, in the sense I am using it here—isn't merely psychophysical; it is also *psychospiritual*. Interestingly enough, there is already beginning to emerge among students of extraordinary encounters and other visionary experiences apparently something of a consensus on the direction this kind of evolution may be expected to take—at least in the long run.[24] In what follows, I would like to outline my own vision of an evolutionary trajectory that is our possible future as a species.

EVOLUTION INTO THE IMAGINAL REALM

My thesis in a nutshell is that in the realm of extraordinary encounters, seeing is destiny. What we see with *imaginal vision* is a representation of our future environment. And when I say "future environment," I am not talking about some purported after-death world (though I am not denying one, either). I mean that it will become our environmental setting *before* death. Indeed, the world of the dead and the world of the living are ones between which there may eventually no longer be a sharp distinction. Veils will be lifted from the face of the nonphysical, and we ourselves will become diaphanous beings, with bodies of light—*if* the speculations about to be offered are a true reading of our future condition and experiential possibilities.

Large claims, indeed, perhaps too extravagant even for a book that has dealt with as many mind-boggling experiences and ideas as this one has—but claims nevertheless that have been made in all seriousness by thinkers who have long pondered where the leading edge of these extraordinary encounters appears to be heading. In drawing on the implications of my own research findings from the Omega Project, however, I find I am led inexorably down the same evolutionary pathway. I believe, in short, that the increasing fascination with and immersion in the domain of extraordinary encounters may well presage the *shamanizing of modern humanity*.

What does this rather grandiose phrase I have just used—*the shamanizing of modern humanity*—actually mean? To make this clear and put it in context for you, consider for a moment the general course of humanity's evolution. What began as physical evolution has obviously and especially with the advent of the neolithic revolution become primarily a cultural evolution. But as cultural evolution has shaped our planet's destiny for the past ten thousand years, there has also been evident a third form of evolution—the evolution of *consciousness* itself. And we have no reason to think that this evolution has ceased, but rather the opposite: It may be that it constitutes the very frontier of humanity's evolution today. If this is so, I would argue that the findings from the Omega Project suggest that we could be in the beginning stages of a major shift in *levels of consciousness* that will eventually lead to humanity's being able to live in *two* worlds at once—the physical and the imaginal. This is of course precisely what the shaman in traditional cultures is trained to do, as I pointed out in the last chapter. And it may be what humanity as a whole is currently learning to do, as a result of its increasing familiarization with extraordinary encounters. This, then, is what I mean by the shamanizing of humanity.

What I am asserting is that the whole range of extraordinary encounters—NDEs, UFOEs, and other mystical and visionary states may be understood as helping to develop our latent capacities for imaginal perception. As these numinous (and luminous!) experiences become more common, the sojourners into these spaces will come to develop and increasingly identify with what has been called "an imaginal body," which will be fully at home in its corresponding imaginal world. Because we are apparently seeing such an influx of these extraordinary encounters, and with them, as our data indicate, a flowering of psychic potentials as well, it can be expected that over time the evolutionary momentum will establish and stabilize these imaginal domains as our shared reality. We shall have a new consensus world, but it won't have anything to do with "the senses." Instead it will be the result of an expanded ability on the part of human beings for imaginal vision. And what *that* would mean is no less than this: Humanity would be led *back* to its true home in the realm of the imagination where it would be liberated to live in mythic time and no longer be incarcerated in the doomed prison of historical time.

In short, Omega revelation again. But not really a new heaven this time so much as an *imaginal earth*.

As I have stated, there are others who have arrived at similar views, and before concluding these remarks of mine, it might be instructive to make brief mention of some of them. One of the earliest and most eloquent partisans of the imaginal life-as-destiny thesis was Terence McKenna, who, like Grosso, has had personal UFO-related experiences and has explored the phenomenon for a long time. McKenna is primarily a student and practitioner of psychedelic shamanism, but in recent years his evolutionary speculations have attracted increasing attention from a much wider audience than those who have journeyed into the realms, physical and metaphysical, that McKenna knows firsthand. In any case, he has held for years that the goal of evolution is "to exteriorize the soul and interiorize the body" and so come to live "in the imagination." [25] Such phrases are typical of McKenna, who in his writing loves to invert the conventions of common thinking in order to bring out his ideas in an arresting way. Here's a little sample, beginning with his perspective on dreams:

> Looking at what people with shamanic traditions say about dreams, one comes to the realization that, experientially, for these people dream reality is a parallel continuum . . .
> I suggest [we] take seriously the idea of a parallel continuum, and say that the mind and the body are embedded in the dream and the dream is a higher-order spatial dimension. In sleep one is released into the real world of which the world of waking is only the surface in a very literal geometrical sense. . . . We are not primarily biological, with mind emerging as a kind of iridescence, a kind of epiphenomenon at the higher levels of organization of biology. We are, in fact, hyperspatial objects of some sort which cast a shadow into matter. The shadow in matter is our physical organism . . .

> . . . The real historical entity that is becoming imminent is the human soul. The monkey body has served to carry us to this moment of release, and it will always serve as a focus of self-image, but we are coming more and more to exist in a world made by the human imagination. This is what the re-

turn to the Father, the transcendence of Physis, the rising out of the Gnostic universal prison of iron that traps light, is. It means nothing less than the transformation of our species.[26]

It would, of course, be easy to continue to cite other proponents of similar views, but my purpose here is not to be exhaustive—or exhausting. Remember, this was to be only a brief excursion into imaginative possibility, and I must be content simply to present my case, not to make it. Nevertheless, it is probably fitting to let Whitley Strieber have the last words here, since he is in fact another of those who appears to see the same kind of evolutionary leap into the imaginal in the making. In reflecting on his experiences with the beings he has encountered in nonordinary realities, Strieber says:

> My impression is that the physical world is only a small instant of a much larger context and that reality is primarily unfolding in a non-physical way. . . . What they are interested in is probably beyond the physical. I think that they are probably midwifing our birth into the non-physical world—which is their origin. . . . The soul of the species—of which we are all a part—will be separated from the physical. . . . However, the physical beings that we are seeing—whether we are perceiving them correctly or not—are probably an evolutionary step beyond ours which has emerged into our world as a result of actions on the non-physical plane.[27]

Regardless of whether these evolutionary projections of mine and other writers are borne out by humanity's actual future, there is one surety about the direct experiential source of their ideas: UFO encounters, near-death experiences, and other anomalies suggestive of contact with a higher, transcendental order are forcing us to think in a new way, as Strieber himself remarks in his interview.[28] Michael Grosso goes even further. He posits that this is the conscious *intent* of Mind at Large:

> My contention is that these different forms of contact are related and that in all likelihood a single source of intelli-

gence is using whatever openings it can find to penetrate our collective mind and modify our basic ideas of how reality works.[29]

Now, once again following Grosso's lead, we shall descend from the heights of our speculations on the evolutionary implications of extraordinary encounters in order to return to the here-and-now of their immediate effects upon us. What lessons, in the end, shall we—all of us who have come to share an interest in these beguiling phenomena—take away from our inquiry into NDEs and UFOEs?

EXTRAORDINARY ENCOUNTERS AS AGENTS OF DECONSTRUCTION

If we return to Jacques Vallee's dictum that served as one of our epigraphs to Chapter 7, we shall find still another important clue to the meaning of the mysteries we have been seeking to understand throughout this book. Speaking of UFOs—though the same point could be made about NDEs—Vallee has advised us to infer intent from effect. From this point of view, then, what seem to be the main effects of these experiences? Vallee himself believes that UFOs are part of a *control system*, helping to regulate belief systems, culture, and even human evolution[30]—a position not all that dissimilar in fact from that of Grosso's Mind at Large formulation, though Vallee doesn't invoke that concept as such.

It is possible, however, to take this type of thinking a step further and to suggest, following the argument developed by another Vallee-influenced thinker, Carl Raschke, that the effect of extraordinary encounters is not merely to control us, but to *confound* us. That is, these experiences are visited upon humanity to loose it from the fetters of its encrusted habits of thought and action, freedom from which is absolutely essential if the next state of human evolution and the reclamation of the planet are to occur. In developing this thesis, based largely on UFO encounters, Raschke has spoken of UFOs as "agents of cultural deconstruction," which I find to be a deliciously apt phrase for their cumulative impact upon us.[31] Here is how he introduces this idea:

> Such experiences tend to be convulsive, perplexing, and *outré* and to conflict strikingly with the habitual thought patterns of the subject. A meeting with a UFO is apt to leave the witnesses' world in upheaval. One must remain curious, therefore, whether the *purpose* of UFO sightings and contacts is mainly to undercut the ingrained human longing for secure knowledge and faith, rather than to gratify it.

> Here then I shall advance a tentative assessment of what UFOs are in point of fact. . . . Our interest in them should center on how the spreading and deepening convictions about them subtly, yet irreversibly, remold not just peripheral religious or metaphysical ideas, but entire constellations of culture and social knowledge. In this connection, UFOs can be depicted as what I would call *ultraterrestrial agents of cultural deconstruction.*[32]

By calling this a process of deconstruction, Raschke of course means to invoke the notion, taken from modern literary criticism, of a gradual but inexorable dismantling of the commonly held structures of thought and values in order to permit a new, more fluid, and open way of being in the world. Deconstruction, then, seeks not to replace one system by another, but to foster a nonrigid openness to experience itself. The result is that the temptation to achieve closure is as incapable of being satisfied as a desert-stuck man who attempts to quench his thirst by drinking deeply from the waters of a mirage.

The intrusion of these deconstructivist forces into the collective consciousness of humanity does more than undermine rational solutions to seemingly scientifically solvable problems, such as the nature of UFOs. Raschke, in common with Vallee, sees the emergence of the UFO phenomenon into history as having an evolutionary purpose, too, namely, "to orchestrate, wittingly or unwittingly, the evolution of consciousness on the planet."[33]

Raschke and Vallee are scarcely isolated thinkers promulgating this deconstructivist view of the meaning of UFOs. They have company, and it includes several of the commentators we have already drawn on earlier in this chapter. Terence McKenna, for example, in advancing his own version of Michael Grosso's Mind at Large theory, also ends up in Raschke's cohort:

> The extraterrestrial is the human oversoul, in its general and particular expression on the planet. . . . The oversoul is some kind of field generated by human beings, but is not under the control of any institution, government or religion. It is actually the most intelligent organism on the planet, regulating human culture through the release of ideas out of eternity and into the continuum of history. The UFO is an idea whose purpose is to confound science, because science has begun to threaten the existence of the human species and the entire ecosystem of the planet. And at this point a shock is necessary for the culture—a shock equivalent to the shock of the Resurrection on Roman imperialism.[34]

Grosso, too, sees a possible deconstructive intent behind the protean and shifting forms of UFOs and other mind-bending encounters. These experiences, he says, have the effect of "shattering our metaphysical complacency."[35]

Whitley Strieber also concurs. His experiences have left him convinced that we have to abandon our accustomed ways of thinking and open ourselves up to modes of cognition that rest on unabashedly indeterministic principles that by definition entirely preclude conventional either/or solutions:

> We haven't yet even begun to think clearly about the whole phenomenon. What we really need to do is to think in a different way. We habitually think in a way that I believe Karl Popper described as linear thinking, that is to say, we think from A to B. But it's not possible to think that way and to deal coherently with this experience. In regard to the presence of the visitors, it is necessary not only to think clearly but also indeterminately. Indeterminate thinking is absolutely essential to even the beginnings of understanding.[36]

All of these thinkers who have been led, often through their own personal experiences, to reflect deeply on the mysteries of extraordinary encounters, especially those connected to UFOs, and have arrived at a deconstructivist interpretation, are helping us finally to discern the principal lesson these baffling phenomena hold out to us: *We are meant to be baffled!* Only by confronting and yielding to the unknowable—by rigorously avoiding both the temptation to deny, or explain away, these phenomena or to try to find some conventional explanation for them—can we, as a species, evolve in consciousness to the point where we may be able to take the steps necessary to avert the grim planetary fate that Berry has warned us will be our lot unless "the dream of the earth" becomes a reality.

Extraordinary encounters, UFOEs, NDEs, and others that disclose something of the mysteries of the transcendent universe, and of ourselves, are conundrums akin to a *koan*. A *koan*—the term comes from Zen Buddhism—is a puzzle that seems to be in the form of a question. The best known of them, at least in the West, is, "What is the sound of one hand (clapping)?" Though phrased as a question, a *koan* is really intended to stump the disciple, to frustrate his rational intellect, to force him to break through to an entirely new mode of understanding, and eventually to realize that he and the universe are—*what?*

Mind at Large has given humanity a cosmic *koan* to dwell upon, for we are all disciples in the mystery school that life itself represents. Science, as we have seen, can take us a part of the way in helping us to understand some aspects of the *koan*, but ultimately we must decondition ourselves from all conventional forms of knowledge and understanding if we are to penetrate into the *koan*'s essence and realize it for ourselves. For some of us, these extraordinary encounters constitute an offering of Mind at Large as one type of *koan* whose unfathomable but irresistible call draws us closer. For all of us, the fate of the earth and our future evolution as a species depend on our unflinching and dedicated determination to open ourselves up to their healing energies.

OMEGA PROJECT BATTERY

NOTE: As explained in Chapter 5, there were four *alternate* forms for the Omega Project Battery: one each for the NDE, NDC, UFOE, and UFOC groups. Even so, most of the questionnaires are either identical or have an identical format so as to be comparable. The illustrative set given below is for the UFOC group. If any researcher is interested in obtaining copies of the Omega Project Battery for other groups, he or she should write to the author at the following address:

> Department of Psychology
> University of Connecticut
> Storrs, Connecticut 06269-1020

OMEGA PROJECT BATTERY

The University of Connecticut

OMEGA PROJECT
Identification Sheet

Name _____

OMEGA PROJECT
Background Information Sheet

1. Sex   M   F

2. Date of Birth _____

3. Race or Ethnic Group

   ____ White

   ____ Black

   ____ Hispanic

   ____ (Native American) Indian

   ____ Oriental

   ____ Other
   (please specify)

4. Current Marital Status

   ____ Single

   ____ Married

   ____ Remarried

   ____ Separated

   ____ Divorced

   ____ Widowed

5. Current Religious Preference/Affiliation

   ____ Catholic

   ____ Protestant

6. Religious Faith You Were Raised In (If Any)

   ____ Catholic

   ____ Protestant

_____ Jewish	_____ Jewish
_____ Moslem	_____ Moslem
_____ Buddhist	_____ Buddhist
_____ Other (please specify)	_____ Other (please specify)
_____ None	_____ None

7. Educational Level

_____ Grade school

_____ Some high school

_____ High school gradu-
ate

_____ Some college or presently attending college

_____ College graduate

_____ Some post-graduate work

_____ Earned advanced degree (please spec-ify)

8. Current Occupation _____

OMEGA PROJECT
Experience and Interest Inventory

In responding to this inventory, you will probably not have to answer all of the questions asked. In any event, please read the following instructions carefully before proceeding.

If you have had a near-death experience (NDE), please answer just the following questions: #1, 2, 3 and 10. Disregard the remainder.

If you have had a UFO-related experience of the kind indicated in #4, please answer just questions #4–9. Disregard the remainder.

If you have had both an NDE and a UFO-related experience of the kind indicated in #4, please answer *all* questions.

If you have never had either an NDE or a UFO-related experience, answer *only* #9 if you have had an interest in UFOs; answer *only* #10 if you have had an interest in NDEs; answer *both* #9 and #10 if both topics have been of interest to you.

1. Have you ever had a near-death experience (NDE)?

    _____ Yes

    _____ No

2. Please indicate the month and year of your NDE below. (If you have had more than one such experience, please list the approximate dates for each one.)

    _____

    _____

    _____

3. Please give a brief description of the circumstances that brought you close to death and an account of the major features of your NDE. (If you have had more than one NDE, please answer this question with respect to your first such experience.) (You may use the back of this page, if necessary, to complete your answer or attach additional sheets if you prefer.)

4. Have you ever had an encounter with a being (or beings) or an intelligence that you believe was connected with a UFO or with a UFO-related phenomenon?

    _____ Yes

    _____ No

5. Please indicate the month and year of this experience below. (If you have had more than one such experience, please list the approximate dates for each one. If you have had too many such experiences to list in this way, please indicate this on the form, but list at least your first such significant experience.)

    _____

    _____

    _____

6. Please give a brief description of the circumstances surrounding your UFO-related experience and an account of the major features of that experience. (If you have had more than one such experience, please answer this question with respect to your first experience of this kind.) You may use the back of this page, if necessary, to complete your answer or attach additional sheets if you prefer.)

7. Did you recall your experience spontaneously and unaided? (That is, without the help of hypnotic regression?)

_____ Yes

_____ No

8. Have you ever been hypnotically regressed in connection with your experience? If so, when did this take place?

_____ Yes   Date _____

_____ No

9. When did you first become seriously interested in the topic of UFOs? What got you interested?

_____ Year of beginning interest

10. When did you first become seriously interested in the topic of NDEs? What got you interested?

_____ Year of beginning interest

Omega Childhood Experience Inventory

This questionnaire inquires into various experiences you may or may not have had as a child or young teenager. Please circle T (True) or F (False) after each of the following items to indicate your response.

1. As a child, a lot of my time was spent in a world of self-created fantasy.   T   F

2. When I was young, I enjoyed reading books about other times and countries.   T   F

3. As a child, I felt that I had a "guardian angel" or special spirit friend that watched over me.   T   F

4. When I was a child, I learned from non-physical beings that there was a special purpose for my life.   T   F

5. As a child, I seemed to know things that were going to happen in the future—and they did.   T   F

6. When I was a child, I was often "off in my own world."   T   F

7. When I was a child, I could see what some   T   F
people call fairies or "the little people."

8. As a child, I was able to see into "other   T   F
realities" that others didn't seem to be
aware of.

9. I can remember being aware before the time   T   F
of my physical birth (that is, I believe I have
memories of events that took place before
I was born into the physical world).

10. When I was a child, I nearly died.   T   F

11. When I was a child, I used to have very   T   F
vivid dreams.

12. As a child, I believed that I had lived be-   T   F
fore—in another body.

13. When I was a child, I relished the time I   T   F
had to myself alone.

14. As a child, I was aware of non-physical   T   F
beings while I was awake.

15. During my childhood, I had out-of-the-body   T   F
experiences.

16. When I was young, I daydreamed a lot.   T   F

17. When I was a child, I was especially fond   T   F
of reading or listening to fairy tales.

18. As a child, I had memories that I had lived   T   F
before.

19. As a child, I had a very vivid imagination.   T   F

20. When I was a child, I had a near-death ex-   T   F
perience.

21. As a child, I often seemed to know what   T   F
others (for example, my parents) were
thinking.

22. As a youngster, I was often ill.   T   F

23. When I was young, a non-physical being   T   F
appeared to me. (If you answered "True"

to this question, at what age did this first
happen? _____)

24.	When I was young, I loved to spend time alone in natural settings.	T	F
25.	When I was a child, I delighted in playing "let's pretend" games.	T	F
26.	When I was a youngster, I read a great deal of fiction.	T	F
27.	As a child, my fantasy world was very rich.	T	F
28.	When I was a child, I was very psychic.	T	F
29.	Even as a child, my intuition was highly developed.	T	F

Omega Home Environment Questionnaire

This questionnaire seeks to determine the general atmosphere of your home when you were a child or teenager and how you felt you were treated by your parents or principal caretaker. (If you were not raised by one or both of your biological parents, please respond to the questions below in terms of the person or persons who had the primary responsibility for your upbringing as a child.) Where a question inquires about the behavior of both of your parents and your parents differed in their behavior, please respond in terms of the parent whose behavior was the more severe or worse.

In responding to these questions, simply circle the appropriate number according to the following definitions:

4 = always
3 = very often
2 = sometimes
1 = rarely
0 = never

To illustrate, here is a hypothetical question:

Did your parents criticize you when you were young?   4 3 2 1 0

If you were rarely criticized, you should circle number 1. Please answer all questions.

1. Did your parents ridicule you?   4 3 2 1 0

2. Did you ever seek outside help or guidance because of problems in your home?   4 3 2 1 0

3. Did your parents verbally abuse each other?   4 3 2 1 0

4. Were you expected to follow a strict code of behavior in your home?   4 3 2 1 0

5. When you were punished as a child or teenager, did you understand the reason you were punished?   4 3 2 1 0

6. When you didn't follow the rules of the house, how often were you severely punished?   4 3 2 1 0

7. As a child, did you feel unwanted or emotionally neglected?   4 3 2 1 0

8. Did your parents insult you or call you names?   4 3 2 1 0

9. To what extent was either of your parents physically mistreated as a child?   4 3 2 1 0

10. Were your parents unhappy with each other?   4 3 2 1 0

11. Were your parents unwilling to attend any of your school-related activities?   4 3 2 1 0

12. As a child, were you punished in unusual ways (e.g., being locked in a closet for a long time or being tied up)? 4 3 2 1 0

13. Were there traumatic or upsetting sexual experiences when you were a child or teenager that you couldn't speak to adults about? 4 3 2 1 0

14. Did you ever think you wanted to leave your family and live with another family? 4 3 2 1 0

15. Did you ever witness the sexual mistreatment of another family member? 4 3 2 1 0

16. Did you ever think seriously about running away from home? 4 3 2 1 0

17. Did you witness the physical mistreatment of another family member? 4 3 2 1 0

18. When you were punished as a child or teenager, did you feel the punishment was deserved? 4 3 2 1 0

19. As a child or teenager, did you feel disliked by either of your parents? 4 3 2 1 0

20. How often did your parents get really angry with you? 4 3 2 1 0

21. As a child, did you feel that your home was charged with the possibility of unpredictable physical violence? 4 3 2 1 0

22. Did you feel comfortable bringing friends home to visit? 4 3 2 1 0

23. Did you feel safe living at home? 4 3 2 1 0

24. When you were punished as a child or teenager, did you feel "the punishment fit the crime"?   4 3 2 1 0

25. Did your parents ever verbally lash out at you when you did not expect it?   4 3 2 1 0

26. Did you have traumatic sexual experiences as a child or teenager?   4 3 2 1 0

27. Did your parents' disapproval of your relationships with the opposite sex ever lead to your physical mistreatment?   4 3 2 1 0

28. Did your parents yell at you?   4 3 2 1 0

29. When either of your parents was intoxicated, were you ever afraid of being sexually mistreated?   4 3 2 1 0

30. To what extent was either of your parents sexually mistreated as a child?   4 3 2 1 0

31. How often were you left at home alone as a child?   4 3 2 1 0

32. Did your parents blame you for things you didn't do?   4 3 2 1 0

33. To what extent did either of your parents drink heavily or abuse drugs?   4 3 2 1 0

34. Did your parents ever hit or beat you when you did not expect it?   4 3 2 1 0

35. Did your relationship with your parents ever involve a sexual experience?   4 3 2 1 0

36. As a child, did you have to take care of yourself before you were old enough?   4 3 2 1 0

37. Were you physically mistreated as a child or teenager?   4 3 2 1 0

38. Was your childhood stressful?   4 3 2 1 0

Omega Psychological Inventory

Please answer these items by circling the appropriate number following each statement according to the following scale:

1 = Strongly disagree
2 = Disagree
3 = Neutral
4 = Agree
5 = Strongly agree

1. Sometimes I have blank spells when I do things without being aware of what I've done.   1 2 3 4 5

2. Sometimes when I'm speaking, my mind goes blank and I lose the thread of what I've been saying.   1 2 3 4 5

3. I have physical symptoms such as heart palpitations or stomach trouble which I can't explain.   1 2 3 4 5

4. I feel like I've been "absent" part of the time.   1 2 3 4 5

5. Other people sometimes tell me I seem to be in a world of my own.   1 2 3 4 5

6. When I want to hear music it usually comes into my mind.   1 2 3 4 5

7. There is a part of me that criticizes what I do by making scathing remarks about me.   1 2 3 4 5

8. I think part of my life has been lived in another realm of time.   1 2 3 4 5

9. I feel as though I have always been able to hypnotize myself.   1 2 3 4 5

10. I spend a lot of time daydreaming.   1 2 3 4 5

11. I can block out all the sounds around me so that I don't hear anything.   1 2 3 4 5

12. I can go to a place where I don't feel anything.   1 2 3 4 5

13. I am afraid I may be epileptic.   1 2 3 4 5

14. Sometimes a part of me just wants to laugh hysterically at everything.   1 2 3 4 5

15. I have had times when I blacked out.   1 2 3 4 5

16. I have had times when my vision became dim or when I couldn't see, but I couldn't explain why.   1 2 3 4 5

17. My ability to daydream, or to detach myself from my surroundings, goes back to when I was a young child (before age 6 or 7).   1 2 3 4 5

18. When I was younger, I had an imaginary companion as a playmate.   1 2 3 4 5

19. I have "come to" in a situation where I didn't understand—even on reflection—how I got there.   1 2 3 4 5

20. There always seems to be something physically (medically) wrong with me.   1 2 3 4 5

21. Sometimes I become quite happy without being able to explain why.   1 2 3 4 5

22. I think I have agreed to having medical treatments I didn't really need. 1 2 3 4 5

23. I have had times when parts of my body were paralyzed or without sensation. 1 2 3 4 5

24. Sometimes my inner voices distract me from what people are saying to me. 1 2 3 4 5

25. Sometimes things just seem silly to me and nothing seems to matter. 1 2 3 4 5

26. I can tell myself to forget something and it will be gone from my mind. 1 2 3 4 5

27. Even though I try to concentrate on what's going on around me, I usually hear an "inner commentary" at the same time. 1 2 3 4 5

28. When I am tense or under a strain, I can relax by blocking everything out of my mind. 1 2 3 4 5

29. Sometimes I become preoccupied with a problem or something that has happened and I "carry it with me" and keep thinking about it. 1 2 3 4 5

30. My inner space seems to expand or contract, depending on my circumstances or mood. 1 2 3 4 5

31. I often forget to do something like an errand when I am in the rush of the day. 1 2 3 4 5

32. Sometimes people say I'm childish or unrealistic. 1 2 3 4 5

33. It's easy for me to really recapture an event in memory and relive it or reexperience it fully.   1 2 3 4 5

34. I hardly ever "talk to myself" silently or have an interior dialogue.   1 2 3 4 5

35. When I learn something in one context, say a particular class or with one group of people, it's usually hard for me to remember it clearly when I'm in a different situation.   1 2 3 4 5

36. When I get scared, I tend to freeze up—all I want to do is be somewhere else.   1 2 3 4 5

37. When I turn my attention inward, my inner world expands.   1 2 3 4 5

38. Most of my thoughts are concerned with concrete, practical matters.   1 2 3 4 5

39. I am frequently thinking about sensations from my body.   1 2 3 4 5

40. I have been hypnotized unintentionally, for example by looking at a lighted sign or listening to a recording.   1 2 3 4 5

Omega Psychophysical Changes Inventory

Please indicate your agreement or disagreement with each of the statements listed below. If you agree or tend to agree with a statement, please circle the letter *A* which follows it. If you disagree or tend to disagree with a statement, circle the letter

D. If you are not sure or have no opinion about a statement, circle the *?*

IMPORTANT: Each statement should be understood as beginning with the phrase, *After I became interested in UFO experiences.*

After I became interested in UFO experiences . . .

1. I came to feel that my nervous system was functioning differently than it had before.   A   D   ?

2. My sensitivity to crystals increased.   A   D   ?

3. I became more sensitive to "other realities, other dimensions."   A   D   ?

4. I seemed to become aware of multiple, overlapping realities at the same time.   A   D   ?

5. My general anxiety level increased.   A   D   ?

6. My tendency to get emotionally upset increased.   A   D   ?

7. I became more psychic than I was before.   A   D   ?

8. My tendency to get angry increased.   A   D   ?

9. My sensitivity to tastes increased.   A   D   ?

10. I felt energy in my hands more often than before.   A   D   ?

11. My tendency to experience time losses or memory lapses increased.   A   D   ?

12. I would sometimes feel a deep ecstatic sensation, something like an orgasm, for no apparent reason.   A   D   ?

13. My ability to tolerate alcoholic beverages decreased.   A   D   ?

14. I often felt that I was flooded with information that I could not absorb.   A   D   ?

15. My interest in learning about new subjects grew.   A   D   ?

16. I found it more difficult to think in strictly linear ways.   A   D   ?

17. I experienced severe or migraine-type headaches more often than before.   A   D   ?

18. My ability to learn increased.   A   D   ?

19. My feelings of being "tagged" or under surveillance increased.   A   D   ?

20. I became aware of energy discharges or currents flowing through my body.   A   D   ?

21. I became more sensitive to fluorescent light.   A   D   ?

22. I would occasionally experience sensations of tickling, itching or tingling on or underneath my skin.   A   D   ?

23. The intensity of my sexual experiences increased.   A   D   ?

24. My metabolic rate decreased.   A   D   ?

25. My blood pressure decreased.   A   D   ?

26. My moods would tend to fluctuate more drastically.   A   D   ?

27. My tendency to grow suspicious of others increased.   A   D   ?

28. My sensitivity to pharmaceutical drugs increased.   A   D   ?

29. My visual acuity increased.   A   D   ?

30. I became allergic or highly sensitive to certain foods that never bothered me before.   A   D   ?

31. I became aware of internal lights or colors.   A   D   ?

32. Telepathic or other forms of psychic awareness between me and others increased.   A   D   ?

33. My tendency to get depressed increased.   A   D   ?

34. My hands often felt hot.   A D ?

35. I would have sensations of extreme heat or cold move through my body more often than before.   A D ?

36. My susceptibility to illness increased.   A D ?

37. My body would occasionally shake, vibrate or tremble for no apparent reason.   A D ?

38. I became more sensitive to light in general.   A D ?

39. My ability to control my autonomic nervous system (e.g., heart rate, blood pressure, bleeding, etc.) seemed to increase.   A D ?

40. My dreams became more interesting.   A D ?

41. I tended to worry more.   A D ?

42. My capacity to absorb information about new things increased.   A D ?

43. Generally, I seemed to have a higher level of energy.   A D ?

44. I felt that I could sometimes heal people by touching them.   A D ?

45. I felt I had flashes of cosmic consciousness at times.   A D ?

46. My hearing acuity increased.   A D ?

47. My normal body temperature decreased.   A D ?

48. I became more aware of other entities or non-physical beings.   A D ?

49. I became more sensitive to humidity.   A D ?

50. My mind became tremendously expanded compared to how it functioned before.   A D ?

51. The amount of time I slept decreased.   A D ?

52. I was able to get along fine on less sleep.   A D ?

53. I came to feel that my brain was actually structurally different somehow.   A   D   ?

54. The frequency of my sexual experiences increased.   A   D   ?

55. My voluntary control over my body decreased.   A   D   ?

56. I became able to channel information from other dimensions.   A   D   ?

57. My intuitive awareness expanded.   A   D   ?

58. I often knew things before they happened—even when there was no natural way for me to know these things.   A   D   ?

59. I found that electric or electronic devices (e.g., car batteries or electrical systems, lights, watches, tape recorders, computers, etc.) more often malfunctioned in my presence than I remember being the case before.   A   D   ?

60. My thinking became more "holistic."   A   D   ?

Omega Life Changes Inventory

An interest in UFO experiences may or may not bring about certain changes in an individual's life. We would like to know in what ways, if any, your interest in UFO experiences affected your life. In responding to the following items all you need do is to circle the appropriate alternative, according to the instructions given below. Each statement should be understood as beginning with the phrase, "Since I became interested in UFO experiences in ____(year of interest)." Consider each statement carefully. For example, consider the following statement:

(Since I became interested in UFO experiences in _____ _____), my interest in the field of medicine has . . .

If you felt your interest had *strongly increased,* you would circle *SI* in the column following this statement. If you felt your interest had *increased somewhat,* you would circle *I* next to the statement. If your interest *hadn't changed,* you would circle *NC.* If your interest had *decreased somewhat,* you would circle *D.* Finally, if your interest had *strongly decreased,* you would circle *SD.*

To summarize: Strongly increase = SI

Increase somewhat = I

No change = NC

Decrease somewhat = D

Strongly decrease = SD

1. My desire to help others has SI I NC D SD
2. My compassion for others has SI I NC D SD
3. My appreciation of "the ordinary things of life" has SI I NC D SD
4. My ability to listen patiently to others has SI I NC D SD
5. My feelings of self-worth have SI I NC D SD
6. My interest in psychic phenomena has SI I NC D SD
7. My ability to love others in an impersonal way has SI I NC D SD
8. My concern with the material things of life has SI I NC D SD
9. My tolerance for others has SI I NC D SD
10. My sensitivity to the suffering of others has SI I NC D SD
11. My interest in creating a "good impression" has SI I NC D SD
12. My concern with spiritual matters has SI I NC D SD

13. My interest in organized religion has   SI   I   NC   D   SD

14. My understanding of myself has   SI   I   NC   D   SD

15. My desire to achieve a higher consciousness has   SI   I   NC   D   SD

16. My ability to express love for others openly has   SI   I   NC   D   SD

17. My insight into the problems of others has   SI   I   NC   D   SD

18. My appreciation of nature has   SI   I   NC   D   SD

19. My competitive tendencies have   SI   I   NC   D   SD

20. My religious feelings have   SI   I   NC   D   SD

21. My concern with the welfare of the planet has   SI   I   NC   D   SD

22. My understanding of "what life is all about" has   SI   I   NC   D   SD

23. My personal sense of purpose in life has   SI   I   NC   D   SD

24. My belief in a higher power has   SI   I   NC   D   SD

25. My understanding of others has   SI   I   NC   D   SD

26. My sense of the sacred aspect of life has   SI   I   NC   D   SD

27. My ambition to achieve a high standard of living has   SI   I   NC   D   SD

28. My self-acceptance has   SI   I   NC   D   SD

29. My desire for solitude has   SI   I   NC   D   SD

30. My sense that there is some inner meaning to my life has   SI   I   NC   D   SD

31. My involvement in my family life has   SI   I   NC   D   SD

32.	My fear of death has	SI	I	NC	D	SD
33.	My concern with the threat of nuclear weapons has	SI	I	NC	D	SD
34.	My desire to become a well-known person has	SI	I	NC	D	SD
35.	My tendency to pray has	SI	I	NC	D	SD
36.	My openness to the notion of reincarnation has	SI	I	NC	D	SD
37.	My empathy with others has	SI	I	NC	D	SD
38.	My concern with ecological matters has	SI	I	NC	D	SD
39.	My interest in the possibility of extra-terrestrial life has	SI	I	NC	D	SD
40.	My interest in self-understanding has	SI	I	NC	D	SD
41.	My inner sense of God's presence has	SI	I	NC	D	SD
42.	My feelings of personal vulnerability have	SI	I	NC	D	SD
43.	My conviction that there is life after death has	SI	I	NC	D	SD
44.	My interest in what others think of me has	SI	I	NC	D	SD
45.	My concern with political matters has	SI	I	NC	D	SD
46.	My interest in achieving material success has	SI	I	NC	D	SD
47.	My acceptance of others has	SI	I	NC	D	SD
48.	My search for personal meaning has	SI	I	NC	D	SD
49.	My concern with questions of social justice has	SI	I	NC	D	SD
50.	My interest in issues related to death and dying has	SI	I	NC	D	SD

Omega Religious Beliefs Inventory

Below you will find a list of statements of religious beliefs. Since your interest in UFO experiences, would you say that you are *now* more or less inclined to agree with the following statements or that you hold the same belief as before? If you are now more inclined to *agree* with a given statement, please write in an *A* in the space provided next to the statement; if you are now more inclined to *disagree* with a statement, write in a *D*; if your opinion is the same as before, write in an *S*.

_____ 1. The essential core of all religions is the same.

_____ 2. I believe there is a heaven and a hell.

_____ 3. No matter what your religious belief, there is life after death.

_____ 4. It is important to attend church regularly.

_____ 5. Private prayer is more important in the religious life of a person than is attendance at public church services.

_____ 6. More and more, I feel at home in any church.

_____ 7. I find the doctrine of reincarnation—the idea that we come back to earth to live in a physical body again—very implausible.

_____ 8. Eternal life is a gift of God only to those who believe in Jesus Christ as savior and Lord.

_____ 9. God is within you.

_____ 10. In order to live a truly religious life, the Church or some such other organized religious body is an essential.

_____ 11. The Bible is the inspired word of God.

_____ 12. A universal religion embracing all humanity is an idea which strongly appeals to me.

Omega Opinion Inventory

In considering the statements listed below, please indicate your own personal opinion for each item according to the following instructions: If you agree or tend to agree with a statement, circle the letter *A* which follows it; if you disagree or tend to disagree with a statement, circle the letter *D*; if you are not sure or have no opinion about a statement, circle the *?*

1. I believe that unless the human race changes significantly for the better, there will be massively destructive geophysical disturbances before the end of the century.   A D ?

2. I believe that the changes I've undergone since becoming interested in UFO experiences are part of an evolutionary unfolding of humanity.   A D ?

3. I believe that humanity may be the object of biological experimentation by extra-terrestrial life forms.   A D ?

4. I believe that my interest in UFO experiences was "arranged" or "designed" by a higher agency or by my higher self.   A D ?

5. Aliens—in the sense of intelligent life forms from other planets or dimensions—are already among us.   A D ?

6. In my opinion, the widespread occurrence of UFO experiences is part of a larger plan to promote the evolution of consciousness on a species-wide scale.   A D ?

7. I believe that I am a more spiritual person now than I was before my interest in UFO experiences.   A   D   ?

8. I believe that alien beings are likely to exert increasing control over human life in years to come.   A   D   ?

9. We are now living through a time of greatly accelerated spiritual evolution.   A   D   ?

10. We are already in or at least on the verge of a New Age.   A   D   ?

11. Evolutionary forces are already at work which will transform humanity at large into a more self-aware, spiritually sensitive species.   A   D   ?

12. I believe that there is a higher power guiding my life.   A   D   ?

13. My own interest in UFO experiences has no "larger" meaning as far as humanity is concerned but only a personal one.   A   D   ?

14. Our home is earth, but our destiny is the stars.   A   D   ?

15. I believe that there are powerful cosmic forces operative today that are working to "spiritualize" the planet.   A   D   ?

16. There is no "higher purpose" to evolution—it just is and does not unfold according to any "higher plan."   A   D   ?

17. I feel that in some way I was "meant" to have an interest in UFO experiences.   A   D   ?

18. There is a plan for our universe.   A   D   ?

19. The goal of human evolution is to transcend physicality as a limit and enter fully into Spirit.   A   D   ?

20. If extra-terrestrial life exists, it does not necessarily bode well for humanity.   A   D   ?

21. There are higher-order intelligences that have a concern with the welfare of our planet.   A   D   ?

22. I believe that my interest in UFO experiences was designed to "program" me to be of service to humanity.   A   D   ?

23. I believe that my interest in UFO experiences occurred so as to awaken me to the existence of larger cosmic forces which are affecting our lives.   A   D   ?

24. Evil as well as good forces are operative in our galaxy.   A   D   ?

25. I believe that massive geophysical disturbances before the end of the century are inevitable—regardless of whatever changes in humanity might take place.   A   D   ?

26. I am here for a purpose.   A   D   ?

27. I feel I have a mission to use what I have learned from my study of UFO experiences to spread God's love to all.   A   D   ?

28. There are higher-order intelligences that are bent on exploiting our planet in some way.   A   D   ?

29. I have come to feel that I am part of a much larger "field of intelligence" than I previously believed.   A   D   ?

30. I believe I have communicated with non-physical entities.   A   D   ?

STATISTICAL TABLES FROM
OMEGA PROJECT

TABLE 1. MEANS FOR SELECTED SCALES OF THE CHILDHOOD
EXPERIENCE INVENTORY

	UFOE	NDE	UFOC	NDC
Fantasy Proneness	6.46	5.79	6.46	5.71
Alternate Realities	2.73	1.66	1.00	0.67
Psychic Sensitivities	2.90	2.01	1.52	0.91

TABLE 2. MEANS FOR COMPONENTS OF CHILDHOOD ABUSE
AND TRAUMA FROM THE HOME ENVIRONMENT INVENTORY

	UFOE	NDE	UFOC	NDC	p
Physical Mistreatment	8.50	8.48	7.26	6.24	$<.02$
Psychological Abuse	10.85	11.11	9.88	8.15	$<.02$
Sexual Abuse	4.40	4.82	2.39	2.77	.005
Neglect	5.48	6.22	3.82	4.26	.0002
Negative Home Atmosphere	15.55	17.02	12.62	11.63	.001

TABLE 3. MEAN DISSOCIATION SCORES

UFOE	NDE	UFOC	NDC
110.78	106.89	105.82	95.82

TABLE 4. PERCENT OF RESPONDENTS ENDORSING ITEM ON
PSYCHOPHYSICAL CHANGES INVENTORY

	UFOE	NDE	UFOC	NDC
Physical Sensitivities increase in:				
light sensitivity	49.5	48.6	25.6	20.4
hearing acuity	25.8	35.1	15.4	7.4
humidity sensitivity	34.0	43.2	15.4	11.1
Physiological Changes decrease in:				
metabolic rate	19.6	17.6	2.6	9.3
body temperature	21.6	17.6	7.7	7.4
blood pressure	25.8	31.1	7.7	11.1
Neurological Changes difference in:				
nervous system	47.4	51.4	12.8	18.5
brain structure	25.1	36.5	7.4	7.7
Energetic Changes increase in:				
energy currents in body	44.3	50.0	20.5	13.0
decrease in:				
sleep time	36.1	39.2	12.8	16.7
Emotional Changes increase in:				
mood swings	34.0	28.4	10.3	13.0
Expanded Mental Awareness increase in:				
mind expansion	48.5	58.1	30.8	27.8
information flooding	56.7	48.6	17.9	20.4
Changes in Paranormal Functioning increase in:				
psychic abilities	51.5	60.8	17.9	31.5
causing electric or electronic malfunction	37.1	24.3	10.3	7.4

TABLE 5. NET PSYCHOPHYSICAL CHANGE SCORES

UFOE	NDE	UFOC	NDC
3.14	−1.78	−28.49	−30.67

TABLE 6. PERCENT ENDORSEMENT OF ITEMS PERTINENT TO THE ELECTRICAL-SENSITIVITY SYNDROME

	UFOE	NDE	UFOC	NDC
More Allergic	21.6	24.3	10.3	7.4
More Psychic	51.5	60.8	17.9	31.5
Healing Gifts	52.6	41.9	23.1	11.1
Sensitivity to Light	49.5	48.6	25.6	20.4
Hearing Acuity	25.8	35.1	15.4	7.4
Mood Fluctuation	34.0	28.4	10.3	13.0

TABLE 7. PERCENT ENDORSEMENT OF ITEMS ON THE KUNDALINI SCALE

	UFOE	NDE	UFOC	NDC
I felt energy in my hands more often than before	37.1	47.3	15.4	14.8
I would sometimes feel a deep ecstatic sensation, something like an orgasm, for no reason	32.0	35.1	15.4	14.8
I experienced severe or migraine type headaches more often than before	34.0	17.6	10.3	9.3

	UFOE	NDE	UFOC	NDC
I became aware of energy discharges or currents flowing through my body	44.3	50.0	20.5	13.0
I would occasionally experience sensations of tickling, itching or tingling on or underneath my skin	54.6	39.2	30.8	3.7
I became aware of internal lights or colors	32.0	43.2	17.9	9.3
My hands often felt hot	24.7	33.8	15.4	11.1
I would have sensations of extreme heat or cold move through my body more often than before	35.1	37.8	10.3	20.4
My body would occasionally shake, vibrate or tremble for no apparent reason	30.9	25.7	10.3	3.7

TABLE 8. NET KUNDALINI SCORES

UFOE	NDE	UFOC	NDC
−0.60	−1.04	−5.03	−6.22

TABLE 9. NET VALUE SHIFTS ON THE LCI

Value Domain	UFOE	NDE	UFOC	NDC
Appreciation for Life	1.19	1.33	0.98	1.02
Self-acceptance	0.92	1.13	0.81	0.80
Concern for Others	0.92	1.21	0.65	0.92
Concern for Impressing Others	0.02	−0.66	−0.06	−0.47
Materialism	−0.37	−0.58	−0.17	−0.39
Concern with Social/Planetary Issues	0.76	0.51	0.65	0.36
Quest for Meaning	1.35	1.27	1.04	1.09
Spirituality	1.21	1.22	0.86	1.09
Religiousness	0.05	−0.17	−0.16	0.33

TABLE 10. NET VALUE SHIFTS ON PLANETARY WELFARE AND ECOLOGICAL CONCERN

	UFOE	NDE	UFOC	NDC
Planetary Welfare	1.44	1.21	1.03	0.86
Ecological Concern	1.29	0.99	0.87	0.79

TABLE 11. PERCENT DISTRIBUTION FOR PLANETARY WELFARE AND ECOLOGICAL CONCERN ITEMS

UFO Sample		
	UFOE	UFOC
My Concern with the Welfare of the Planet Has		
Strongly increased	58.8	30.8
Increased	26.8	41.0
Not changed	11.3	28.2
Decreased	2.1	—
Strongly decreased	—	—

UFO Sample		
	UFOE	UFOC
My Concern with Ecological Matters Has		
Strongly increased	47.4	25.6
Increased	33.0	35.9
Not changed	18.6	38.5
Decreased	—	—
Strongly decreased	1.0	—
NDE Sample		
	NDE	NDC
My Concern with the Welfare of the Planet Has		
Strongly increased	37.8	20.4
Increased	41.9	44.4
Not changed	17.6	31.5
Decreased	—	1.9
Strongly decreased	—	—
My Concern with Ecological Matters Has		
Strongly increased	27.0	14.8
Increased	43.2	48.1
Not changed	28.4	35.2
Decreased	—	—
Strongly decreased	—	—

TABLE 12. UNIVERSALISTIC SPIRITUAL SHIFT SCORES ON THE RBI

UFOE	NDE	UFOC	NDC
6.46	5.45	5.12	5.19

TABLE 13. PERCENT OF AGREE AND DISAGREE RESPONSES TO
"EVOLUTIONARY ITEMS" OF THE OPINION INVENTORY

Item	UFOE		NDE		UFOC		NDC	
	A	D	A	D	A	D	A	D
I believe that the changes I've undergone since my UFO experience are part of an evolutionary unfolding of humanity	62.9	8.2	54.1	16.2	56.4	20.5	55.6	14.8
In my opinion, the widespread occurrence of UFO experience is part of a larger plan to promote the evolution of consciousness on a species-wide scale	60.8	9.3	52.7	14.9	56.4	7.7	50.0	13.0
We are already in or at least on the verge of a New Age	71.1	7.2	67.6	10.8	71.8	10.3	53.7	9.3
Evolutionary forces are already at work which will transform humanity at large into a more self-aware, spiritually sensitive species	62.9	11.3	59.5	8.1	66.7	15.4	38.9	13.0

TABLE 14. PERCENT OF AGREE AND DISAGREE RESPONSES TO "PURPOSIVENESS ITEMS" OF OPINION INVENTORY

Item	UFOE		NDE		UFOC		NDC	
	A	D	A	D	A	D	A	D
I believe that my UFO experience was "arranged" or "designed" by a higher agency or by my higher self	59.8	11.3	63.5	18.9	43.6	20.5	44.4	25.9
I believe that my UFO experience occurred so as to awaken me to the existence of larger cosmic forces which are affecting our lives	56.7	16.5	50.0	20.3	51.3	17.9	44.4	22.2
I feel I have a mission to use what I have learned from my UFO experience to spread God's love to all	27.8	29.9	58.1	27.0	28.2	30.8	50.0	31.5

TABLE 15. PERCENT OF AGREE AND DISAGREE RESPONSES TO "EXTRATERRESTRIAL INFLUENCE ITEMS" OF OPINION INVENTORY

Item	UFOE		NDE		UFOC		NDC	
	A	D	A	D	A	D	A	D
I believe that humanity may be the object of biological experimentation by extraterrestrial life forms	68.0	7.2	18.9	41.9	56.4	12.8	9.3	50.0

TABLE 15. (*Continued*)

Item	UFOE		NDE		UFOC		NDC	
	A	D	A	D	A	D	A	D
I believe alien beings are likely to exert increasing control over human life in years to come	38.1	28.9	16.2	36.5	41.0	23.1	11.1	55.6
There are higher order intelligences that are bent on exploiting our planet in some way	17.5	40.2	13.5	41.9	28.2	23.1	3.7	61.1
There are higher order intelligences that have a concern with the welfare of our planet	76.3	2.1	48.6	9.5	71.8	0.0	44.4	9.3

NOTES

PREFACE

1. D. Royce, "The NDE: A Survey of Clergy's Attitudes and Knowledge," *Journal of Pastoral Care*, 39 (March 1985), pp. 31–42. R. M. Orne, "Nurses' Views of NDEs," *American Journal of Nursing*, 86 (1986), pp. 419–420. B. A. Walker and R. D. Russell, "Assessing Psychologists' Knowledge and Attitudes Toward Near-Death Phenomena," *Journal of Near-Death Studies*, 8 (1989), pp. 103–110. E. R. Hayes and L. D. Waters, "Interdisciplinary Perceptions of the Near-Death Experience: Implications for Professional Education and Practice," *Death Studies*, 13 (1989), pp. 443–483.

2. For the most complete statement of this hypothesis, see his book, *The Final Choice* (Walpole, N. H.: Stillpoint, 1985).

CHAPTER 1: ANOTHER ROAD TO OMEGA

1. Stanton T. Friedman, "Who Believes in UFOs?" *International UFO Reporter*, 14 (January/February 1989), pp. 6–10.

2. These were Budd Hopkins's *Intruders* (New York: Random House, 1987) and Gary Kinder's *Light Years* (New York: Atlantic Monthly Press, 1987).

3. Strieber himself objects strenuously to the term *abductee* because of its connotation of victimization. I use this term here only to maintain linguistic continuity with the discussion that has preceded it.

4. Lawrence Fawcett and Barry J. Greenwood, *Clear Intent* (Englewood Cliffs, N. J.: Prentice-Hall, 1984).

CHAPTER 2: VARIETIES OF UFO ENCOUNTERS

1. All respondents in this study signed an informed-consent statement and were promised that their questionnaire materials would be kept confidential and their actual identities would remain anonymous.

2. See, for example, Thomas E. Bullard, *Comparative Analysis of UFO Abduction Reports* (Mt. Rainier, Maryland: Fund for UFO Research, 1987); Hopkins, *Intruders;* Jenny Randles, *Abduction* (London: Robert Hale, 1988). A cautionary note is necessary here, however: While a perusal of the foregoing books will provide ample evidence that tales of identically described diminutive figures as my respondents claim to have seen abound in contemporary UFO narratives, there are many accounts that clearly indicate that distinctly *different* humanoid figures have appeared to other witnesses. Thus, the type that is featured in my own narratives seems to represent only *one species of UFO entity*. In the world of UFO parlance, this type is usually spoken of simply as "the greys."

CHAPTER 3: CLOSE ENCOUNTERS OF THE FOURTH KIND

1. See, for example, the work of Thomas E. Bullard, especially his article, "Hypnosis and UFO Abductions: A Troubled Relationship," *Journal of UFO Studies,* 1 (1989), pp. 3–40.

2. Strieber, in his book *Communion* (New York: Beech Tree/William Morrow, 1987), makes a point of talking about the frequency and significance of triangular markings on the bodies of persons who have had UFO visitations. I myself have seen such a pattern, in the form of a purplish welt, on the hand of a woman I interviewed who described a close encounter of the fourth kind to me.

3. See, for example, Bullard's work, *Comparative Analysis of UFO Abduction Reports*.

CHAPTER 4: NEAR-DEATH EXPERIENCES

1. Standard works on the NDE, in addition to Moody's initial book, now include: Kenneth Ring, *Life at Death* (New York: Coward, McCann and Geoghegan, 1980) and *Heading Toward Omega* (New York: William Morrow, 1984); Michael B. Sabom, *Recollections of Death* (New York: Harper & Row, 1982); Bruce Greyson and Charles P. Flynn, eds., *The Near-Death Experience* (Springfield, Illinois: Charles C. Thomas, 1984); Margot Grey, *Return from Death* (London: Arkana, 1985); Charles P. Flynn, *After the Beyond* (Englewood Cliffs, N. J.: Prentice-Hall, 1986); Carol Zaleski, *Otherworld Journeys* (New York: Oxford University Press, 1987); P.M.H. Atwater, *Coming Back to Life* (New York: Dodd, Mead, 1988); Raymond A. Moody, Jr., *The Light*

Beyond (New York: Bantam, 1988); and D. Scott Rogo, *The Return from Silence* (Wellingborough, England: Aquarian Press, 1989). In addition to these books, there is a scholarly quarterly periodical, *The Journal of Near-Death Studies*, edited by Dr. Bruce Greyson, which (though formerly called *Anabiosis*) has been in print since 1981.

2. See Gallup's book, *Adventures in Immortality* (New York: McGraw-Hill, 1982).

3. See Kalweit's book, *Dreamtime and Inner Space* (Boston: Shambhala, 1988), p. 94.

4. For a careful study of these matters in a sample of sixty-three persons who reported out-of-body experiences in conjunction with NDEs, see the article by J. M. Holden, "Visual Perception During Naturalistic Near-Death Out-of-Body Experiences," *Journal of Near-Death Studies*, 7 (1989), pp. 107–120.

5. For some impressive examples, see especially the work of Sabom in *Recollections of Death*, particularly Chapter 7, as well as his article, "The Near-Death Experience: Myth or Reality?" *Anabiosis*, 1 (1981), pp. 44–56. Moody, in his book *The Light Beyond*, provides an intriguing anecdotal case involving a blind woman who allegedly had veridical perception during an NDE (see pp. 134–135). For a real mind-blower in this regard, however, be sure to see Kimberly Clark's article "Clinical Interventions with Near-Death Experiencers" in Greyson and Flynn, op. cit. pp. 242–255.

6. For a readable summary of some of this evidence, see David Chamberlain's book *Babies Remember Birth* (Los Angeles: J. P. Tarcher, 1988) as well as his article "The Expanding Boundaries of Memory," *Revision*, 12 (1990), pp. 11–20.

7. The best studies of childhood NDEs have been carried out by a pediatrician, Melvin Morse, and his colleagues and are summarized in his recent book, *Closer to the Light* (New York: Villard Books, 1990). See also, however, Morse's article, "A Near-Death Experience in a Seven-Year-Old Child," *American Journal of Diseases in Children*, 137 (1983), pp. 959–961, Morse et al., "Childhood Near-Death Experiences," *American Journal of Diseases in Children*, 140 (1986), pp. 1110–1114, as well as "Near-Death Experiences in a Pediatric Population," *American Journal of Diseases in Children*, 139 (1985), pp. 595–600. Moody also presents a summary of such cases in his book, *The Light Beyond*. Additional cases have been reported by Nancy Bush in her article, "The Near-Death Experience in Children: Shades of the Prison-House Reopening," *Anabiosis*, 3 (1983), pp. 177–193, by William J. Serdalehy in his report, "Pedriatic Near-Death Experiences," *Journal of Near-Death Studies*, 9 (1990), pp. 33–39, and in a book by Glen Gabbard and Stuart

Twemlow, *With the Eyes of the Mind* (New York: Praeger, 1984), pp. 154–166.

8. See the article by David B. Herzog and John T. Herrin, "Near-Death Experiences in the Very Young," *Critical Care Medicine*, 13 (1985), pp. 1074–1075.

9. Although it is not altogether rare for there to be reports of encounters with distinct religious personages, such as Christ, in NDEs, it is quite common, as is implied in this instance, that there is some ambiguity in these reports concerning what exactly is seen and what is *inferred*. I have even come across cases where an NDEr makes it clear that the being perceived in no way resembled our modern artistic representations of Christ, but was nevertheless sure that it *was* Christ.

10. For some detailed case material on NDErs' emotional reactions and personal difficulties following their NDEs, see my book, *Heading Toward Omega*, pp. 90–99. On this same point, Atwater's book *Coming Back to Life* is perhaps the most useful general reference.

CHAPTER 5: THE OMEGA PROJECT

1. Ted Bloecher, Aphrodite Clamar, and Budd Hopkins, "Summary Report on the Psychological Testing of Nine Individuals Reporting UFO Abductions," in *Final Report on the Psychological Testing of UFO "Abductees"* (Mt. Rainier, Maryland: Fund for UFO Research, 1985).

2. See the discussion in the paper I co-authored with Christopher J. Rosing, "The Omega Project: A Psychological Survey of Persons Reporting Abductions and Other UFO Encounters," *Journal of UFO Studies*, 2 (1990), pp. 59–98.

3. "Hypnotic and Psychic Implications in the Investigation of UFO Reports," in Coral Lorenzen and Jim Lorenzen, eds., *Encounters with UFO Occupants* (New York: Berkley, 1976), pp. 256–329.

4. "Personality Characteristics of Persons Who Claim UFO Experiences," *Journal of UFO Studies*, 2 (1990), pp. 45–58.

5. For example, Berthold Schwarz. See, especially, his *UFO Dynamics: Psychiatric and Psychic Aspects of the UFO Syndrome* (Moore Haven, Florida: Rainbow Books, 1983).

6. For example, J. A. Meerloo, "The Flying Saucer Syndrome and the Need for Miracles," *Journal of the American Medical Association*, 203 (1968), p. 70; R. A. Gordon, "People Who See Flying Saucers," *Science*, 171 (1971), p. 957; and Lester Grinspoon and A. D. Persky, "Psychiatry and UFO Reports," in C. Sagan and T. Page, eds., *UFOs: A Scientific Debate* (Ithaca, New York: Cornell University Press, 1972), pp. 223–246.

7. See, for example, Gallup, *Adventures in Immortality,* or my book, *Heading Toward Omega,* Chapter 2.

8. See Wilson and Barber's article, "The Fantasy-Prone Personality: Implications for Understanding Imagery, Hypnosis and Parapsychological Phenomena," in A. Shiekh, ed., *Imagery: Current Theory, Research and Application* (New York: John Wiley, 1983), pp. 340–387.

9. Robert A. Baker, "Are UFO Abductions for Real? No, No, A Thousand Times, No!" *Journal of UFO Studies,* 1 (1989), pp. 104–110; Keith Basterfield and Robert Bartholomew, "Abductions: The Fantasy-Prone Hypothesis," *International UFO Reporter,* 13 (May-June 1988), pp. 9–11; Budd Hopkins, Letters, *International UFO Reporter,* 13 (May-June 1988a), pp. 22–23, (July-August 1988b), pp. 20–21; Martin Kottmeyer, "Abduction: The Boundary Deficit Hypothesis," *Magonia,* 37 (1988), pp. 3–7; Kenneth Ring, "Toward an Imaginal Interpretation of UFO Abductions," *Revision,* 11:2 (1989), pp. 17–24; D. Scott Rogo, Letter, *International UFO Reporter,* 13 (July-August 1988), p. 20.

10. See the article by Robert Bartholomew and Keith Basterfield, "Abduction States of Consciousness," *Internationl UFO Reporter,* 13 (March-April 1988), pp. 7–9, 15.

11. See the works of Schwarz and Sprinkle, previously cited, as well as Jacques Vallee's *Dimensions* (Chicago: Contemporary Books, 1988).

12. Randles, *Abduction.*

13. Bruce Greyson, "Increase in Psychic Phemonena Following Near-Death Experiences," *Theta,* 11 (1983), pp. 26–29; Richard Kohr, "Near-Death Experiences, Altered States, and Psi Sensitivity," *Anabiosis,* 3 (1983), pp. 157–176; Kenneth Ring, *Heading Toward Omega*; Margot Grey, *Return from Death*; Phyllis Atwater, *Coming Back to Life*; Cherie Sutherland, "Psychic Phenomena Following Near-Death Experiences," *Journal of Near-Death Studies,* 8 (1990), pp. 93–102.

14. See the articles of Kohr and Sutherland, previously cited.

15. See Evans, *Alternate States of Consciousness* (Wellingborough, England: Aquarian Press, 1989) as well as my papers, "An Imaginal Interpretation of UFO Abductions," previously cited, and "Near-Death Experiences, Imaginal Worlds, and Light After Death," in Gary Doore, ed., *What Survives?* (Los Angeles: J. P. Tarcher, 1990), pp. 204–215.

16. For example, Evans, *Alternate States of Consciousness.*

17. For example, Joseph Nyman (personal communication, February 1988); Rima Laibow, "Dual Victims: The Abused and the Abducted," *International UFO Reporter,* 14 (May-June 1989), pp. 4–9; and Thomas E. Bullard, "The UFO Abduction Phenomenon: Past Research and Future Prospects," paper presented at the First Conference on Treatment

and Research on Experienced Anomalous Trauma, Fairfield, Connecticut, May 1989.

18. This has been suggested to me, for example by NDErs Ellen Stoia (May 1987) and Barbara Harris (September 1987) in personal communications as well as indicated by the findings of a pilot study carried out by Sherry Stewart and Mary Lou Carrione, "The Chosen Few," unpublished term paper for Advanced Seminar in Near-Death Studies, University of Connecticut, Storrs, Connecticut, May 1987.

19. See, for example, *Heading Toward Omega,* Chapter 9, and Bruce Greyson's recent chapter, "Scientific Commentary," in Barbara Harris and Lionel C. Bascom's book, *Full Circle* (New York: Pocket Books, 1990), pp. 251–270.

20. See, for example, the previously mentioned books by me, Atwater, Flynn, and Grey.

21. Lorraine Davis, "A Comparison of UFO and Near-Death Experiences as Vehicles for the Evolution of Human Consciousness," *Journal of Near-Death Studies,* 6 (1988), pp. 240–257.

22. My research was funded by grants from the University of Connecticut Research Foundation and the Bernstein Brothers Foundation in Pueblo, Colorado.

23. In this connection, I am indebted to abduction researchers Budd Hopkins and Joseph Nyman for their referrals, as well as to Whitley Strieber, Leo Sprinkle, and John White for providing me with lists of additional candidates for my study.

24. The full set of questionnaires is presented in Appendix I.

25. For example, in *Heading Toward Omega,* in the Davis study, previously cited, and in the research of Barbara Sanders et al., "Correlates of Dissociation in a College Population," *Journal of Dissociation,* 2 (1989), pp. 17–23.

26. For reasons that will be indicated in full in the following chapter, individuals reporting abduction experiences were not distinguished for the purposes of this study from those who had other kinds of UFO encounters.

27. I am deeply indebted to my project coordinator, Christopher J. Rosing, for the enormous task of designing and running the programs necessary for the computer analysis of our data, as well as for his overall expert administration of the Omega Project from start to finish. In addition, I would also like to express my heartfelt thanks to my students, Barbara Rosen, Kevin Nelson, Gretchen Gaugler, and Kristie Davis, for their invaluable help on other aspects of the data coding and analysis.

CHAPTER 6: CHILDHOOD ANTECEDENTS OF EXTRAORDINARY ENCOUNTERS

1. Many UFO respondents indicated that they had had more than one such experience, but those included in this category were individuals who had listed or implied so many that it was not possible to determine the primacy of any one encounter.

2. For the statistically minded, we used a series of one-way analyses of variance on the measures derived from our inventories.

3. The exact items comprising this scale will be found in Appendix II.

4. All of the major statistical findings of the Omega Project will be presented in this appendix. However, if rows of numbers tend to give you a pronounced condition of mental vertigo, fear not. I will always summarize the gist of my findings in the text. The tables in the appendix are provided for those who are interested in examining particular findings more closely and, of course, for professionals.

5. An analysis of variance (ANOVA) shows that this difference is significant at well over the .0001 level, meaning that far less than one time in ten thousand would a difference as large as this or larger occur by chance.

6. The correlation (r) was .73.

7. The probability of the difference (p) was once more $\ll$ .0001.

8. Randles, *Abduction*, pp. 87, 104.

9. Ibid., p. 208.

10. Ibid., p. 205.

11. Evans, *Gods, Spirits, Cosmic Guardians* (Wellingborough, England: Aquarian Press, 1987), p. 188.

12. Evans, *Visions, Apparitions, Alien Visitors* (Wellingborough, England: Aquarian Press, 1984), p. 156.

13. The HEI was devised by Barbara Rosen, a graduate student working on the Omega Project, my wife, Dr. Barbara Sanders (who has used it in her own research), and me.

14. p <.001.

15. p <.0001.

16. A technical note here is necessary for our NDEr sample: Since some NDErs (n=6) had their NDEs during childhood, a more valid comparison is one that excludes them. When this is done, however, the effect for the NDE sample still holds up (p=.002).

17. Using one such criterion, we found that approximately half of our experiential respondents reported a "significant" amount of abuse compared to slightly less than a third of our controls (p <.005), but I would caution against giving much weight to such arbitrarily derived figures. Indeed, arriving at generally agreed upon criteria for what constitutes child abuse is one of the persisting unresolved issues in that field of concern. (On this point, see Murray A. Straus et al., *Behind Closed Doors: Violence in the American Family* [Garden City, New York: Anchor, 1980]).

18. Michael Wogan, "A New Test for Dissociation," *Journal of Experimental and Clinical Hypnosis* (in press).

19. For example, see the previously cited study by Barbara Sanders et al., "Correlates of Dissociation in a College Population."

20. See again the article by Sanders et al., just cited, as well as the studies by Sanders and Giolas, "Dissociation and Child Abuse in Disturbed Adolescents," *American Journal of Psychiatry*, 14 (1991), pp. 50–54; and by Chu and Dill, "Dissociative Symptoms in Relation to Childhood Physical and Sexual Abuse," *American Journal of Psychiatry*, 147 (1990), pp. 887–892. See, for example, Kluft, *Childhood Antecedents of Multiple Personality* (Washington, D.C.: American Psychological Association, 1985) and the article by Roberta Sachs, "A Comparison of Experienced Anomalous Trauma and Satanic Cult Experiences," paper presented at the Second Conference on Treatment and Research on Experienced Anomalous Trauma, Blacksburg, Virginia, 1990.

21. See his book, *Alternate States of Consciousness*.

22. The difference between experiential and control groups is significant at p <.02, while the UFO/ND difference is just barely significant (p <.05).

23. Sanders et al., previously cited.

24. p <.0001.

25. Of course it's obvious, as many of our close encounter narratives have amply demonstrated, that alternate realities don't necessarily induce positive experiences. This is an important point, which we will take up later, but in this context I am speaking more of the motivational impetus to seek those realities than their content per se.

26. Evans, *Alternate States of Consciousness*, p. 233.

27. I am referring here to some still unpublished work of Barbara Sanders, "Dissociation, Imaginative Involvement, and Child Abuse," manuscript in preparation, University of Connecticut; however, there is already evidence from the research of Wilson and Barber, previously cited, that also points to a connection between child abuse and tendencies toward psychological absorption.

28. See Peter L. Nelson, "Personality Factors in the Frequency of Reported Spontaneous Preternatural Experiences," *Journal of Transpersonal Psychology,* 21 (1989), pp. 193–209.

29. For example, E. W. Mathes, "Mystical Experiences, Romantic Love, and Hypnotic Susceptibility," *Psychological Reports,* 50 (1982), pp. 701–702; N. P. Spanos and P. Moretti, "Correlates of Mystical and Diabolical Experiences in a Sample of Female College Students," *Journal for the Scientific Study of Religion,* 27 (1988), pp. 105–116.

30. Here see especially the work of H. J. Irwin, particularly his book *Flight of Mind* (Metuchen, New Jersey: Scarecrow Press, 1985).

31. James B. Council and Bruce Greyson, "Near-Death Experiences and the Fantasy-Prone Personality," paper presented to the American Psychological Association, Los Angeles, California, August 1985.

32. D. Scott Rogo, *Alien Abductions* (New York: Signet, 1980).

CHAPTER 7: PSYCHOPHYSICAL CHANGES FOLLOWING EXTRAORDINARY ENCOUNTERS

1. Again, the full questionnaire will be found in Appendix I.

2. $F = 76.62$, $p \ll .0001$.

3. Grey, op. cit., p. 162.

4. Randles, *Mind Monsters* (Wellingborough, England: Aquarian Press, 1990), pp. 177–178.

5. *The Communion Letter,* 2 (Spring 1990), p. 4.

6. Michael Shallis, *The Electric Connection* (New York: Amsterdam, 1988).

7. Wilson, "In Search of the Elusive Chi," *Newsletter of the International Society for the Study of Subtle Energy and Energy Medicine,* 1 (1990), pp. 8–9.

8. See especially his books, *The Body Electric* (New York: William Morrow, 1985) and *Cross Currents* (Los Angeles: J. P. Tarcher, 1990).

9. Becker, "The Relationship Between Bioelectromagnetics and Psychic Phenomena," *ASPR Newsletter,* 16 (Spring 1990), pp. 11–14.

10. Shallis, p. 76 ff.

11. Persinger's position is explicated in his book, *Space-Time Transients and Unusual Phenomena,* co-authored with G. Lafreniere (Chicago: Nelson-Hall, 1977), and in such papers as "Modern Neuroscience and Near-Death Experiences," *Journal of Near-Death Studies,* 7 (1990), pp. 233–239, and "The 'Visitor' Experience and the Personality: The Temporal Lobe Factor," in Dennis Stillings, ed., *Cyberbiological Studies of the Imaginal Component in the UFO Contact Experience* (St.

Paul: Archaeus Project, 1989), pp. 157–171. Randles draws on Persinger's general formulation in developing her own explanatory framework in *Mind Monsters,* Chapter 7. A brief statement on this same issue by Gotlib, with specific reference to abductions, which also mentions Shallis's research, will be found in his commentary, "EM Fields Affect Consciousness," *Bulletin of Anomalous Experience,* 1 (June-July 1990), pp. 2–3.

12. James Hardt, "Kundalini and Biofeedback," paper presented to the Second Spiritual Emergence Network Conference, Pacific Grove, California, March 1990. Valerie Hunt, personal communication, April 1990.

13. For discussions of the possible role of kundalini activation in NDEs, see my book, *Heading Toward Omega*; Grey's *Return From Death*; Atwater's *Coming Back to Life*; and Greyson's "Scientific Commentary" in Harris and Bascom's book, *Full Circle.*

14. For useful case studies of persons who have undergone kundalini awakening, see the books by Lee Sanella, *Kundalini: Psychosis or Transformation?* (San Francisco: H. S. Dakin, 1977) and Bonnie Greenwell, *Energies of Transformation* (Cupertino, California: Shakti River Press, 1990).

15. For those interested in knowing more about this important concept, see the books by Emma Bragdon, A *Sourcebook for Helping People in Spiritual Emergency* (Los Altos, California: Lightening Up Press, 1988) and *The Call of Spiritual Emergency* (San Francisco: Harper & Row, 1990), as well as the volume edited by Stanislav and Christina Grof, *Spiritual Emergency* (Los Angeles: J. P. Tarcher, 1989).

16. See the summary remarks about his kundalini research on NDErs by Greyson in his "Scientific Commentary" in *Full Circle,* pp. 268–270.

17. $F = 60.68$, $p << .0001$.

18. Greyson, "Scientific Commentary," p. 270.

19. Gopi Krishna (1903–1984), who himself had a profound kundalini awakening in 1937, wrote more than a dozen books on this subject in which he compellingly articulated the evolutionary significance of this phenomenon. In his view, which has increasingly come to be shared by many students of kundalini, it is kundalini that activates a biological mechanism in the human body that in turn is responsible for mystical and religious experiences, psychic abilities, creativity, higher states of consciousness in general, and even genius. His best known books are *Kundalini* (Berkeley, California: Shambhala, 1970); *The Biological Basis of Religion and Genius* (New York: NC Press, 1971); *The Awakening of Kundalini* (New York: Dutton, 1974); and *Higher Consciousness and Kundalini* (Flesteron, Ontario: F.I.N.D. Research Trust, 1974).

20. White, *Kundalini, Evolution and Enlightenment* (Garden City, New York: Anchor, 1979), pp. 17.

21. I know this for a fact since when I visited England in the summer of 1984, I brought Margot an advance copy of *Heading Toward Omega.* At the same time she asked me to read a copy of the manuscript she was then preparing for publication. We were both astonished to discover that not only were our NDE findings extremely similar, but our conclusions were virtually identical.

22. Grey, p. 168.

23. Greyson, "Scientific Commentary," p. 270.

CHAPTER 8: BELIEFS AND VALUE SHIFTS FOLLOWING EXTRAORDINARY ENCOUNTERS

1. As before, the full versions of both these value questionnaires will be found in Appendix I.

2. $p < .05$.

3. See, for example, the books by Grey (1985), Flynn (1986), and Atwater (1988).

4. The virtual identity of Hazel's observations to those characteristic of NDErs will be obvious to anyone who takes the trouble to read Chapter 6 of my book, *Heading Toward Omega,* which deals with religious and spiritual orientations following NDEs.

5. For a good summary of this period, see the book by David Jacobs, *A History of the UFO Controversy in America* (Bloomington, Indiana: Indiana University Press, 1975), Chapter 5.

6. See *Heading Toward Omega,* Chapter 8, for an account and interpretation of these visions. For an update, also see my article, "Prophetic Visions in 1988: A Critical Reappraisal," *Journal of Near-Death Studies,* 7 (1988), pp. 4–18.

7. Strieber, *Communion,* p. 288.

8. For further information on this scale and its component items, see *Heading Toward Omega.*

9. $p < .0001$. Although there is a suggestion here that the experiential groups show this effect more strongly than the controls, the difference is not significant.

10. As indicated earlier, some items were worded slightly differently in alternate forms of the OI so as to be appropriate to each of the four groups. Those given in this section and in the corresponding tables in Appendix II are taken from the UFOE battery.

11. As implied, this is a not a *universal* position among our respondents. A particularly vehement objection to it was lodged by Claire Cham-

bers, whose terrifying ordeals with other entities were described in Chapter 3 (see pages 79–80). She expostulates heatedly: "It is a *dread-ful* insult to those of us who have been kidnapped and endured torture at the hands of the aliens to suggest that this is a 'spiritual experience' and that the aliens are 'higher-order intelligences'—they are not. *I have suffered from them for 20 years.*"

12. Again, this is highly consistent with my previous findings on the meaning ascribed to NDEs by experiencers. See especially the last chapter of *Heading Toward Omega* on this point.

13. See the article by Lorraine Davis, "A Comparison of UFO and Near-Death Experiences as Vehicles for the Evolution of Consciousness."

CHAPTER 9: HEADING TOWARD OZ: DEMYSTIFYING EXTRAORDINARY ENCOUNTERS

1. See his books, *Earth Lights* (Wellingborough, England: Turnstone, 1982) and *Earth Lights Revelation* (London: Blandford, 1989).

2. Devereux, *Earth Lights Revelation,* p. 14.

3. See, for example, his account in *Communion,* pp. 156–157.

4. Devereux, *Earth Lights Revelation,* p. 19.

5. Devereux, "The 'Earth Lights' Approach to the UFO Problem," *Journal of UFO Studies,* 2 (1990), pp. 102–103.

6. See especially Devereux's *Earth Lights Revelation* for a good summary of his findings.

7. Ibid., p. 163.

8. For a good recent summary of Persinger's position, see his article, "The Tectonic Strain Theory as an Explanation for UFO Phenomena: A Non-Technical Review of the Research, 1970–1990," *Journal of UFO Studies,* 2 (1990), pp. 105–137.

9. Persinger, ibid., pp. 110.

10. Persinger, ibid., p. 122.

11. For a useful, if technical, account of Persinger's argument here and the data that appear to support it, see his article, "The 'Visitor' Experience and the Personality: The Temporal Lobe Factor."

12. See, for example, *The Journal of Near-Death Studies,* Vol. 7 (No. 4), which is entirely concerned with a presentation and evaluation of such neurological models for the NDE. Melvin Morse's recent book, *Closer to the Light,* also presents his own version of such a model (see Chapter 5).

13. Devereux, *Earth Lights Revelation*, p. 213.

14. Persinger, "Modern Neuroscience and Near-Death Experiences: Expectancies and Implications. Comments on 'A Neurobiological Model for Near-Death Experiences.' "

15. Persinger, "The Tectonic Strain Theory," pp. 130–131.

16. Devereux, *Earth Lights Revelation*, p. 209.

17. Persinger, "The Tectonic Strain Theory," p. 130.

18. Persinger, "The 'Visitor' Experience and the Personality," pp. 161–163.

19. Persinger, "The Tectonic Strain Theory," p. 131.

20. Persinger, "The 'Visitor' Experience and the Personality," p. 166.

21. In *Communion*, Strieber describes such a smell in connection with the beings he encountered during his initial abduction episode.

22. Devereux, *Earth Lights Revelation*, p. 205.

23. See, for example, the books of Jacques Vallee, especially *Passport to Magonia* (Chicago: Henry Regnery, 1969) and *Dimensions*, as well as Devereux's *Earth Lights Revelation*, Jenny Randles's *Beyond Explanation?* (New York: Bantam, 1987), and Hilary Evans's *Visions, Apparitions, Alien Visitors* and *Gods, Spirits, Cosmic Guardians*. In connection with the airship mystery of 1896–1897, the articles by Jerry Clark in the *International UFO Reporter* are very much worth reading (16 [January/February 1990], pp. 4–23 and 16 [March/April 1991], pp. 20–21, 23–24).

24. See Stanton Friedman's article, "Who Believes in UFOs?"

25. Méheust, *Science Fiction et Soucoupes Volantes* (Paris: Mercure de France, 1978).

26. Vallee, *Confrontations* (New York: Ballantine, 1990), p. 179.

27. See Evans's *Visions, Apparitions, Alien Visitors*, pp. 278–283.

28. See Kottmeyer's article, "Gauche Encounters: Badfilms and the UFO Mythos." *Zontar*, 9 (in press).

29. See John G. Fuller's account of this famous case in *The Interrupted Journal* (New York: Dell, 1966).

30. On this point, see the article. "Extraterrestrial Hybridization Unlikely," by Michael Swords, *MUFON UFO Journal*, November 1988, pp. 6–10.

31. Kottmeyer, "Gauche Encounters," p. 12.

32. Bullard, "UFO Abduction Reports: The Supernatural Kidnap Narrative Returns in Technological Guise," *Journal of American Folklore*, 102 (1989), p. 164.

33. See, for example, Carol Zaleski's seminal study of medieval NDEs, *Otherworld Journeys,* or the cases mentioned in Holger Kalweit's book on shamanism, *Dreamtime and Inner Space.*

34. For example, Moody, *The Light Beyond*; Ring, *Life at Death,* and *Heading Toward Omega.*

35. Kalweit, op. cit., p. 17.

36. Zaleski, op. cit., p. 13.

37. For example, Kalweit, op. cit; Zaleski, op cit; Roger Walsh, *The Spirit of Shamanism* (Los Angeles: J. P. Tarcher, 1990); Michael Harner and Gary Doore, "The Ancient Wisdom in Shamanic Cultures," in Shirley Nicholson, ed., *Shamanism* (Wheaton, Illinois: Theosophical Publishing House, 1987), pp. 3–16; Ring, "Near-Death and UFO Encounters as Shamanic Initiations," and "Shamanic Initiation, Imaginal Worlds and Life After Death."

38. Persinger, "Modern Neuroscience and Near-Death Experiences," pp. 237–238.

39. Devereux, *Earth Lights Revelation,* p. 223.

40. Zaleski, op. cit., p. 4.

41. See, for example James Hillman, *Revisioning Psychology* (New York: Harper & Row, 1975); Henry Corbin, *Mundus Imaginalis or the Imaginal and the Imaginary* (Ipswich, England: Golgonooza Press, 1972); Roberts Avens, *Imagination Is Reality* (Dallas: Spring Publications, 1980); Jeanne Achterberg, "The Shaman: Master Healer in the Imaginary Realm," in Shirley Nicholson, ed., *Shamanism,* pp. 103–124; Michael Harner and Gary Doore, "The Ancient Wisdom in Shamanic Cultures"; Jean Houston, "The Mind and Soul of Shamanism," in Shirley Nicholson, ed., *Shamanism,* pp. vii–xii; Richard Noll, "The Presence of Spirits in Magic and Madness," in Shirley Nicholson, ed., *Shamanism,* pp. 47–61; Carol Zaleski, *Otherworld Journeys*; Terence McKenna, "New Maps of Hyperspace" (San Francisco: Harper-Collins, in press); Kenneth Ring, "Toward an Imaginal Interpretation of UFO Abductions" and "Shamanic Initiation, Imaginal Worlds, and Light After Death"; Dennis Stillings, ed., *Cyberbiological Studies of the Imaginal Component in the UFO Contact Experience*; Michael Talbot, *The Holographic Universe* (New York: HarperCollins, 1991); Fred Alan Wolf, *The Eagle's Quest* (New York: Summit Books, 1991).

42. See his seminal work, *Mundus Imaginalis or the Imaginal and the Imaginary,* previously cited.

43. Corbin, ibid., p. 17; italics are Corbin's.

44. Corbin, ibid., p. 9.

45. Randles, *Mind Monsters,* pp. 169–170.

CHAPTER 10: OMEGA REVELATION: ECOLOGICAL AND EVOLUTIONARY IMPLICATIONS OF EXTRAORDINARY ENCOUNTERS

1. Grosso, "The Symbolism of UFO Abductions," *UFO Universe* (Fall 1988), p. 45.

2. Grosso, "UFOs and the Myth of the New Age," in Dennis Stillings, ed., *Cyberbiological Studies of the Imaginal Component in the UFO Contact Experience*, p. 97.

3. Grosso, ibid., p. 62.

4. Grosso, "The Symbolism of UFO Abductions," p. 45, italics mine.

5. For example, Grosso has devoted a great deal of attention to Marian visions—i.e., apparent apparitions of the Virgin Mary—and to how they may also be interpreted according to a Mind at Large perspective. On this, see his book, *The Final Choice*, as well as his intriguing article, "The Riddle of the 'Falling Sun' at Fatima—Was It a Space Craft?" *UFO Universe* (Winter 1989), pp. 50–52.

6. Grosso, "The Near-Death Experience: Is It a Clue to the UFO Mystery and the Message of the Contactees?" *UFO Universe* (Fall 1989), pp. 49–50.

7. Data from a recent study by Bruce Greyson indicate that approximately 10 percent of NDErs may fall into this category. See his article, "Near-Death Encounters with and Without Near-Death Experiences: Comparative NDE Scale Profiles," *Journal of Near-Death Studies*, 8 (1990), pp. 151–161.

8. See *Heading Toward Omega*, Chapter 8. And for a followup and reassessment of these findings, see also my article, "Prophetic Visions in 1988: A Critical Reappraisal."

9. For example, see Margot Grey's *Return from Death*, pp. 122–133.

10. I had actually first proposed the idea of a planetary near-death experience in a similar context in my book, *Heading Toward Omega*, see p. 260. What Grosso has done is to extend this idea to a spectrum of extraordinary encounters suggestive of extramundane contact.

11. That is, the view that the earth itself is a self-regulating living system.

12. Grosso, "The Near-Death Experience," pp. 49–50.

13. Strieber, *Communion*, p. 288.

14. Fowler, *The Watchers* (New York: Bantam, 1990), p. 119.

15. Ibid., p. 348.

16. Ibid., p. 354, 357.

17. *The Dream of the Earth* (San Francisco: Sierra Club Books, 1988), Chapter 5.

18. Ibid., p. 206, 209.

19. Ibid., p. 211–212.

20. See, for example, John W. Perry's book, *The Heart of History* (Albany, New York: State University of New York Press, 1987).

21. See *Heading Toward Omega*, Chapter 10.

22. White, *The Meeting of Science and Spirit* (New York: Paragon, 1990), pp. 172, 248.

23. Richard Dabb and Michael Peter Langevin, "An Interview with Whitley Strieber," *Magical Blend* (January 1990), pp. 39–41, 102–104.

24. In addition to the writers I have already drawn on, such as Grosso, Strieber, and White, I mean also to allude to the formulations of thinkers such as Terence McKenna in *The Archaic Revival,* Michael Talbot in *The Holographic Universe,* and Fred Alan Wolf in *The Eagle's Quest.*

25. McKenna, "New and Old Maps of Hyperspace" (audiocassette) (Big Sur, California: Dolphin Tapes, 1982).

26. McKenna, "New Maps of Hyperspace," pp. 2–3, 11.

27. "An Interview with Whitley Strieber," p. 41. I have rearranged slightly some of the quotes that comprise this excerpt.

28. Ibid., p. 102.

29. Grosso, "The Near-Death Experience," p. 50.

30. On Vallee's views in this respect, see his books *The Invisible College* (New York: E. P. Dutton, 1975), p. 6, and *Dimensions,* pp. 271–281.

31. See his article, "UFOs: Ultraterrestrial Agents of Cultural Deconstruction," in Dennis Stillings, ed., *Cyberbiological Studies of the Imaginal Component in the UFO Contact Experience,* pp. 21–32.

32. Raschke, ibid., p. 25.

33. Raschke, ibid., pp. 30–31.

34. McKenna, "Oversoul Takes Shape in an Archetypal UFO," *California UFO,* 2:2 (1987), p. 17.

35. Grosso, "The Ultradimensional Mind," *Strange* magazine, 7 (April 1990), p. 11.

36. Dabb and Langevin, "An Interview with Whitley Strieber," p. 102.

BIBLIOGRAPHY

Achterberg, Jeanne. "The Shaman: Master Healer in the Imaginary Realm." In Nicholson, Shirley, ed., *Shamanism*. Wheaton, Illinois: Theosophical Publishing House, 1987, pp. 103–24.

Atwater, P. M. H. *Coming Back to Life*. New York: Dodd Mead, 1988.

Avens, Roberts. *Imagination Is Reality*. Dallas: Spring Publications, 1980.

Baker, Robert A. "Are UFO Abductions for Real? No, No, a Thousand Times No!" *Journal of UFO Studies*, 1 (1989) 104–10.

Bartholomew, Robert E., and Keith Basterfield. "Abduction States of Consciousness." *International UFO Reporter*, 13 (March–April, 1988) 7–9, 15.

Basterfield, Keith, and Robert E. Bartholomew. "Abductions: The Fantasy Prone Hypothesis." *International UFO Reporter*, 13 (May–June 1988) 9–11.

Becker, Robert O. *The Body Electric*. New York: William Morrow, 1985.

———. *Cross Currents*. Los Angeles: J. P. Tarcher, 1990.

———. "The Relationship between Bioelectromagnetics and Psychic Phenomena." *ASPR Newsletter*, 16 (Spring 1990) 11–14.

Berry, Thomas. *The Dream of the Earth*. San Francisco: Sierra Club Books, 1988.

Bloecher, Ted, Aphrodite Clamar, and Budd Hopkins. "Summary Report on the Psychological Testing of Nine Individuals Reporting UFO Abduction Experiences." In *Final Report on the Psychological Testing of UFO "Abductees."* Mt. Rainier, Maryland: Fund for UFO, 1985.

Bragdon, Emma. *A Sourcebook for Helping People in Spiritual Emergency*. Los Altos, California: Lightening Up Press, 1988.

———. *The Call of Spiritual Emergency*. San Francisco: Harper & Row, 1990.

Bullard, Thomas E. *Comparative Analysis of UFO Abduction Reports*. Mt. Rainier, Maryland: Fund for UFO Research, 1987.

———. *UFO Abductions: The Measure of a Mystery,* 2 vols. Mt. Rainier, Maryland: Fund for UFO Research, 1987.

———. "Hypnosis and UFO Abductions: A Troubled Relationship." *Journal of UFO Studies,* I (1989) 3–40.

———. "UFO Abduction Reports: The Supernatural Kidnap Narrative Returns in Technological Guise." *Journal of American Folklore,* 102 (1989) 147–70.

———. "The UFO Abduction Phenomenon: Past Research and Future Prospects." Paper presented at the First Conference on Treatment and Research on Experienced Anomalous Trauma, Fairfield, Connecticut, May 1989.

Bush, Nancy E. "The Near-Death Experience in Children: Shades of the Prison-House Reopening." *Anabiosis,* 3 (1983) 177–93.

Chamberlain, David. *Babies Remember Birth*. Los Angeles: J. P. Tarcher, 1988.

———. "The Expanding Boundaries of Memory." *Revision,* 12 (1990) 11–20.

Chu, James A., and Diana L. Dill. "Dissociative Symptoms in Relationship to Childhood Physical and Sexual Abuse." *American Journal of Psychiatry* 147 (1990) 887–92.

Clark, Jerome. "Airships." *International UFO Reporter* 16 (January/February 1991) 4–23 and 16 (March/April 1991) 20–21, 23–24.

Clark, Kimberly. "Clinical Interventions with Near-Death Experiencers." In Bruce Greyson and Charles P. Flynn, eds., *The Near-Death Experience*. Springfield, Illinois: Charles P. Thomas, 1984, pp. 242–55.

Corbin, Henry. *Mundus Imaginalis or the Imaginal and the Imaginary*. Ipswich (England): Golgonooza Press (originally published in Spring 1972).

Council, James, and Bruce Greyson. "Near-Death Experiences and the Fantasy-Prone Personality." Paper presented to the American Psychological Association, Los Angeles, California, August 1985.

Dabb, Richard, and Michael Peter Langevin. "An Interview with Whitley Strieber." *Magical Blend* (January 1990): 39–41, 102–4.

Davis, Lorraine. "A Comparison of UFO and Near-Death Experiences as Vehicles for the Evolution of Human Consciousness." *Journal of Near-Death Studies*, 6 (1988): 240–57.

Devereux, Paul. *Earth Lights*. Wellingborough (England): Turnstone, 1982.

———. *Earth Lights Revelation*. London: Blandford, 1989.

———. "The 'Earth Lights' Approach to the UFO Problem. *Journal of UFO Studies*, 2 (1990) 100–104.

Evans, Hilary. *Visions, Apparitions, Alien Visitors*. Wellingborough (England): Aquarian Press, 1984.

———. *Gods, Spirits, Cosmic Guardians*. Wellingborough (England): Aquarian Press, 1987.

———. *Alternate States of Consciousness*. Wellingborough (England): Aquarian Press, 1989.

Fawcett, Lawrence, and Barry J. Greenwood. *Clear Intent*. Englewood Cliffs, New Jersey: Prentice-Hall, 1984.

Flynn, Charles P. *After the Beyond*. Englewood Cliffs, New Jersey: Prentice-Hall, 1986.

Fowler, Raymond E. *The Andreassen Affair*. Englewood Cliffs, New Jersey: Prentice-Hall, 1979.

———. *The Watchers*. New York: Bantam, 1990.

Friedman, Stanton T. "Who Believes in UFOs?" *International UFO Reporter*, 14 (January/February 1989) 6–10.

Fuller, John G. *The Interrupted Journey*. New York: Dell, 1966.

Gabbard, Glen O. and Stuart W. Twemlow. *With the Eyes of the Mind*. New York: Praeger, 1984.

Gallup, George, Jr., *Adventures in Immortality*. New York: McGraw-Hill, 1982.

Gordon, R. A. "People Who See Flying Saucers" (letter). *Science*, 171 (1971) 957.

Gotlib, David. "EM Fields Affect Consciousness." *Bulletin of Anomalous Experience*, 1 (June–July 1990) 2–3.

Greenwell, Bonnie. *Energies of Transformation*. Cupertino, California: Shakti River Press, 1990.

Grey, Margot. *Return from Death*. London: Arcana, 1985.

Greyson, Bruce. "Increase in Psychic Phenomena Following Near-Death Experiences." *Theta*, 11 (1983) 26–29.

———. "Scientific Commentary." In B. Harris, and L. C. Bascom, eds. *Full Circle*. New York: Pocket Books, 1990, pp. 251–70.

———. "Near-Death Encounters with and Without Near-Death Experiences: Comparative NDE Scale Profiles." *Journal of Near-Death Studies*, 8 (1990) 151–61.

Greyson, Bruce, and Charles P. Flynn, eds. *The Near-Death Experience*. Springfield, Illinois: Charles C. Thomas, 1984.

Grinspoon, Lester, and A. D. Persky. "Psychiatry and UFO Reports." In C. Sagan, and T. Page, eds. *UFOs: A Scientific Debate*. Ithaca, New York: Cornell University Press, 1972, pp. 223–46.

Grof, Stanislav, and Christina Grof, eds. *Spiritual Emergency*. Los Angeles: J. P. Tarcher, 1989.

Grosso, Michael. *The Final Choice*. Walpole, N. H.: Stillpoint, 1985.

———. "The Symbolism of UFO Abductions." *UFO Universe* (Fall 1988) 44–45, 62–63.

———. "UFOs and the Myth of the New Age." In Dennis Stillings, ed. *Cyberbiological Studies of the Imaginal Component in the UFO Contact Experience*. St. Paul: Archaeus Project, 1989, pp. 81–98.

———. "The Riddle of the 'Falling Sun' at Fatima—Was it a Space Craft?" *UFO Universe* (Winter 1989) 50–52.

———. "The Ultradimensional Mind". *Strange* magazine, 7 (April 1990) 10–13.

Hardt, James. "Kundalini and Biofeedback." Paper presented to the Second Spiritual Emergence Network Conference, Pacific Grove, California, March 1990.

Harner, Michael, and Gary Doore. "The Ancient Wisdom in Shamanic Cultures." In Nicholson, Shirley, ed. *Shamanism*. Wheaton, Illinois: Theosophical Publishing House, 1987, pp. 3–16.

Harris, Barbara. Personal Communication, September 1987.

Hayes, Evelyn R., and Linda D. Waters. "Interdisciplinary Perceptions of the Near-Death Experience: Implications for Professional Education and Practice." *Death Studies*, 13 (1989) 443–53.

Herzog, David B., and John T. Herrin. "Near-Death Experiences in the Very Young." *Critical Care Medicine,* 13 (1985) 1074–75.

Hillman, James. *Revisioning Psychology.* New York: Harper & Row, 1975.

Holden, Janice M. "Visual Perception During Naturalistic Near-Death Out-of-Body Experiences." *Journal of Near-Death Studies,* 7 (1989): 107–20.

Hopkins, Budd. *Intruders.* New York: Random House, 1987.

———. Letter. *International UFO Reporter,* 13 (May–June, 1988) 22–23.

———. Letter. *International UFO Reporter,* 13 (July–August 1988) 20–21.

Houston, Jean. "The Mind and Soul of Shamanism." In Nicholson, Shirley, ed. *Shamanism.* Wheaton, Illinois: Theosophical Publishing House, 1987, vii–xiii.

Hunt, Valerie. Personal Communication, April 1990.

Irwin, Harvey J. *Flight of Mind.* Metuchen, New Jersey: Scarecrow Press, 1985.

Jacobs, David M. *A History of the UFO Controversy in America.* Bloomington, Indiana: Indiana University Press, 1975.

Kalweit, Holger, *Dreamtime and Inner Space.* Boston: Shambhala, 1988.

Kinder, Gary. *Light Years.* New York: Atlantic Monthly Press, 1987.

Kluft, Richard P., ed. *Childhood Antecedents of Multiple Personality.* Washington, D.C.: American Psychological Association, 1985.

Kohr, Richard L. "Near-Death Experiences, Altered States and Psi Sensitivity." *Anabiosis,* 3 (1983) 157–76.

Kottmeyer, Martin. "Gauche Encounters: Badfilms and the UFO Mythos." *Zontar,* 9 (in press).

———. "Abduction: The Boundary Deficit Hypothesis." *Magonia,* 37 (1988) 3–7.

Krishna, Gopi. *Kundalini.* Berkeley, California: Shambhala, 1970.

———. *The Biological Basis of Religion and Genius.* New York: NC Press, 1971.

———. *The Awakening of Kundalini.* New York: Dutton, 1974.

——. *Higher Consciousness and Kundalini*. Flesterton, Ontario: F.I.N.D. Research Trust, 1974.

Laibow, Rima E. "Dual Victims: The Abused and the Abducted." *International UFO Reporter,* 14 (May–June 1989) 4–9.

Mathes, E. W. "Mystical Experiences, Romantic Love, and Hypnotic Susceptibility." *Psychological Reports* 50 (1982) 701–2.

McKenna, Terence. "New and Old Maps of Hyperspace" (audio-cassette). Big Sur, California: Dolphin Tapes, 1982.

——. "Oversoul Takes Shape in an Archetypal UFO." *California UFO,* 2:2 (1987) 17.

——. "New Maps of Hyperspace." In Terence McKenna. *The Archaic Revival: Essays and Conversations.* San Francisco: HarperCollins, in press.

Meerloo, J. A. "The Flying Saucer Syndrome and the Need for Miracles" (letter). *Journal of the American Medical Association,* 203 (1968) 70.

Méheust, Bertrand. *Science Fiction et Soucoupes Volantes.* Paris: Mercure de France, 1978.

Moody, Raymond A., Jr. *Life After Life.* Atlanta: Mockingbird Books, 1975.

——. *The Light Beyond.* New York: Bantam, 1988.

Morse, Melvin. "A Near-Death Experience in a Seven-Year-Old-Child." *American Journal of Diseases in Children,* 137 (1983) 959–61.

——. *Closer to the Light.* New York: Villard Books, 1990.

Morse, Melvin, Doug Conner, and Donald Tyler. "Near-Death Experiences in a Pediatric Population." *American Journal of Diseases in Children,* 139 (1985) 595–600.

Morse, Melvin, et al. "Childhood Near-Death Experiences." *American Journal of Diseases in Children,* 140 (1986): 1110–14.

Nelson, Peter L. "Personality Factors in the Frequency of Reported Spontaneous Praeternatural Experiences." *Journal of Transpersonal Psychology,* 21 (1989) 193–209.

Noll, Richard. "The Presence of Spirits in Magic and Madness." In Nicholson, Shirley, ed. *Shamanism.* Wheaton, Illinois: Theosophical Publishing House, 1987, pp. 47–61.

Nyman, Joseph. Personal Communication, February 1988.

Orne, Roberta M. "Nurses' Views of NDEs." *American Journal of Nursing*, 86 (1986) 419–20.

Parnell, June O., and R. Leo Sprinkle. "Personality Characteristics of Persons Who Claim UFO Experiences." *Journal of UFO Studies*, 2 (1990) 45–58.

Perry, John Weir. *The Heart of History*. Albany, New York: State University of New York Press, 1987.

Persinger, Michael A. "The Tectonic Strain Theory as an Explanation for UFO Phenomena: A Non-Technical Review of the Research, 1970–1990." *Journal of UFO Studies*, 2 (1990) 105–37.

———. "Modern Neuroscience and Near-Death Experiences." *Journal of Near-Death Studies*, 7 (1990): 233–39.

———. "The 'Visitor' Experience and the Personality: The Temporal Lobe Factor." In D. Stillings, ed. *Cyberbiological Studies of the Imaginal Component in the UFO Contact Experience*. St. Paul: Archaeus Project, 1989, pp. 157–71.

Persinger, Michael A., and G. Lafreniere. *Space-Time Transients and Unusual Phenomena*. Chicago: Nelson-Hall, 1977.

Randles, Jenny. *Beyond Explanation?* New York: Bantam, 1987.

———. *Abduction*. London: Robert Hale, 1988.

———. *Mind Monsters*. Wellingborough (England): Aquarian Press, 1990.

Raschke, Carl. "UFOs: Ultraterrestrial Agents of Cultural Deconstruction." In D. Stillings, ed. *Cyberbiological Studies of the Imaginal Component in the UFO Contact Experience*. St. Paul: Archaeus Project, 1989, pp. 21–32.

Ring, Kenneth. *Life at Death*. New York: Coward, McCann and Geoghegan, 1980.

———. *Heading Toward Omega*. New York: William Morrow, 1984.

———. "Prophetic Visions in 1988: A Critical Reappraisal." *Journal of Near-Death Studies*, 7 (1988) 4–18.

———. "Near-Death and UFO Encounters as Shamanic Initiations." *Revision*, 11: 1 (1989): 14–22.

———. "Toward an Imaginal Theory of UFO Abductions." *Revision* 11: 2 (1989), 17–24.

———. "Shamanic Initiation, Imaginal Worlds, and Light After

Death." In Doore, Gary, ed. *What Survives?* Los Angeles: J. P. Tarcher, 1990, pp. 204–15.

Ring, Kenneth, and Christopher Rosing. "The Omega Project: A Psychological Survey of Persons Reporting Abductions and Other UFO Encounters." *Journal of UFO Studies,* 2 (1990): 59–98.

Rogo, D. Scott, ed. *Alien Abductions.* New York: Signet, 1980.

———. Letter. *International UFO Reporter,* 13 (July–August 1988) 20.

———. *The Return from Silence.* Wellingborough (England): Aquarian Press, 1989.

Royce, David. "The Near-Death Experience: A Survey of Clergy's Attitudes and Knowledge." *Journal of Pastoral Care,* 39 (March 1985) 31–42.

Russell, Alene B., and Cynthia M. Trainor. *Trends in Child Abuse and Neglect: A National Perspective.* Denver: The American Humane Association, 1984.

Sabom, Michael B., *Recollections of Death.* New York: Harper & Row, 1982.

———. "The Near-Death Experience: Myth or Reality?" *Anabiosis,* 1 (1981) 44–56.

Sachs, Roberta. "A Comparison of Experienced Anomalous Trauma and Satanic Cult Experiences." Paper presented at the Second Conference on Treatment and Research on Experienced Anomalous Trauma, Blacksburg, Virginia, February 1990.

Sanders, Barbara. "Correlates of Dissociation in a College Population." *Journal of Dissociation,* 2 (1989) 17–23.

———. "Dissociation, Imaginative Involvement and Child Abuse." Manuscript in preparation, University of Connecticut, 1991.

Sanders, Barbara, and Marina Giolas. "Dissociation and Child Abuse in Disturbed Adolescents." *American Journal of Psychiatry* 14 (1991) 50–54.

Sanella, Lee. *Kundalini: Psychosis or Transformation?* San Francisco: H. S. Dakin, 1977.

Schwarz, Berthold E. *UFO Dynamics: Psychiatric and Psychic Aspects of the UFO Syndrome,* 2 vols. More Haven, Florida: Rainbow Books, 1983.

Serdalehy, William J. "Pediatric Near-Death Experiences." *Journal of Near-Death Studies,* 9 (1990) 33–39.

Shallis, Michael. *The Electric Connection.* New York: Amsterdam, 1988.

Spanos, N. P., and P. Moretti. "Correlates of Mystical and Diabolical Experiences in a Sample of Female University Students." *Journal for the Scientific Study of Religion,* 27 (1988) 105–16.

Sprinkle, R. Leo. "Hypnotic and Psychic Implications in the Investigation of UFO Reports." In Coral Lorenzen and Jim Lorenzen, eds. *Encounters with UFO Occupants.* New York: Berkley, 1976, pp. 256–329.

Stewart, Sherry, and Mary L. Carrione. "The Chosen Few." Unpublished term paper for Advanced Seminar in Near-Death Studies, University of Connecticut, Storrs, Connecticut, May 1987.

Stillings, Dennis, ed. *Cyberbiological Studies of the Imaginal Component in the UFO Contact Experience.* St. Paul: Archaeus Project, 1989.

Stoia, Ellen. Personal Communication, May 1987.

Straus, Murray A., Richard J. Gelles, and Suzanne K. Steinmetz, *Behind Closed Doors: Violence in the American Family.* Garden City, N.Y.: Anchor Books, 1980.

Strieber, Whitley. *Communion.* New York: Beech Tree Books, 1987.

Strieber, Whitley, and James Kunetka, *Warday.* New York: Holt, Rinehart & Winston, 1984.

———. *Nature's End.* New York: Warner Books, 1986.

Sutherland, Cherie. "Changes in Religious Beliefs, Attitudes and Practices Following Near-Death Experiences: An Australian Study." *Journal of Near-Death Studies,* 9 (1990) 21–31.

———. "Psychic Phenomena Following Near-Death Experiences." *Journal of Near-Death Studies,* 8 (1990) 93–102.

Swords, Michael D. "Extraterrestrial Hybridization Unlikely." *MUFON UFO Journal* (November 1988) 6–10.

Talbot, Michael. *The Holographic Universe.* New York: HarperCollins, 1991.

Vallee, Jacques. *Passport to Magonia.* Chicago: Henry Regnery, 1969.

———. *The Invisible College.* New York: E. P. Dutton, 1975.

————. *Dimensions*. Chicago: Contemporary Books, 1988.

————. *Confrontations*. New York: Ballantine, 1990.

Walker, Barbara A., and Robert D. Russell. "Assessing Psychologists' Knowledge and Attitudes Toward Near-Death Phenomena." *Journal of Near-Death Studies*, 8 (1989) 103–10.

Walsh, Roger N. *The Spirit of Shamanism*. Los Angeles: J. P. Tarcher, 1990.

White, John. *The Meeting of Science and Spirit*. New York: Paragon, 1990.

————, ed. *Kundalini, Evolution and Enlightenment*. Garden City, New York: Anchor, 1979.

Wilson, Edgar. "In Search of the Elusive Chi." *Newsletter of the International Society for the Study of Subtle Energy and Energy Medicine*, 1 (1990) 8–9.

Wilson, Sheryl, and Theodore X. Barber. "The Fantasy-Prone Personality: Implications for Understanding Imagery, Hypnosis and Parapsychological Phenomena." In A. Shiekh, ed. *Imagery: Current Theory, Research, and Application*. New York: John Wiley, 1983, pp. 340–87.

Wogan, Michael. "A New Test for Dissociation." *Journal of Experimental and Clinical Hypnosis* (in press).

Wolf, Fred Alan. *The Eagle's Quest*. New York: Summit Books, 1991.

Zaleski, Carol. *Otherworld Journeys*. New York: Oxford University Press, 1987.

INDEX